DATE DUE

DEMCO 38-296

HOSPITABLE
PERFORMANCES

HOSPITABLE PERFORMANCES

*Dramatic Genre and Cultural Practices
in Early Modern England*

DARYL W. PALMER

PURDUE UNIVERSITY PRESS
West Lafayette, Indiana

Printed in the United States of America

Book and jacket design by Susan Miller

Library of Congress Cataloging-in-Publication Data

Palmer, Daryl W.
    Hospitable performances : dramatic genre and cultural practices in early modern England / by Daryl W. Palmer.
        p.   cm.
    Includes bibliographical references and index.
    ISBN 1-55753-014-9 (cloth : alk. paper)
    1. English drama—Early modern and Elizabethan, 1500–1600—History and criticism. 2. English drama—17th century—History and criticism. 3. Hospitality—England—History—16th century. 4. Hospitality—England—History—17th century. 5. Courts and courtiers in literature. 6. Manners and customs in literature. 7. Hospitality in literature. 8. Pageants—England. I. Title.
    PR658.H64P35 1991
    822'.309355—dc20   91-16223
                                                                              CIP

For my parents

CONTENTS

ACKNOWLEDGMENTS

As Thomas Nashe would explain, scholars rise early, contend with the cold, and converse with scarcity. It goes without saying that scholarship depends on hospitalities, and I have had the best hosts. My debt to David M. Bergeron comes first and exceeds my power to thank. When I might have settled for scraps, he has offered great tables and been the best teacher and friend. At the University of Kansas, Jack Oruch, Michael L. Johnson, Cheryl Lester, and Ben Sax were superb readers of the first versions of this work. At the University of Exeter in England, Gareth Roberts inspired my work with Nashe and plebeian revelry. Like so many others, I am grateful to Stephen Orgel for his inspiration and careful reading. Coppélia Kahn's commentary on the earliest version of this study was timely and provocative. Steven Mullaney, James Yoch, and Charles Ross read final versions of the manuscript with brilliance and energy. Their labors taught me much.

I am certainly grateful to Djelal Kadir, the former chairman of the editorial board at Purdue University Press, for finding virtue in my rough beginnings. No one could have had better editors than Margaret Hunt and Verna Emery. Margaret manages everything with care and wit, two scarce commodities. Verna has been my salvation, comma by comma. Graphic designer Susan Miller made it all look beautiful.

Of course, a scholar's hospitalities take a thousand forms. Here and in England, a number of institutions have been particularly helpful: the British Library, The Folger Shakespeare Library, Bierce Library of the University of Akron, Watson Library of the University of Kansas, the Department of Special Collections, Spencer Research Library, University of Kansas.

The hospitalities of many friends and colleagues made distinct impressions on the course of my labors. I happily thank G. Douglas Atkins, Bernard Hirsch, Thomas Hudson, Martha O'Brien, Barbara Paris, Geraldo Sousa, Robert Stein and his colleagues at Washburn University, and Raymond L. Williams. From the first drafts of this project, Nina Molinaro has been between the lines, as Paz might say, *una voz mágica.* Thank you.

Finally, my colleagues at the University of Akron have made closure both possible and delightful. Thanks to Claibourne E. Griffin, Dean of Buchtel College of Arts and Sciences, and Eric Birdsall, Head of the Department of English, for support and research time to finish. Dawn Trouard gets the last word for being the best. Thank you for expression, everything to express.

NOTE ON TEXTS

In the interest of readability and to in no way create an erroneous antiquity for the many unedited primary texts used in this study alongside Shakespeare and others, I have modernized spelling and (infrequently) punctuation. Readers familiar with McKerrow's grand edition of Thomas Nashe's works will take notice that I have taken the same liberty with Nashe's texts in Chapter 4.

References to the works of Shakespeare appear parenthetically in the text and come from *William Shakespeare: The Complete Works*, edited by Alfred Harbage (New York: Viking/Pelican, 1969).

References to the three volumes of John Nichols, *The Progresses and Public Processions of Queen Elizabeth* (London, 1823), and to his four volumes of *The Progresses, Processions, and Magnificent Festivities of King James, the First* (London, 1828) have been abbreviated as follows: Nichols, *Elizabeth;* Nichols, *James*.

1

Hospitalities:
Practices and Representations

William Vaughan spoke for the age of Elizabeth and James when he wrote: "Hospitality is the chiefest point of humanity, which an householder can show, not only unto his friends, but also unto strangers & wayfaring men."[1] Looking back at the age of Elizabeth and James from the end of the seventeenth century, George Wheler defined hospitality succinctly as "a liberal entertainment of all sorts of men, at one's house, whether neighbors or strangers, with kindness, especially with meat, drink, and lodgings. Hospitality is an excellent Christian practice."[2] Caleb Dalechamp preached what amounts to a grammar of hospitable practice, dividing the idea into "act" and "object" and adducing an obligatory schema of *earnest invitation, cheerful entertainment, faithful protection,* and *courteous dismission or deduction.*[3]

For men such as Henry Wotton and Christopher Wandesford, hospitality was more than Christian practice; it was a natural law.[4] Regardless of its authority, hospitality practically defined English manners for a chorus of commentators.[5] From the ground-breaking political criticism of L. C. Knights to the innovative critique of popular culture and drama by Michael Bristol, literary scholars have long recognized the ubiquity of these hospitable ideals and their uncertain connection to the crucial social, aesthetic, and ideological issues of the period; yet despite such consistent attention, hospitality remains for most studies a passing citation, a glance at roast beef, ale, and merriment.[6] This study seeks to define hospitality in dynamic relation to the age's ideology and theater.

Perhaps the most troubling aspect of hospitality for both the historian and the literary scholar has been the question of hospitality's verisimilitude, of what actually took place between hosts and guests. Without a doubt, the practice of hospitality goes back to the dim origins of human consciousness, but for Elizabethans and Jacobeans, the mention of hospitality conjured up visions of a golden age. Did such a golden age exist? Did a significant decline in the practice of hospitality occur in early modern England? To put the question most precisely, *what is the difference between the practices of hospitality and the representations of hospitable practice?* If we mean to study the relationship between Shakespeare's *Macbeth* and Renaissance hospitality, do we intend to analyze the play in relation to a historically verifiable practice or to other contemporary representations of that practice? We may well attempt both courses, but it will be important to make initial distinctions between the two registers of data and to maintain those distinctions as we read the literary text. Any serious study of literature and its cultures must begin with such questions and such caveats.

For this reason, the following chapter introduces hospitable practices separately from their contemporary representations. In discussing practices, I focus on incidents involving historical figures, "documented" by reports, payments, and contemporary conversation. Whom did Archbishop Parker entertain in 1573? What were the qualities of Lady Hoby's hospitalities around Hackness? How were Norwich's plans for hosting the queen different from those of Sittingborne? Source material for this kind of summary is slight and always fragmentary, but with the publication of Felicity Heal's monumental *Hospitality in Early Modern England*, it should be clear that serious scholarship can proceed from the identification of concrete (albeit neglected) social practices.[7] Turning to representations of hospitality, I want to consider the plethora of sixteenth- and seventeenth-century texts that elaborate an idea of hospitality through narrative, collocation of historical data, and an awareness of a reading public. How did John Stow represent the hospitalities of England's nobility and clergy? In what sense did certain "pamphlet conventions" govern the texts of writers such as Vaughan and Tusser?[8] How might we articulate the relationship between John Savile's role as pamphleteer and King James's royal part in an entertainment at Theobalds?

At the outset, I admit to having no hope of discovering some real Elizabethan and Jacobean hospitality. Trenchers and possets have quite passed away. My separation of practice and representation has, then, nothing to do with latent nostalgia. Instead, I have become painfully aware of the intricacy of hospiliti*es* in the period and have determined that only by imposing parameters on the discussion can I meaningfully record patterns of dominance, parasitism, and resistance that take shape under the auspices of hospitality.

The very notions of *host* and *guest* contain inherent equivocations that upset easy assumptions. The word *host* derives from the Latin *hospes* and *hospitis*. In these etymological origins and in Renaissance usage, the single term *host* signifies both host and guest. *Hosting* means both the offering and the receiving of hospitality.[9] The role of host thus commits one to a rather volatile chain of metonymy. The entertained remains a host and the host a guest. Motives remain in constant abeyance and authority in doubt. Does the host entertain to be entertained? Does the host entertain only to be displaced in the manner of Agammenon, Odysseus, Gloucester, King Lear, Camillo in *The White Devil,* and the more ordinary Arden of Feversham? Does the guest want more than hospitality, as Leontes suspects in *The Winter's Tale?* Such a motive certainly animates Don John in *Much Ado about Nothing* or Cocledemoy in John Marston's *The Dutch Courtesan.* Like the Host in Thomas Middleton's *A Trick to Catch the Old One,* a Renaissance wit may always play with the ambiguous Latin phrase *Hic et haec hostis.*[10]

To make matters even more opaque, hospitality meant (as Wheler suggests in his definition) *entertainment,* a term whose etymology elucidates its social function: *inter* and *tenere,* to hold together. While much has been written about Renaissance notions of the Great Chain of Being, little has been said concerning hospitable entertainments as the human "glue" of this chain. Moreover, if Kevin Sharpe is correct in his suggestion that *access* to powerful men determined the allocation of power as much as degree, then entertainment was certainly one of the chief practices supporting, holding together, the existing order. Hospitality maintains chains of access.[11] Not surprisingly, under Elizabeth and James, hospitality and entertainment are nearly interchangeable terms, marking the accepted interdependence of householding and theater, domestic and political practice. At the inception of Renaissance theater in England, hospitality was "the first condition" of the interlude. In his prologue to *Staple of News,* Jonson is busy developing this sensibility by framing his audience as "guests."[12] The "real" Renaissance hospitality was, even for the Elizabethans, an unstable amalgam of practices thriving at the heart of English rule.

In practice and in representation, hospitality seemed to many people in the Renaissance the very essence of English custom and proper hierarchy. Ironically, this salutary form, almost by definition, turns hosts into beggars and beggars into courtiers. As we enter the great hall, we imagine magnificence and generosity; we may well find parasitism and parodies of communion. On returning to the streets, who will be surprised to find the whole converted into news and sport, the possibility of economic advantage?

Hospitable Practices

Throughout England's age of expansion, aesthetic achievement, and civil revolution, hospitality existed as a code of exchange between competing, often conflicting, orders of society: between the poor and rich, noble and plebeian, noble and noble, male and female, patriarch and family, family and society, English and non-English, Anglican and Puritan. Although a modern perception of hospitality may amount to little more than food and drink exchanged between equals, the Renaissance mind, as Heal suggests, found the most diverse relationships united by hospitable practice:

> Since the poor were among those who were made the responsibility of the householder, the whole problem of domestic charity and the continuity of private beneficence in the age of the Poor Laws is raised. Obligations to the poor also comprehend issues of community and neighbourhood: peculiarly sensitive problems in the troubled England of the early seventeenth century. Further extension of the idea includes the potentially threatening figure of the stranger, and may serve to reveal something of English attitudes to the outsider. And the location of entertainment within the household may facilitate understanding of the changing nature of the family in these centuries.[13]

Household accounts from medieval and early modern England confirm Heal's observation as they record charitable giving with *pro hospicii* and *in nomine hospicii*.[14] Everyone from monarch to beggar participated in a logic of obligation and reciprocity that is both very old and absolutely current, a cultural pattern primarily studied by anthropologists whose scholarship suggests the universality of ritualistic welcomes and care. One of the great authorities on the subject, Marcel Mauss, reminds us that such patterns persist today: "Invitations have to be offered and have to be accepted."[15] Unfortunately, the vestigial customs *we* recognize hardly prepare us to judge the significance of dishes served to nobility centuries ago, especially when the significance of a dry trencher tossed to a hungry beggar outside a merchant's house has everything to do with that merchant's identity and power.

This interpretive challenge is perhaps best embodied in a dove. When Queen Elizabeth visited Norwich in the summer of 1578, part of her entertainment included a "Princely Maske" of Mercury and other gods, authored by Henry Goldingham. As the evening's supper waited just outside the hall, the pageant moved forward via the presentation of gifts, none being more beautiful than that of Venus "whose gift was a whyte Doue."[16] Garter's account of the performance lingers for a moment on the beauty of the giving: "The Doue being caste off, ranne directly to the Queene, and being taken vppe and set vppon the Table before hir Maiestie sate so quietyly, as if it had bin tied" (p. 274). In this moment the writer has captured delicately the fluttering obedience manifested in successful hospitality. Governing this moment is the archaic system of exchange described by Mauss as "prestation":

> In the systems of the past we do not find simple exchange of goods, wealth and produce through markets established among individuals. For it is groups, and not individuals, which carry on exchange, make contracts, and are bound by obligations. Further, what they exchange is not exclusively goods and wealth, real and personal property, and things of economic value. They exchange rather courtesies, entertainments, ritual, military assistance, women, children, dances, and feasts; and fairs in which the market is but one element and the circulation of wealth but one part of a wide and enduring contract. Finally, although the

> prestations and counter-prestations take place under a
> voluntary guise they are in essence strictly obligatory,
> and their sanction is private or open warfare. (p. 3)

In the gift of the dove, Norwich means to succeed in this complex
system, negotiating wealth, authority, and power with a seemingly frivolous token. As Lewis Hyde explains, the motion of the gift,
unlike the motion of the commodity, means ongoing increase instead of one-time profit.[17] No mere commodity, the dove is immediately "used up," but the "feeling-bonds" it engenders (to borrow
Hyde's term) only continue to increase.

In discussing hospitable practice, we appear to be talking of
simple matters of food and lodging when in fact we are approaching the fundamental nature of social connection in the culture.
Viewed from the revisionist perspective of historian Kevin Sharpe,
the pressures of nascent capitalism and changing modes of governance on this system of prestation appear as a problem of communication, of how to entertain fiercely independent familial,
religious, and political factions in a common language.[18] Much remains to be done in the elaboration of the older system and
its transformations.

The task will be especially difficult because so much of the
material culture that animated these practices is lost that the whole
undertaking may appear at first glance to be foolhardy. If my consideration of the practice of hospitality escapes this fault, it will be
because I claim only to adduce some of the complex agendas behind the roast goose and dry trencher. We need, among other
things, a terminology for the distinctive operations of a long-term
host like William Cecil and a thwarted host like Leicester, of a
humble yeoman and a climbing merchant. The best distinction, I
think, would be one that focuses on method. I want, then, to follow the example of Michel de Certeau, who proposes that we divide practices according to their modes of deployment. He
suggests the terms *tactics* and *strategies*.[19] Tactics are "seized opportunities," maneuvers made possible because of a temporary configuration of circumstances. Time always runs out on a particular
tactic. The practitioner plays the situation as it appears, exploits
the vulnerable elements, and then moves on. In contrast, strategies
get deployed over time. They involve a series of actions planned
in advance, and they depend on the strategist's ability to config-
ure situations to his or her advantage.

In the practice of hospitality, tactics abound. At one extreme, the host may distract the guest in order to murder him. Meanwhile, the guest may seek hospitality as an improvised delay in some larger course of events. In the midst of an entertainment, a guest may lean on the protocols of hospitality in order to displace another guest. Host and guest may easily don masks in order to play out roles that would otherwise be constrained by their community. The list is seemingly endless and certainly includes what Frank Whigham has called "tropes of personal promotion," tactics used by the individual "to argue his (or another's) membership in the [dominant] group."[20] On the other hand, hospitality seems to encourage principally what Whigham calls "tropes of social hierarchy," strategies that mystify the constructedness of hierarchical rule (p. 63). In other words, hospitable practice means strategies of ideological shaping, a term for all the ways in which hospitality's protocols of earnest invitation, cheerful entertainment, faithful protection, and courteous dismission can be used to cast and recast the ideological commitments of hosts, guests, and onlookers. Hospitable practice is about the production of fantasies.

Thomas Greene's commentary on court spectacle sums up the status of hospitable practice: "Perhaps court spectacle can best be regarded as a vulnerable institution, vulnerable always to the suspicion of manipulation but struggling intermittently to earn its idealizations, to transcend a vulgarity of motive it can never permanently exorcise."[21] A brief foray through the hierarchies of Renaissance England will suggest the ubiquity of these practices as well as their idealizations and vulgarities. It will also hint at the dramatic energy to be mined from the persistent tension between time-constrained tactics and long-term strategies.

From the beginning of Elizabeth's reign, courtly comment marked her hosting. In 1559, an observer noted of one such occasion: "There was extraordinary cheer at supper, and, after that as goodly a banquet as had been seen, with all manner of music and entertainment till midnight."[22] That same year the queen authorized "a goodly banqueting-house for her Grace, made with fir poles, and decked with birch branches, and all manner of flowers, both of the field and garden, as roses, July flowers, lavender, marigolds, and all manner of strewing herbs and rushes; there were also tents for the kitchen, and for the officers, against tomorrow, with provision laid in of wine, ale, and beer."[23]

Throughout her reign, Elizabeth took care to arrange strewing herbs and rushes when the occasion warranted. She played hostess to her clergy, her gentry, and her foreign visitors. If need be, she borrowed guild halls and enlisted her nobles as surrogate hosts. In 1601, Elizabeth determined to entertain a party of French nobility in Winchester. With two days notice, the people of Southampton produced 140 beds. Local nobility proffered habitations. And the queen commented that "she had done that in Hampshire, that none of her ancestors ever did, neither that any Prince in Christendom could do: that was, she had in her Progresses at her subjects' houses, entertained a Royal Ambassador, and had royally entertained him."[24] When the Archduke of Austria's ambassador Ludovic Verreyken arrived in England, Sir Walter Ralegh was pressed into service as a surrogate host. Chamberlain describes how Ralegh "attends the ambassador much by the Quenes appointment, and carries him up and downe to see sights and rarities hereabout. . . . This day he is feasted at the Lord Treasurers, and to morrow at the Lord Chamberlaines."[25] In sum, the vital construction of feminine rule (so much discussed by recent commentators) always included attention to matters of hospitality.

Both Elizabeth and James made subtle alterations in their royal households in order to carry out hospitable practices and political aims. Elizabeth, for example, altered household custom in order to make the *bouche of court* a breakfast affair whose invitation meant beef with the queen and revealed significant gradations of honor, rank, and royal favor. In this fashion, Elizabeth could shape the way courtiers approached her for gifts. Had they not already entered into the ritual logic (clarified by anthropological studies) which holds that "the spirit of a gift is kept alive by its constant donation"?[26] To expect favor in this context means taking responsibility for a double donation. The life of power is coextensive with habit of donation. For his part, James created the office of master of the ceremonies to oversee hospitality for visiting ambassadors.[27] Always priding himself on his ability to make peace in the world, James made certain that diplomatic relations would not lose the shaping force of hospitality's proper deployment.

Royal proclamations from Elizabeth, James, and Charles attempt to enforce hospitality. Elizabeth commands:

> Her majesty is particularly informed of some intentions of sundry persons, of ability to keep hospitality in their countries, to leave their said hospitalities, and to come to the city of London and other cities and towns corporate, thereby leaving the relief of their poor neighbours, as well for food, as for good rule, and with covetous minds to live in London, and about the city privately, and also in other towns corporate, without charge or company. For withstanding whereof her majesty chargeth all manner of persons, that shall have any such intention during the time of this dearth, not to break up their households nor to come to the said city or other towns corporate; and all others that have of late time broken up their households to return to their houses again without delay.[28]

The queen makes hospitality central to her country's welfare. Like her less powerful contemporaries, Elizabeth recites in proclamation the age's belief that hospitality embraces the whole notion of communal responsibility to the poor. Simultaneously, this endorsement serves other ends. Since the court seemed to hold out greater prospects for advancement, Elizabeth practiced a careful policy of containment, restricting the marriages of nobility and overseeing their alliances. By holding this ancient householding practice up to her aristocracy, by reiterating the link between noble status and the practice of hospitality, the queen encouraged the dispersal of England's powerful householders; their compliance would confirm their true aristocracy. The queen, in a sense, confined the nobility in their imaginations of themselves. In 1600, Sir Thomas Egerton affirmed this position in a speech to Star Chamber. John Chamberlain reported to Dudley Carleton that the lord keeper had charged the justices of the peace to look "to gentlemen that leave hospitalitie and housekeping and hide themselves in Cities and Borough-townes."[29]

King James elaborated on his predecessor's demands with special vigor. In 1603, the new monarch complained of the "great numbers of the principall Gentlemen" who had left their country households so that "both th'execution of things incident to their charge is omitted, and Hospitalities exceedingly decayed."[30] By 1615, the royal manner became more urgent. James admonished his subjects "to live in the steps and examples of their worthy Ancestours, by keeping and entertaining Hospitalitie, and charitable relieving of the poore according to their estate and meanes, not thinking themselves borne for themselves, and their families alone, but for the publique good and comfort of their Countrey."[31] Failure to live up to this canonical statement of hospitable practice would mean "Our indignation and displeasure" and the "uttermost perils."[32] In 1616, James addressed the Star Chamber, explaining that "as every fish lives in his own place, some in the fresh, some in the salt, some in the mud: so let everyone live in his own place, some at Court, some in the Citie, some in the Countrey."[33] The nobility would simply have to return to the country and maintain the proper hospitality.

In proclamations of 1626, 1627, 1630, and 1632, King Charles faithfully echoed the terms of his father's proclamations,[34] but Charles never matched James's special commitment to the practice of hospitality and to its strategic utility. The maneuverings of the early 1620s suggest the contours of James's policy. In 1620, Chamberlain communicated to Carleton that "divers gentlemen are called in question there, for lying here in town and not keeping houses in Christmas, as they were enjoined by a certain proclamation two or three years since."[35] As Christmas approached in 1622, James grew more distressed that in a time of scarcity and celebration hospitality might be neglected. His resulting policy meant the transplantation of as many as 7,000 families.[36] Meanwhile, the Venetian ambassador saw through the language of open hearths, explaining that James was simply using hospitality as an excuse to depopulate a London full of people anxious to discuss and criticize the Spanish marriage proposal.[37] Hospitable practice among the powerful is always laced with strategies and tactics—real and imagined.

Membership in England's elites meant vigorously cultivating such strategic possibilities, a fact illustrated most dramatically by the career of Cardinal Wolsey. England has rarely known a more powerful person with a more lowly beginning. When Henry VIII was preparing for war with France in 1513, the commoner Wolsey impressed the monarch with an amazing capacity for planning. In a sense, Wolsey undertook the provisioning of Henry's troops as a massive act of hospitality, ordering the slaughter of 25,000 oxen and making careful arrangements for the transportation of beer. As Charles W. Ferguson points out, Wolsey's plans were guided by the "hankerings" of English soldiers, the need to entertain them properly if the war effort would have any possibility of success. The importance of the war aside, Wolsey succeeded in winning Henry's respect: "Every single phase of his task led sooner or later to a firmament thick with detail that came like stars out of the darkness."[38] Wolsey could cater. His common origins vanished among so many stars. His management of a fantastic hospitality demonstrated political savvy and clearly shaped the royal perspective.

Ever aware of his low-born origins, Wolsey seems to have defined his career through the lavish imitation of aristocratic hospitality. Stephen Greenblatt's *Renaissance Self-Fashioning* opens with an account, through the eyes of More, of one of Cardinal Wolsey's hospitalities. As Greenblatt explains, Wolsey's hospitality carefully orchestrated the shaping of the cardinal's own powerful position. "The point," Greenblatt argues, "is not that anyone is deceived by the charade, but that everyone is forced either to participate in it or to watch it silently."[39] In part because of the rigorous code of respect imposed upon the guests, hospitality particularly suits such a strategic program. But I think Wolsey's hospitable successes, beginning with his amazing preparations in response to the English soldiers' hankerings, reveal a more profound dimension of the English manipulation of ideology. For generations, the essence of English authority seemed to lie in the *consent of the governed*. As Sharpe explains, "In the sixteenth century, the co-operation of a leading magnate with central government was of vital importance and could go far towards securing the support of a region in which he possessed his estates and of the clients who followed him."[40] To govern in the language of hospitality, as Wolsey did, was to make use of this cherished custom. Hospitality could be put to decidedly English uses because the need to win consent was so decidedly English.[41]

No one understood this fact better than William Cecil, Lord Burghley and treasurer under Elizabeth. Like Wolsey, Cecil came to power as the result of careful fashioning; he retained power for the same reason. As Sanford and Townsend point out in *The Great Governing Families of England*, "The Cecils have a great ancestor [William], but no pedigree."[42] How ironic that Cecil's enemies tried to slander him by saying that his grandfather had "kept the best inn in Stamford,"[43] for like Wolsey, Cecil supplied elements of a missing pedigree with genteel hosting. As he kept his hands on every matter of government, Cecil maintained a constant correspondence with Kemp, his household steward.

For Cecil and for his astute son Robert, who improved his own position under James, political practice always meshed with household matters. When Henry was on progress into Dorsetshire in 1552, enjoying the hospitality of the countryside, Cecil used the change of household; he "was in the way of observing that certain persons, having the ear of the King, and being bent on the further plunder of Church property, were busy to instill into the King's mind that the Bishops were too rich."[44] Cecil quietly prepared Cranmer for the challenge. The counsellor was developing a hospitable practice that, by 1561, meant choreographing the entertainment of the Privy Council, gentry, and queen: "Here her [Elizabeth's] Council waited on her, with many Lords and Knights, and Ladies, and great cheer made till midnight; and then her Grace rode back to the Charterhouse, where she lay that night."[45]

It is not surprising then that no house beckoned to the sovereign imaginations of Elizabeth and James more than the Burghleys' Theobalds. Understanding the lord treasurer's influence over Elizabeth means understanding her fascination with being a guest—especially at Theobalds. With her first visit, Burghley commenced a program of building. Theobalds, Burghley explained, "was begun by me with a mean measure; but increased by occasion of her Majesty's often coming: whom to please, I never would omit to strain myself to more charges than building it. And yet not without some especial direction of her Majesty."[46] As the monarch entered the grand household, she passed through a series of courtyards which represented the hierarchical ordering of her kingdom; the progress flattered the royal guest with the "height" of the most distant rooms. In this setting, Cecil's entertainment gave a shape to the authority of every guest: one slept in a location encoded with one's authority.[47]

Over the years, Theobalds emerged as a concrete expression of Elizabethan rule through hospitality. Peck's *Desiderata Curiosa* eulogizes the edifice, its owner, and the royal guest

> there at his Lordship's charge sometimes three weeks or a month, or six weeks together. Sometimes she had strangers or ambassadors come to her thither, where she has been seen in as great royalty, and served as bountifully and magnificently as at any other time or place, all at his Lordship's charge, with rich shows, pleasant devices, and all manner of sports that could be devised, to the great delight of her Majesty and her whole train, with great thanks from all who partook of it, and as great commendations from all that heard of it abroad. His Lordship's extraordinary charge in entertaining of the Queen was greater to him than to any of her subjects. But his love to his Sovereign, and joy to entertain her and her train, was so great, that he thought no trouble, care, or cost, too much, but all too little, so it were bountifully performed to her Majesty's recreation, and the contentment of her Train.[48]

Theobalds offered everything Elizabeth could desire from the practice of hospitality, and this long passage does much to explain why. As Cecil's guest she could indulge in royal whim, staying for three weeks or six, hunting when it suited, seeking drama when her tastes changed. What makes this passage particularly revealing is the writer's constant return to *the reception of hospitable practices*. The hospitality of Theobalds succeeds because Cecil's entertainment finds "great thanks" and "great commendations." Above all, it contents not simply Elizabeth but the whole train. As rival courtiers plotted around him, Cecil had to understand the importance of contenting as many as possible.

In the confines of Theobalds, this powerful host had a significant amount of royal time at his disposal. He could mount long-term strategies, as he did with respect to the queen's consideration of the Duke d'Alençon as a candidate for marriage. In the final years of the 1560s, he could keep the plotting Duke of Norfolk and Earl of Arundell at bay by keeping Elizabeth in his own house where timing (and hence tactics) were everything.[49] Occasionally, we get a glimpse of the lord's tactical bite, as in this undated journal entry for June 1566: "Fulsharst, a Foole, was suborned to speak slanderously of me at Greenwich to the Queen's Majesty; for which he was committed to Bridewell."[50] More often than not, Cecil's journal records hospitable practice as simply another administrative task: "The Queen's Majesty at my house." But Elizabeth thought the house and its manners no ordinary retreat; she visited on twelve separate occasions, remaining for weeks, as her fancy pleased.

After his own fashion, James set his heart upon the Cecils' household. Robert Cecil, like his father, played host and so consolidated his power under the Scottish king, who eventually received the house as a "present" from Cecil. The Cecils may have been the most powerful hosts to entertain Elizabeth, but they competed with no small company of imitators. Indeed, how one exercised hospitality dictated much of one's "courtly" success. Consequently, Elizabeth's court could regularly seek the hospitality of the great Elizabethan householders. Frequently, the queen and her retinue descended on a series of frightened hosts, exposing the household staff to much discomfort and the grounds to near destruction. The host, nevertheless, had an opportunity to follow in Wolsey's footsteps. Theatrical performances blended smoothly with household decorums and the very real political exigencies of royal favor. This reality was not lost on the age's premier critic of architectural fashion, Sir Henry Wotton, who considered "every man's proper mansion" to be "the *theater* of his hospitality."[51] In the hands of skilled courtiers, the fusion of householding and entertainment in hospitality could be obligatory, often consummate.

In the midst of those elites contending for the monarch's favor with banquet tables and spectacles, the Anglican clergy occupied a constantly contested position. Indeed, during Henry's progress alluded to earlier, the principal "slanders" Cecil reported to Cranmer were that "the Bishops were too rich; that they neglected the hospitality." Such attacks came regularly, throughout the early modern period. Bishops were painted first as too greedy and then as too worldly and generous.[52] Cecil himself complained that "the bishops and clergy that shuld by ther teachyng and devotion and speciallye by hospitallyte and releyvng of the poore men wyn creditt amyngst the people, ar rather despised than reverenced and beloved."[53]

The prelates themselves certainly took some care to maintain their own theater of hospitality. In his biography of Archbishop Whitgift, George Paule revelled in the great man's ecclesiastical hospitalities.[54] During the reign of Elizabeth, Archbishop Parker made lesser hospitalities pale. When he entertained the queen at Lambeth in the spring of 1573, Parker "made a great dinner; at his own table sat down nine Earls and seven Barons; at the other table, the Comptroller of the Queen's Household, her Secretary, and many other Knights and Esquires; besides the usual table for the great Officers of State."[55] In turning to Parker for the year 1573, Strype provocatively locates the prelate's authority in "two great capacities: *viz.* To be the Queen's Host, and his Church's Visitor." Parker embodies both host and guest. Strype goes on to suggest that during this summer "the Archbishop's chief care was to give an Entertainment to her Majesty at his house, when she would come to Canterbury, that might answer his own figure, and obtain a gracious acceptation from her."[56] Good hospitality for a prelate of Parker's stature can be defined as an appropriate echoing of the host's figure and a gracious reception of the entertainment.

Of course, few householders could command the £1,000 to £2,000 Burghley spent every time the queen came to enjoy his "theater." No one *but* Parker could offer Lambeth. One could perhaps aspire, like the Earl of Arundell, to the position of a royal "housekeeper." When the progressing Elizabeth arrived at Nonsuch on 5 August 1559, the earl played host: "There the Queen had great entertainment with banquets, especially on Sunday night, made by the said Earl; together with a mask; and the warlike sounds of drums, and flutes, and all kinds of music, till midnight."[57]

The patronage of acting companies offered another alternative to the would-be host. Leo Salingar has argued that the "indirect provision of plays at court" by the great lords of Elizabeth's household "was a form of tribute to their sovereign, an extension of the principle of entertaining her when on progress, much cheaper no doubt but possibly for that reason, very competitive."[58] In this way, the host could seek out his most powerful guest in the royal household at Christmas and on other important occasions. The role of host and the capacity to shape were more than flexible, being always subject to substitution.

Whatever the tack, no aristocratic host could afford to ignore the practice of hospitality. Tempted as scholars have been to study the careers of the age's most glittering figures, men such as Cecil and Wolsey, evidence continues to mount that persons occupying positions throughout the strata of government exercised real impact on the shapes of authority.[59] By studying the ways in which these lesser hosts and guests attempt to gain influence, we begin to capture the full, tremulous practice of government. From such a position of dependence, Edward Panton counselled that the elite of one level must "visit, honour and follow them [more powerful elite], taking part in their Interests, esteeming them as your Master."[60] Access is everything; therefore, no one seeking power could afford to *appear* parsimonious with his or her hospitality.

With this fact in mind, one contemporary explained to a sparing Francis Willoughby, "Wherefore I think it best for you not to defray Her Majesty, but rather that you should give her some good present of beefs muttons, and to keep a good table yourself in some place, if you have any convenient room for it, two mess of meat. But do herein as you shall think best, but you had need to consider how your provision of drink, etc. may hold out."[61] An ominous quality pervades such communications. The countryside knows the queen is coming, can do nothing to stop her, must not defray her. Any accurate discussion of hospitable practice must remark this difficult side of hosting with its especially fraught sense of the inexorable.

That authority and power in the Renaissance obtained in some curious fashion through hosting, both the giving and receiving of entertainment, was hardly the privileged information of England's highest elites. Whether powerful merchant, diligent baker, or mere husbandman, one's claim to holding a position in the community, perhaps even to *being English,* could be said to rest in part on the practice of hospitality.

In the case of wealthy gentlemen, we may better understand their position through the pamphlets they read for advice and the records of particular hospitable occasions, which described the music and the meal. For example, Nicholas Yonge's *Musica Transalpina* (1588) is addressed to "Gentlemen and Merchants" who, feeling the obligation to host, will pay for instruction in the making of hospitable madrigals.[62] What these men lacked in social standing, they could attempt to mend with accomplishments, an elegant lute song after cakes or a fine discussion of counterpoint's rules. And evidence suggests that men who were willing to depend on acquired skills and venture money were not unwilling to venture hospitable resources.

In January of 1571, the famous merchant Sir Thomas Gresham hosted Elizabeth. Two years later, Gresham entertained Elizabeth at Mayfield during one of the queen's progresses. On 16 July 1607, the Merchant Taylors welcomed James, Prince Henry, and other nobility to their hall, "where they were royally and joyfully feasted and entertained."[63] In 1622, the Virginia Company hosted its own gathering at the Merchant Taylors' Hall.[64] In 1623, Ralph Freeman, a future lord mayor, hosted Prince Charles and Buckingham at the same hall because his house was too small to accommodate his designs.[65] Guilds, such as the bricklayers and the bakers in York, exchanged formal hospitalities, offering dinner and minstrels throughout the period.[66] Elizabeth and James were each hosted on many occasions by the Inns of Court and by the universities.

Meanwhile among the lower orders, a whole panoply of hospitable practice was taking place, patterns of welcome and feasting that rarely found their way into records. This is not to say, however, that some golden, plebeian hospitality has escaped recording; indeed, the fragmentary evidence of these other hospitalities suggests as much ambivalence over proper action as that experienced by the elites.[67] What can be said, matter of factly, is that a powerful sense of obligation to practice hospitality coupled with an always-ambivalent will to make the practice succeed were present at every level of the culture.

Somewhere between the hosting of nobility and the hospitalities offered by England's communities, a skein of woman's hospitable practice existed. In any system of prestation, woman is viewed as a nexus of exchange.[68] In terminology and responsibility, this position in early modern England reflects the dominant male version, yet for the contemporary scholar, the triumphs and gambits and nurture of women remain just out of reach, having never been subject to the patriarchal order's passion for recording their own entertainments. We know enough of women's hospitalities, nevertheless, to remark their appropriation and manipulation in literary genres controlled by men. Queen Elizabeth hosted and her female subjects followed suit. Now and then we sight a lavish hospitality, as when in 1614 Queen Anne hosted the wedding of Lord Roxburgh and Jane Drummon at Somerset House. For the most part, we must settle for glimpses into the everyday—some glittering, some ordinary.

The diaries of Lady Anne Clifford, daughter of the gallant courtier George Clifford, for example, offer splendid portraits of hospitable concourse at the beginning of James's reign: "From Mr Dutton's we went to Barton, one Mr Dormer's, where Mrs Humphrie, her Mother & she entertained us with great kindness."[69] At times, the accounts foreshadow the comic touch of Jane Austen: "While we lay at Barton I kept so ill a Diet with Mrs Carey & Mrs Kinson on eating Fruit so that I shortly fell into the same sickness" (p. 26). On other occasions, we are treated to royal entertainment: "Went by Barge to Greenwich & waited on the King and Queen [James and Anne] to Chapel & dined at my Lady Bedford's where I met Lady Hume, my old acquaintance. After dinner we went up to the Gallery where the Queen used me exceeding well" (p. 38).

Mostly, the diaries show an emerging modernity (especially in scale) in hospitable practice, as in the following entry from the winter of 1616: "Upon the 14th, my Lord supp'd at the Globe—upon the 15th my Lord & I went to see the young Lady Arundel, & in the afternoon my Lady Willoughby came to see me. My Lady Gray brought my Lady Carr to play at Glecko with me, when I lost £15 to them; they two & my Lady Grantham & Sir Geo. Manners supping with me" (p. 29). Such entries record a comfortable pattern of exchange and cooperation. We learn, for example, that "one day the Queen went from Basingstoke and dined at Sir Hy. Wallop's where my Lady, my Aunt and I had lain 2 or 3 nights before and did help to entertain her" (p. 26).

Above all, what emerges out of Lady Anne Clifford's diaries is this sense of the writer's secure place in a web of cooperative entertainments, a mood confirmed by the more sparing Lady Hoby in her diary of the same period. The North Riding of Yorkshire, it seems, offered the same patterned contentment: "After praier I talked with Mr Smith and/dimed: afterward I was visited by my Socine Sthnope, and, when he was gone, I went to priuat praier and then to suppoer wth my lord of limbrick who Came to vs."[70] On the eighth day of the same month, after prayer, we find her off "to my lord bourleys, beinge invited thether." And we discover this hostess practicing the same kind of extended hospitality prescribed for the male householders of the day by the pamphlet texts: "After, I praied, and so I dined and bestowed the after none in goinge about and takinge order for the entertaining strangers" (p. 141). Women of rank clearly knew hospitable practice well; it formed a vital part of their lives.

It could also, as in the case of male hosts, be a mode of contestation. Lady Anne recalls such a scene from amid the tableaux of Jacobean progresses:

> From thence the Court removed & were banqueted with great Royalty by my Father at Grafton where the King & Queen were entertained with Speeches and delicate presents at which time my Lord & the Alexanders did run a Course at the field where he hurt Henry Alexander very dangerously. Where the Court lay ths night I am uncertain. At ths time of the King's being at Grafton my Mother was there, but not held as Mistress of the house by reason of the Difference between my Lord & her which was grown to a great height. (p. 24)

Lady Anne's depiction of this intersection of marital dispute and political negotiation is priceless. The chance to host this king and queen together had to be the opportunity of a lifetime; but partridge and trencher have become awkward pawns in a contest for authority in the household, a joust the woman seems to have lost in the diary's passively voiced summary.

With more tactical success, Lady Hatton, wife of Sir Edward Coke, seems to have managed a genuine coup with her hosting. On 8 November 1617, she hosted King James and others at a splendid dinner. Following the conventions of the day, the gates would have been closed and bells rung; but against the custom of the day, this hostess excluded her husband from participation.[71] In this way, woman's hospitality managed to combine the calm maintenance of communal rhythms with a tactical propensity for gendered tilts. Aware of this phenomenon, the critic of representations in early modern England can only marvel at the wealth of untold stories—but more of this in the coming pages.

In forming the lists of hospitality's best champions, no scholar can neglect the hopeful yet burdened communities of the age.

When royalty visited towns such as Norwich, Bristol, and Wells, the cities offered welcome, gifts, lodging, supper, and theater. Renaissance towns in England jostled with the forms and resources of the country's noble hosts. It is fascinating to note that in its entertainment of the queen in 1574 Bristol spent approximately the same amount Burghley spent on a typical royal visit to Theobalds.[72] No less than courtiers, these communities felt the economic burden of entertaining royalty, as the Norwich *Assembly Minute Books* for 1578 show. The city fathers found the monarch's impending visit cause for raising "great som*m*es of mony," even if the money had to be borrowed. Less than a year later, we find the city selling off "somoche of the apparrell & other stuff & thin*ge*s that were prepared for shewes ageynst the Quenes maiestes com*m*ying."[73]

Like courtiers, towns took pride in their hosting, a characteristic attested to by Edward VI, who praised Southampton for being "handsome, and for the bignesse of it as faire houses as be at London. The Citizens made great cheer, and many of them kept costly tables."[74] In the same vein, Norwich in 1578 offered the queen a steady diet of supper and spectacle that inspired pamphlet praise for the city.[75] Only by recognizing the activity of these amorphous political entities and their asymmetrical competition with the glittering personalities of the period can we accurately gauge patterns of dominance and authority during the period. Only in the context of such expenditures can we value the distinctive show of liberality extended by a town like Harwich, whose entertainment of Elizabeth in 1561 included lodging in a house on the town's High Street. At the moment of her "dismission," Elizabeth asked the townspeople what they wanted from her in return for her entertainment. When the magistrates simply wished her a good journey, Elizabeth responded, "A pretty Town, and wants nothing."[76] A courtier like Cecil would have valued the town's expression of largess, its successful formation of giving and receiving, of wanting but not needing, under the guise of "courteous dismission."

In addition to economic burden, community records typically show special ordinances enforcing the repair of houses, painting, and the sanding of streets. In 1561, Ipswich charged that "all the inhabitants of the towne shall be assessed to the cost and charges for the entertainment of the Queen."[77] In 1571, Saffron Walden paid for, among other things, a "podd of oysters" and "3 sugar-loves, presented to my L. of Leyester, my L. Burleigh, and Sir Thomas Smyth."[78] In 1608, in preparation for the coming of James, Northampton even moved its sheep market. In 1612, Nottingham dispatched agents to purchase a gift for the royal guest and to inquire in other communities about the proper entertainment for a monarch.[79]

With a similar sense of obligation, communities went about preparing hospitalities for other visiting officials, even for themselves. When, for example, the judges for the Oxford assizes arrived at Banbury, the famous Banbury cakes were served to the authorities. Marking the connection between authority and hospitality in the currency of the day, the corporation accounts record the expenditure of £2 3s. 6d. for cakes.[80] This same spirit governs the yearly payments for food, music, and theater in Norwich in celebration of Perambulation Day. Each year the citizens "beat the bounds" of the city in celebration of their propriety; and each year a record such as the following appears: "Payed to Robert Golthorpp the xxj daye of Iune for the dynner of certeyne Aldermen the Chambleynes Councellers the olde & new ffestmakers & diuerse other that ded ryde the perambulacion with the trumpiter charge & the waytes & the charge of one that ryd before to laye ope the waye."[81] As no other form of evidence does, these records, especially in their clerically uniform structure, demonstrate the community's hospitable linkage of seemingly discrete ideological spheres—food preparation, performance, chorographical authority, and seasonal festivity.

Faced with such a welter of detail, the historian of cultural practices will nonetheless struggle to calculate the efficacy of any single hospitality. But the lack of quantification (in whatever form that could possibly take) hardly diminishes the significance or the remarkable complexity of these heterogeneous attempts at shaping and mystifying Elizabethan and Jacobean rule. Traces of outcomes abound. When Francis Willoughby departed the queen's entertainment at Kenilworth before a proper dismission, he lost an easy opportunity to become a knight.[82] On the other hand, one gathers that, with his brilliant entertainment of the queen at Cowdray in 1591, the Catholic Lord Montague defused some of Elizabeth's suspicions concerning his loyalty. Sir Nicholas Bacon, father of the famous Francis, seems to have reversed the queen's displeasure with successful hospitality in 1577. And Bacon's accomplishment is quite overshadowed by the Earl of Hertford's hosting of Elizabeth at Elvetham in 1591. Hertford, after making (what appeared to Elizabeth as) a subversive marriage to the queen's cousin Katherine Grey, had weathered the monarch's wrath. With a new wife by his side, the host offered a brilliant spectacle that appears to have mollified the queen. If they do not exactly prove the efficacy of hospitality, such tales seem to confirm the attractiveness of the practice to those in need of political agency.

Theories of Representation and Appropriation

Practices do not cease in the practicing. No theoretical insight has been more important to contemporary criticism of Renaissance drama (and to the present study) than this recognition. In speaking of hospitality, then, the scholar can never assume that "courteous dismissal" terminates the tactical and strategic workings of the particular occasion. Renaissance hospitalities were like so many stones falling into stately pools. The guests departed, but successes and failures rippled for some time. Hospitality hardly ceases in the practicing. While these claims do not need new theories to justify their force, they certainly require some explanation of how the critic might move from practices to representations of practices.

Before turning to specific representations of hospitality, I want to consider my dependence on new historicism, cultural materialism, and cultural history for their lucid articulations of the many ways in which this "rippling" occurs. This study owes a great debt to the works of Stephen Greenblatt, who, after the example of Kenneth Burke, has clarified the nagging conundrum of mediation, defined succinctly by Fredric Jameson as "the relationship between the levels or instances, and the possibility of adapting analyses and finding from one level to another. Mediation is the classical dialectical term for the establishment of relationships between, say, the formal analysis of a work of art and its social ground, or between the internal dynamics of the political state and its economic base."[83]

Literature borrows something from distinct cultural forms (institutions, alliances, etc.); but, as we all know, these cultural forms take something back from literature. Dramatic literature may borrow the practices of hospitality, but surely those practices will occur differently thanks to the borrowing. Such exchanges may appear as propaganda, coercion, abuse, subversion—the list goes on and on. The difficulty with these fundamental recognitions arises when we attempt to *interpret* the origins, values, and impacts of specific instances of mediation. Obviously, no one wants to slip into mundane allegory, the tendency to produce what Richard Levin calls "The King James Version" of works written under James I.[84] How to proceed?

Greenblatt's most compelling answer to this question has been to deesentialize the crucial cultural forms, i.e., theater, monarchy, play text. If the boundaries that define these forms are *made,* then they must be permeable, open to negotiation and manipulation. Next, in light of the constructedness of these forms, Greenblatt wants to study the "circulation of social energy" between them. We ought to study

> how collective beliefs and experiences were shaped, moved from one medium to another, concentrated in manageable aesthetic form, offered for consumption. We can examine how the boundaries were marked between cultural practices understood to be art forms and other, contiguous, forms of expression. We can attempt to determine how these specially demarcated zones were invested with the power to confer or excite interest or generate anxiety.[85]

It must be pointed out that this superbly articulated program may come down to the straightforward statement offered by Louis A. Montrose in a now-classic discussion: "This is because 'text' and 'context' define and illuminate each other."[86] Greenblatt's project remains radical, nevertheless, because of his insistence on the deesentialized nature of forms that make up text and context. In Greenblatt's version, every exchange between text and context can alter the very structure of the interacting forms—so much so that the old forms replicate (almost virus-like) in surprising mutations.

If we grasp the boundaries between cultural practices in detail, we may read provocatively for both literary innovation and cultural conflict. Presuming that the critic is convinced of this account of mediation, a large task remains—*how to isolate in some detail the myriad of boundaries that both constitute and separate cultural forms.*

Leeds Barroll has made an eloquent plea for this kind of focus in the work of historicist criticism of Shakespeare.[87] Similarly, outside the field of literary criticism, Sharpe, in his announced "revisionist" return to "sources," signals a useful corrective.[88] My choice of a single group of cultural practices—hospitality—is intended to answer, in part, these demands. My own methodological proposal for studying this dense but limited sampling derives from Bakhtin's notion of *speech genres.* According to this now-famous voice of carnival, the boundaries that separate cultural practices may be viewed as boundaries between a collection of fairly stable types of utterances, or speech genres, that

> include short rejoinders of daily dialogue (and these are extremely varied depending on the subject matter, situation, and participants), everyday narration, writing (in all its various forms), the brief standard military command, the elaborate and detailed order, the fairly variegated repertoire of business documents (for the most part standard), and the diverse world of commentary (in the broad sense of the word: social, political).[89]

Speech genres "contain" the daily practices of every level of a culture.

Bakhtin calls these ubiquitous practices *primary genres,* suggesting that the uniqueness of a given level of cultural organization appears through its adherence to a particular repertoire of utterances. In the reasonably stable habits of welcome and care alive in sixteenth- and seventeenth-century England, hospitality coheres as a group of primary genres we might commonly list with terms such as "seasonal cycles," "table conversation," "cooking," "welcoming," "purveying," "touring," and "inviting." Every nuance available in a specific practice may be traced to the discreteness of a primary speech genre. Likewise, every nuance in the re-presented practice will be marked, highlighted, by the still-discreet genre's inclusion in a literary text. Attention to the appropriation and transformation of speech genres makes it possible to scrutinize social energy with some particularity.

Indeed, according to Bakhtin, literary genres, too, exist as complex collections of speech genres: "During the process of their formation [literary genres], they absorb and digest various primary (simple) genres that have taken form in unmediated speech communion" (p. 62). This is a most radical revision of traditional genre scholarship.[90] For Bakhtin, literary works may be subject to generic grouping, but genres arise out of interaction between otherwise separate cultural domains. Genre is thus a product of accretion, a building up of hundreds of micro-genres that are busy enabling practice in the artist's culture. Consequently, a portion of what materialist criticism calls mediation, Bakhtin isolates as *digestion*. This theory of genre is particularly useful because it explains *how* hospitality and a given theatrical genre might engage each other. Bakhtin certainly envisioned this application when he concluded that "speech genres are the drive belts from the history of society to the history of language" (p. 65). In other words, genre exists as a register of mediation.[91]

The chapters that follow suggest in detail how the representation of the practice of hospitality in dramatic texts is marked by the inclusion of primary genres of welcome, entertainment, and departure that, to borrow Bakhtin's terminology, digest with varying degrees of difficulty depending on their ties to conflicting ideological agendas of the period. And because the boundaries between these represented practices can be isolated, I will aim for "thick descriptions" of what can be gained and lost by a given class interest at particular generic intersections. My contention, to be demonstrated in the following chapters, is that the representation of hospitality both stabilizes and destabilizes literary genres. In certain cases, hospitality renews tired generic conventions. In many other cases, because of its collective engagement, hospitality admits lower orders into the hall of the play, into the circles of the ruling elite, creating powerful challenges (often ignored by scholarship) to the work's generic resolution. Hospitality in drama means admitting outsiders who threaten decorums of sexuality and marriage otherwise preserved by generic customs.

I will not, therefore, offer elaborate models that "explain" whole strata of Elizabethan and Jacobean society through the reading of a single play. My more humble goal is to locate, say, at the intersection of a heterodox nobility and the genre of romantic comedy, successful and failed attempts at appropriation, *moments when a representation of hospitality becomes useful, strategically and tactically, for a narrowly defined class interest which either succeeds or fails at turning (appropriating) that representation for its own ends.*

We are now at no little distance from the first part of this chapter, a rather traditional excavation of hospitable artifacts from Elizabethan and Jacobean England. I have chosen to undertake this particular project because, no matter how much we claim to the contrary, our ability to recover a true hospitality remains, obviously, limited. It thus becomes far more interesting to consider how the ruling powers of the period gained from the assertion of a particular version of hospitality. As Heal notes above, hospitality was appropriated in part to *imitate* the social and political strategies of those in authority. How were such versions produced? Whom did they include and exclude? Did the lower orders merely consume such versions (along with hospitality's meat and drink), or did they shape their own stories of hospitality? Finally, more theoretically, how is the idea of hospitality appropriated by writers working in major as well as minor genres? In such analyses, the final toting of who gains and who loses will always be provisional, awaiting the already forming revision of imminent reappropriations. And although the critic could find fault for such limited explanatory power, I in fact find the whole project more stimulating and rewarding for the way it forces us back, to borrow Sharpe's language, to the unstable world of sources.

Hospitality emphatically did not cease in the practicing. From its interaction with dramatic texts, it left marks as perceptible as the blackened stones of an ancient hearth. In turning to these marks, I pursue a theoretical clarification of the theories of mediation so provocatively set forth by recent historicist criticism. At the same time, I seek provisional but detailed readings of dramatic texts that offer up something of what could be won and lost in the representation and appropriation of Elizabethan and Jacobean practices.

Representations and Appropriations of Hospitality

It goes without saying that dramatic genres were hardly alone in their representation of hospitable practices. Pamphleteers, preachers, poets, and historians, to name a few, all competed for the most convincing appropriation of those primary genres that define hospitality in practice. So it seems essential that, before turning to dramatic texts, we situate those forms in this furious marketplace, an arena whose circulation of social energy allowed whole strategies of authority and resistance to emerge.

Nowhere were images of abuse and prosperity more intricately drawn than in the great flood of pamphlet literature, carefully chronicled by Heal, that complained of the present age's loss of ancient hospitality and attempted to elaborate the proper practice.[92] (The scholar of Renaissance literature would do well to pause over the dates of this publication explosion, 1580–1630, which coincide precisely with the height of literary accomplishment in England.) Drawing sustenance from classical authors such as Martial and Juvenal and from Old and New Testament sources, these publications anatomized contemporary culture in moral, economic, and religious terms.[93] In ways unavailable to theater, pamphleteers claimed for their representations the status of reportage, of a simple presentation of the manifold versions of hospitable practice, its successes and failures.

Complaint always took the form of comparison with the past. In *Grevious Groans for the Poor* (1621), the author claims to recall a time when men "hunted after worship and credit by good housekeeping, and therein spent great part of their revenues: but now commonly, the greater part of their livings is too little to maintain us and our children in the pomp of pride: and yet all is well if we may maintain that, though no hospitality be maintained therewithal."[94] Revenue no longer supports housekeeping; even when it could, "all is well" when pomp comes first and hospitality is forgotten. The essence of noble identity was supposed to hinge on housekeeping, that being the most conspicuous sign of a nobleman's worth. If hospitality was declining, then so was the state of England's gentry.

Such analyses were aimed at every strata of English society. Alongside the pleas for proper noble householding, the historian of Renaissance pamphleteering will find texts like *The Brewer's Plea: Or a Vindication of Strong-Beer and Ale*, an anonymous pamphlet which contends that only England's brewers endure as a source of hospitality for strangers and beggars.[95] No friend of the alehouse, Caleb Dalechamp argued that the chief responsibility of

bishops was hospitality, an obligation explored in detail by Heal.[96]
From yet another vantage point, the Reverend Mr. Newbury could
preach to the yeomen of Kent that "it has always been that at a
yeoman's table you might have as good entertainment as at the
best Gentlemans, not for variety of messes, but for solid sufficiency
and hearty welcome."[97] *The movement from hospitable practice to the
representation of hospitality nearly always meant a competition over the
subject position of host and how the proper casting of host determined
communal order.* This representational pattern will prove crucial for
understanding the appropriation of hospitality in the age's drama;
for when a playwright introduces a host, questions of societal order and survival are automatically invoked.

Representations of hospitality enable nothing less than a total
mystification of the culture's patterns of dominance, thereby accomplishing what Raymond Geuss in his introduction to Habermas and the Frankfurt school calls the manipulation of "epistemic
properties" in order to produce false consciousness.[98] In particular,
hospitality encourages a benign description of the world, even as
it supports strategies of exploitation. For all its appropriations in
the name of Christian care, hospitality actually legitimates "the unequal allocation of wealth that makes magnanimity a virtue."[99] As
Raymond Williams pointed out some time ago, Ben Jonson's "To
Penshurst" may be the most enduring nondramatic version of this
cultural production. In the country-house poem, Jonson reproduced the Sidney home

> whose liberal boord doth flow
> With all, that hospitalitie doth know!
> Where comes no guest but is allow'd to eate,
> Without his feare, and of thy lords owne meate:
> Where the same beere, and bread, and selfe-same wine,
> That is his Lordships shall be also mine.
> And I not faine to sit (as some this day
> At great mens tables) and yet dine away.[100]

In fact, hospitable practice knows more than its representations
show. It knows that the lordship's bountiful charity depends on
others having less, on others laboring to make possible the feasting. It knows that the relationships the genre claims as "natural"

are constructions of a ruling order intent on preserving "great men's tables."

At the same time, one of the things the pamphlet literature teaches the reader of Renaissance drama is how closely connected were ideas of hospitality and cultural indictment. If the practice of hospitality occasioned vast opportunities for ideological shaping, then the representation of hospitality seems to have ensured a mood of complaint toward what was being shaped. In *A Compendious or Brief Examination of Certain Ordinary Complaints*, the Doctor describes the householder of moderate means: "In times past and within & the memory of a man, he hath been accounted a rich and wealthy man and well able to keep house among his neighbours . . . but in these our days the man of that estimation, is so far in the common opinion from a good housekeeper, or a man of wealth, that he is reputed the next neighbour to a beggar."[101]

Looking critically at hospitality meant examining the instability of traditionally fixed roles. In this instance, the traditional historian's question of whether householders were actually becoming beggars in great numbers pales beside a far more intriguing question: to what extent did the pamphleteer's critical use of hospitality help to support and undermine the existing social structure? In what ways did the movement from practice to representation habitually lead to indictment of existing social hierarchies? My contention concerning the age's dramatic genres is that the representation of hosts and guests always implies subtexts of complaint and indictment, impulses that frequently disturb generic closure.

Of course, the movement into representation is not by definition "counter." In fact, when pamphlet texts represent the lower orders' participation in hospitality, whole new strategies of ideological shaping come into play. In representing hospitality, writers could codify a "screening of the poor." At first glance, dozens of pamphlet texts, largely inspired by biblical injunctions such as Hebrews 13:2, seem to demand care for all comers. In his *Five Hundred Points of Good Husbandry*, Thomas Tusser emphasizes hospitality as a version of charity:

> Of all other doings housekeeping is chief,
> for daily it helpeth the poor with relief.[102]

Yet behind Tusser's simple agenda lurks a careful sorting of the deserving and undeserving poor, of the known poor and the unknown poor, of the "lozells" and the needy.[103] More than one writer acknowledged the difficulty of determining the worth of strangers, an admission that ought to warn the contemporary scholar about the "empirical" nature of this sorting.

In reality, the ancient practices of the hearth were being appropriated in various discourses to construct categories that reinforced the evolving schemes for public care of the poor and the changing needs of an evolving economy. Household responsibility could be lessened, and the poor better ordered. Thomas Harman aims at nothing else in *A Caveat for Common Cursitors* (1566), complaining to Elizabeth, Countess of Shrewsbury, that beggars succeed through feigning "to the utter deluding of the good givers, deceiving and impoverishing of all such poor householders"[104] Harman claims to speak from personal experience: "And for that I, most honourable lady, being placed as a poor gentleman, have kept house these twenty years, whereunto poverty daily hath and doth repair, not without some relief, as my poor calling and ability may and doth extend, I have of late years gathered a great suspicion that all should not be well, and, as the proverb saith: 'Something lurk and lay hid that did not plainly appear'" (pp. 81–82). If householders could only begin to see that which "lay hid," Harman contends, "then shall it encourage a great number of gentlemen and others, seeing this security, to set up houses and keep hospitality in the country, to the comfort of their neighbours, relief of the poor, and to the amendment of the commonwealth" (p. 83).

In these discourses, English society has begun to create an other, a plebeian pool with a tendency for feigning and lurking, capable of taking over a menial role in the culture's nascent industrialization. Simultaneously, an institution of surveillance and measurement evolves that claims empirical truth in order to take away gradually the individual voices of the lower classes by quantifying them in controllable masses as the "indigent" or "labor" or, to borrow Harman's phrase, a "rowsey, ragged rabblement" (p. 81). Throughout this study, I want to attend moments in plays and criticism when the shape of the lower orders is formed in terms of hospitable ideals.

What made these texts particularly resonant to the early
modern mind was the uniform use of cherished pictures of open
hearths, of great feasts for nobility and beggars alike. In other
words, these texts thrived on primary genres drawn from the daily
practice of English hospitality. Donald Lupton's *London and the
Country Carbonadoed and Quartered* (1632) suggests this strategy:

> He [hospitality] always kept his greatness by his
> charity: he loved three things, an open cellar, a full
> hall, and a sweating cook: he always provided three
> dinners, one for himself, another for his servants, the
> third for the poor: any one may know where he kept
> house, either by the chimney's smoke, by the freedom
> at gate, by want of whirligig jacks in the kitchen, by
> the fire in the hall, or by the full furnished tables.[105]

In a manner consistent with the age's imagining, Lupton incarnates hospitality as a congenial and all-encompassing relation
between every order of England's society. Chimneys, fires, halls,
and tables make up a repertory of emblems used to recollect this
golden age. Primary genres animate the passage, as indicated by
"furnished tables," "at the gate," and "an open cellar." Even the
syntax of the passage becomes mimetic as the author serves practice after practice to his reader. In sum, hospitable practices have
been digested into a story of an old man's love.

In his *Survey of London*, John Stow lent to such mythic tales
the air of historical accuracy: "I myself, in that declining time of
charity, have oft seen at the Lord *Cromwell's* gate in London, more
than two hundred persons served twice every day with bread,
meat and drink sufficient, for he observed that ancient and
charitable custom as all prelates, noble men, or men of honour
and worship his predecessors had done before him."[106] Stow goes
on to cite (or perhaps *construct*) a genealogy of hospitable practice
that includes the Venerable Bede; Ethelwald, Bishop of Winchester in the tenth century; Walter de Suffilde, Bishop of Norwich in
the thirteenth century; Robert Winchelsey, Archbishop of Canterbury at the same time; Henry II; Henry III; and so on. From Stow's
account one gathers that hospitable practices practically define
temporal authority and its successes and failures.

At the same time, hospitality defined life in London. In "Honour of Citizens and Worthiness of Men," Stow offers a litany of London citizens who have lived hospitable lives. The writer can recall the hospitality of the priors of Christ Church in Aldgate ward: "I myself have seen in my childhood: at which time the Prior kept a most bountifull house of meat and drink, both for rich and poor, as well within the house, as at the gates, to all comers according to their estates" (1:141). No less fantastic in its descriptions than the pamphlet literature, the *Survey* elaborates this vision by telling of how Ethelwald "sold away all the sacred vessels of his Church, for to relieve the almost starved people" (1:89).

Whereas Lupton and his familiars were content to emplot hospitality, Stow adds historical heroes to his narratives. In a passage that deserves quoting at length because of its lively prose and because it counters the age's low opinion of London hospitality, Stow continues:

> In so much that as any man might come into their church to prayer, so might they enter the hall at meal times and fill their bellies, and at all times of the day come to the buttery and cellar and have bread and drink, or to the kitchen in the forenoon and require of the cook a piece of beef, which should be given him roast or sod on his knife or dagger's point, and so to bear it abroad, whither he would for himself and his friends. The liberality of this house, as I have heard and partly seen, is rather to be wondered at than reviled of them that have not seen the like. (1:141n)

This wonderful image of beggars demanding their choice of beef to be carried away on dagger point is surely worthy of old Hospitality himself. Like Harman, the author cultivates historical verisimilitude: *I myself have seen.* In this way, hospitality exists in the *Survey* as a tradition of exchange stretching from the life of the author back to the beginnings of English civilization. Like most pamphlet writers, however, Stow notes evidence of decline.

To Puritan writers, ideas of a diminishing age were too tempting to avoid. If Elizabeth and her nobility could attempt an ideological shaping through their practice of hospitality, the Puritans could surely accomplish something in the same vein. Richard

Greaves has noted how quickly this marginalized group appropriated hospitable practices, infusing them "with a special religious mission, akin to the exhortations they were supposed to give recipients of alms. Hospitality required not only a liberal and cheerful bestowal of food and clothing but also edification, exhortation, church attendance, and (on Sundays) sabbath observance."[107] One pamphlet writer described the aim with a clear simile: "That every householder should be the same in his own house, as the preacher is in the pulpit, or in God's house."[108] Lest we dismiss such strategies as antiquated fancies of a single sect, it is important to note, as Paul Hollander has done, the same uses of hospitality by Cuba and Nicaragua in the twentieth century.[109] While the success of such ventures remains tenuous, we may nonetheless remark the ways that such texts represent guests being inserted *willingly or not* into positions of indoctrination.

In a sense the very successes of these representations have ensured their neglect by historically minded scholarship. Even though the practices writers like Stow and Lupton claim to "record" have in fact been meticulously shaped in the re-presenting, scholars have taken these writers at their word. Analysis comes down to a debate over whether or not the authors got their historical perceptions right. William A. McClung points out the ancient echoes of these complaints and their ideas of a golden world, concluding that "the pamphlet literature of complaint in his [Ben Jonson's] time gives a distorted view of the changes in country life."[110] Noting the existence of a powerful "literary stereotype," Heal concludes: "From the troubadour literature of twelfth-century Provence to the writings of Samuel Johnson good housekeeping has always been believed to be in decline and the golden age of the good host has always just disappeared."[111] As a basis for her conclusions, Heal suggests that

> family biographies, for example, often single out only one or two generations of men who were good hosts among the many ancestors that are the subjects of their concern. Moreover, in these biographies there is no necessary sense of development away from generous entertainment during the course of the sixteenth century: hospitality often appears as a virtue prompted by personal taste and perhaps some desire to emulate the

> leaders of society, fed by resources that were all too
> easily dissipated by its lavish exercise. (p. 91)

I think that this kind of recognition is both essential and incomplete: essential because it reigns in the seductive capacities of Renaissance rhetoric, incomplete because it does not consider the affective force of representational strategies. In other words, the discursive and ontological status of Stow's text differs little from the many texts by "literary figures" that were simultaneously representing hospitable practices alongside the age's dramatic texts.

Although I have limited myself to a consideration of certain theatrical genres, these other genres must be remarked. Writers of significance—Nashe, Greene, Dekker, Sidney, James I, to name a few—elaborated their own competing versions of hospitality. The seventeenth century spawned the country-house poem, a genre devoted, in part, to eulogizing ancient hospitable practices. King James himself turned to poetry in order to reshape his subjects' householding practice.[112] For their part, the Stuarts loved the masque. The intense interest in the form since Stephen Orgel's work with Jonson's masques makes the area rich for inquiry. Jonson himself toyed with the language of social custom in *Pleasure Reconciled to Virtue* (1618). Hercules meditates on the earth's sheltering of monsters:

> Is earth so fruitful of her own dishonor?
> Or 'cause his vice was inhumanity,
> Hopes she by vicious hospitality
> To work an expiation first?[113]

Suddenly, in this most spectacular of genres, the courtly audience must consider the timely possibility that hospitality is either a means of expiation or a breeder of its own subversion. Even heroes cannot be certain. What pamphleteers debated, Hercules ponders. Somewhere in the shadows of mediation hovers the ongoing practice of hospitality; the Jacobean court confronts spectacle.

Approaching dramatic texts with an eye for their representations of hospitable practices means becoming attuned to the competition between representational strategies rather than thirsting for clarifications of "real" hospitable conflicts. Typically, the reader will find low-level conflicts over ideological shaping, positioned in counterpoint to the work's main action. Visions of the dominant order jostle. At any point in a drama, it is possible that a character will see through hospitality's shapings. At such a moment, the figures of authority become quite vulnerable. One may rule in confidence until the guest stays too long. Pressing early modern theatrical genres, the everyday commentary of pamphlets counselled caution.

Gilbert Walker's *A Manifest Detection of Dice-Play* (1552) is illustrative, suggesting much about the production of vulnerability on the Renaissance stage. In the pamphlet, a speaker R. recounts a chance meeting and hospitable invitation "in the church of Paul's" to an interlocutor M. R. recalls that the kind gentleman said, "'I shall now and then show you a lesson worth the learning; and to th'end hereafter each of us may be the bolder of the other, I pray you, if ye be not otherwise bespoken, take a capon with me at dinner. Though your fare be but homely and scant, yet a cup of good wine I can promise you, and all other lacks shall be supplied with a friendly welcome.'"[114] No facet of hospitable care is overlooked by this gentle host. He orders his wife, "'Bid this gentleman welcome.'" He chides her for the lateness of the meal. He even offers entertainment: "'You shall see my house the while. It is not like your large country houses. . . . Nevertheless, assure yourself that no man is welcomer than you to such cheer as ye find'" (pp. 33–34). With every hospitable speech genre in place, the house becomes a scene of entrapment and disillusionment: "With this and that like talk, consumed was our dinner. And, after the table was removed, in came one of the waiters with a fair silver bowl, full of dice and cards" (p. 35). R. has fallen among rogues, and the moral seems clear. Hospitality's shaping makes a person vulnerable; it calls for detection.

I find the paradigmatic example of hospitable shaping, its capacity for violence and dissolution, in the opening scenes of *Macbeth,* a dramatic situation discussed in detail in Chapter 6. The King praises the hospitable dwelling of the Macbeths. Lady Macbeth plays hostess and welcomes her royal guest with a revealing version of Scotland's allocation of resources:

> All our service
> In every point twice done, and then done double,
> Were poor and single business to contend
> Against those honors deep and broad wherewith
> Your Majesty loads our house. For those of old,
> And the late dignities heaped up to them,
> We rest your hermits. (1.6.14–20)

The dwelling is hospitable. As in Walker's pamphlet text cited above, primary genres of welcome familiar to every level of English society flesh out the speech. Consequently, however the critic wants to define the play's main conflict, hospitable responsibility has become an ancillary element; and in the representation, hospitality can be imagined *otherwise*. In terms of dramatic construction, a character's awareness of discrepancies between real practice and shaped ideals affords him or her a tactical advantage, the possibility of using hospitality against the host, playing on the host's willing suspension of disbelief. Barabas, Don John, the Macbeths, and Lear's evil daughters all serve to illustrate this representational course.

By mentioning Lady Macbeth, I raise a particularly difficult question for a study of hospitality's appropriations in the theater of early modern England, a problem already confronted in this chapter: what to do with the role of hostess? As the diaries of Lady Anne Clifford and Lady Hoby show, English women were no strangers to the tradition's tactical and strategic possibilities. Henry Percy, ninth Earl of Northumberland, singled out English women for their unusual authority at hospitable occasions. On the other hand, James I seems to have focussed increasingly on the potential for impropriety in women's householding.[115]

When I first considered this topic in connection with Shakespeare's *The Winter's Tale*, without making the distinction between practice and representation, I found powerful hostesses in Paulina and Perdita. At the time, I thought Shakespeare's representation of hospitality seemed to accord with Western civilization's emphasis on "woman as care-giver."[116] I found Peter B. Erickson's argument for two kinds of giving in the play a convincing argument not only for *The Winter's Tale* but for early modern theater as a whole. Erickson sees Hermione's restoration of "bounty" at the play's end as dependent on the work's "distinguishing male and female kinds of gift giving. Male gift giving is institutionalized, though it has its 'natural' source in the pastoral image portrayed by Polixenes. Female bounty, in contrast, is analogous to nature, grounded in giving birth and nurturance to infants."[117] The men in the play turn to Perdita as the obvious source of hospitality and this special "female bounty." Florizel encourages Perdita:

> See, your guests approach.
> Address yourself to entertain them sprightly,
> And let's be red with mirth. (4.4.52–54)

The Shepherd elaborates on this speech with a message of responsibility and in doing so suggests a tradition of hosting with woman at the center:

> Fie, daughter! When my old wife lived, upon
> This day she was both pantler, butler, cook,
> Both dame and servant; welcomed all, served all;
> Would sing her song and dance her turn; now here
> At the upper end o' th' table, now i' th' middle;
> On his shoulder, and his; her face o' fire
> With labor, and the thing she took to quench it
> She would to each one sip. (55–62)

Surprisingly, Perdita's example and the men's recognition of her responsibility turn out to be a rather striking anomaly, as much a part of generic closure as the age's investment in depicting a world of happy prestation. Finding representations of hostesses carrying out ancient customs with passion and delight and authority proves to be difficult. The sensibility of order alive in Lady Anne's diary has been largely repressed. In its place exists what Catherine Belsey has described as "a series of contests for the place of women in the family and in society, which may in turn be understood as struggles to install women as subjects."[118] Representations of hospitality, it seems, constitute a special arena for such contests in which woman's agency is refashioned.

An explanation of this phenomenon may be found in Merry E. Wiesner's "Spinsters and Seamstresses: Women in Cloth and

Clothing Production," in which the author explains how women who had occupied positions of authority in the clothing trade in early modern Germany were systematically replaced by men. Ultimately, only the most menial positions were left to women from the lower orders.[119] I suggest that in the contest for subject positions in hospitable domains the hostess experienced the same fate as the women in clothing production—a consistent and class-determined usurpation of their authoritative roles. A kind of domestic competition would necessarily obtain, but the contest would not be fought in the great hall. What men accomplished by direct intervention in workplaces, representations produced by men enabled in the household. In her discussion of "women as subjects," Belsey contends that "women as subjects had a place— in the home, in the bosom of the family" (p. 192). If my hypothesis is correct, this subject position in the home was posited representationally even as it was emptied of the implicit and explicit authority of hosting. Women certainly stood by their men in the hosting, but in the reckoning of gains and losses, only the position of the male host "counted." To voice the language of Lady Anne, women cease to be "held as Mistress[es] of the House."[120]

As we consider the age's drama in this respect, it will become apparent that playwrights appropriated the idea of hospitality consistently with this process of cultural displacement. Both Coppélia Kahn and Stephen Orgel have argued for such a process of usurpation in *King Lear* and *The Tempest*, respectively. In persuasive accounts of these important plays, Kahn and Orgel describe how Lear and Prospero seek to acquire woman's culturally determined roles by displacing women.[121] In representations of hospitality in other dramas, a similar situation obtains. When a woman assumes the authority of hostess, the play quickly comes to center on woman's power. In George Peele's *The Old Wives Tale* (1595), for example, Madge plays the part of hostess and demonstrates a fantastic power of storytelling that incarnates its characters before the guests. By the turn of the next century, the woman who takes charge of hosting is Lady Macbeth. Women who host appear dangerous and deserve displacement. My suggestion here is tentative and necessarily hypothetical; only more detailed research from both feminist and materialist positions will clarify the situation.

Another reason for proposing this process of usurpation so tentatively is rank. As Peter Stallybrass and Allon White have argued, matters of gender and class almost always intersect.[122] That Perdita's example does not repeat throughout the age's drama must be partially explained by the very language of the Shepherd's description of the model hostess singing and dancing, her face on fire with labor. Surely this model hostess belongs in a painting by Breughel as part of a peasant affair. Perdita's blood is royal; and she sits, not surprisingly, "retirèd, / As if you were a feasted one and not / The hostess of the meeting" (4.4.62–64). Seen against the pattern of usurpation I have just described, one could appropriately cite the old adage for this minor conflict: blood will tell. Hostesses who perspire play butler and servant for shepherds. Householders host with spectacle. Meanwhile, the woman of rank hosts on the fringe of the drama's action. It is, finally, Paulina's secret and decorous hospitality offered to Hermione and her public welcome of Leontes that saves the day: "you have vouchsaf'd . . . my poor house to visit" (5.3.4,6).

Study the representations of hospitable practices in dramatic texts and the plethora of strategic and tactical maneuvers on the fringe of the work's main action may prove overwhelming. Violent contrasts emerge between the noisy jocularity of male hospitalities and the murmured allusions to female hospitalities. The repression of latent contestations for political and social advantage—sharpened by differing rank, gender, profession, and opportunity—turn out to be the very means of dramatistic closure. Nevertheless, the problem for the scholar interested in these representational phenomena lies in the fragmentary nature of hospitable entertainments as appropriated by Renaissance drama. Approached in terms of the still-powerful tradition of New Criticism and its valorization of "readings," the project seems to falter, since no body of major plays exists that one can label "plays about hospitality." Any search for hospitality as a "unifying theme" or a "dominant motif" seems doomed to failure. Indeed, the impracticality of making these kinds of formalist claims may explain hospitality's neglect in literary studies. (One wonders whether fascinating social and ideological analyses have been ignored because they could not endure the painstaking totalization of a New Critical reading.) Perhaps we are gradually freeing ourselves to discover these projects.

NOTES

1. Vaughan, *The Golden-grove*, sig. P6r.
2. Wheler, *The Protestant Monastery*, 173.
3. Dalechamp, *Christian Hospitality*, 5–7, 18.
4. Wotton, *The Elements of Architecture*, 82; Wandesford, *A Book of Instructions*, 83. Sir Philip Sidney uses this terminology in his *Arcadia:* "If it be so that innocency shall not be a stop for fury; if it be so that the law of hospitality (so long and holily observed among you) may not defend a stranger fled to your arms for succour . . ." (384–85).
5. See, for example, Wotton, 70–71; Humphrey, *The Nobles*, bk. 2: vi.
6. See Knights, *Drama and Society in the Age of Jonson*, 111–17. Bristol in his *Carnival and Theater* observes: "If there is an idea about which Elizabethans professed unanimity, it is the image of an idyllic country hospitality rather than philosophical abstractions of hierarchy and the chain of being" (82).

The neglect of hospitality in literary studies is hardly the rule in other fields. Fascinating studies in sociology, theology, and anthropology consider hospitality in its past and present forms. See, for example, Harry William Murray, "Isaiah's Fast: The Practice of Hospitality in the Catholic Worker Movement" (Ph.D. diss., Syracuse University, 1988); and Lois Beck, "Nomads and Urbanites, Involuntary Hosts and Uninvited Guests," *Middle Eastern Studies* 18 (1982): 426–44.

7. Heal's *Hospitality in Early Modern England* (hereafter referred to as *Hospitality*) combines and expands on a series of studies that she devoted to matters of hospitality in early modern England: "The Crown, the Gentry and London," in *Law and Government under the Tudors*, 211–26; "Hospitality and Honor in Early Modern England," 21–50; "The Idea of Hospitality in Early Modern England," 66–93; and "The Archbishops of Canterbury and the Practice of Hospitality," 544–63.

8. Obviously, my division is more pragmatic than theoretically verifiable. No practice comes to the scholar in an unmediated form. Thucydides pointed this fact out long ago. Our own ancestors of Vico, Hayden White, Michel Foucault, Michel de Certeau, the new historicists and cultural materialists—all have done their part to make us acutely aware of the artificiality of this kind

of separation. My hope is that, by keeping these insights in front of the reader, the clarity derived from such a readerly strategy will not come at the expense of ideological responsibility.

    9.   Shakespeare makes use of the term in both senses. See, for example, *The Comedy of Errors*, 1.2.9 and *All's Well That Ends Well*, 3.5.94. For a discussion of the etymological confluence, consult Eric Partridge, *Origins: A Short Etymological Dictionary of Modern English* (London: Routledge, 1966), 296-97.

    10.   Middleton, *A Trick to Catch the Old One*, 1.2.51.

    11.   Sharpe, "Crown, Parliament and Locality," in Sharpe, *Politics and Ideas in Early Stuart England*, 77–87.

    12.   Moeslein, introduction, in *The Plays of Henry Medwall*, 6. Medwall's production of theater out of household resources perfectly illustrates the culture's fusion of these two terms. For Jonson's use of the term "guests," see "The Prologue for the Stage" in *The Staple of News, Ben Jonson*, 6:282.

    13.   Heal, "The Idea of Hospitality in Early Modern England," 67.

    14.   Mertes, *The English Noble Household*, 158.

    15.   Mauss, *Gift*, 64. See also Ruth Benedict, *Patterns of Culture* (New York, 1934) and Hyde, *Gift*.

    16.   The text of this little pageant appears in Bernard Garter's *The Joyful Receiving of the Queen's Most Excellent Majesty into Her Highness' City of Norwich*, 273.

    17.   Hyde, *Gift*, 24–37. See also Hyde's "Some Food We Could Not Eat," 32–60. Bordieu brilliantly describes this process of increase in *Outline of a Theory of Practice*, 12.

    18.   Sharpe, "Crown, Parliament and Locality," 321–50. See also Levy, "How Information Spread Among the Gentry, 1550–1640," 11-34.

    19.   Certeau, *The Practice of Everyday Life*, xix-xx.

    20.   Whigham, *Ambition and Privilege*, 88.

    21.   Thomas M. Greene, "Magic and Festivity at the Renaissance Court," 657.

    22.   Nichols, *Elizabeth*, 1:67.

    23.   Ibid., 73.

    24.   Quoted by Nichols, *Elizabeth*, 1:xxxi.

    25.   Chamberlain, letter 26, of *The Letters of John Chamberlain*, 91.

    26.   Hyde, *Gift*, xiv.

27.   Chambers, *The Elizabethan Stage*, 1:51, 53.

28.   Elizabeth I, *The Late Tudors, 1588–1603*, 3:171–72.

29.   Chamberlain, "To Dudley Carleton," 13 June 1600, letter 29 of *The Letters of John Chamberlain*, 1:97.

30.   James I, *The Royal Proclamations of James I, 1603–1625*, 1:21–22.

31.   Ibid., 357.

32.   Ibid., 358. Cf. James's subsequent proclamation of 1617, 1:369–71.

33.   James I, *The Works of the Most High and Mighty Prince, James*, 567. Throughout his reign, James made hospitable practice part of political strategy. See, for example, Marcus, *Puzzling Shakespeare*, 148–59.

34.   Charles I, *The Royal Proclamations of Charles I, 1625–1640*, 2:112–13, 170–72, 292–96, 350–53.

35.   Dated 12 Feb. 1620, letter 347, 2:289. In subsequent letters to Sir Dudley Carleton in 1622 and 1623, Chamberlain observes that little has changed in the face of royal proclamations. See letters 419 and 427. For the relevant proclamation, see *The Royal Proclamations of James I, 1603–1625*, 1:561–62.

36.   James I, *The Royal Proclamations of James I, 1603–1625*. Editors Larkin and Hughes provide an excellent commentary on this proclamation; see 1:561 n. 1. For a discussion of this exodus and a comparison of enforcement under Charles, see Heal, *Hospitality*, 119–20 and Heal, "The Crown, the Gentry and London," 211–26.

37.   *Calendar of State Papers Venetian*, 17:530, 538. For a discussion of the proclamation's enforcement and a moderate interpretation of James's motives in issuing the document, see Heal, "The Crown, the Gentry and London," 224. Even though Charles's enforcement was less rigorous than his father's, the Venetian ambassador once again entertained doubts about the English monarch's motives. See *Calendar of State Papers Venetian*, 23:38.

38.   Ferguson, *Naked to Mine Enemies*, 100. Wolsey's ability to orchestrate hospitable practice successfully, even for the most ordinary guests, deserves the scholar's attention because it won the monarch's favor. Disasters of scale were everywhere waiting to happen. In 1552, for example, Henry set out on progress into Dorsetshire. The retinue blossomed to four thousand in a region whose forage could support less than two hundred. For a discussion of the resulting dilemma, see Nares, *Memoirs of the Life and Administration of the Right Honourable William Cecil, Lord Burghley* (hereafter referred to as *Memoirs of William Cecil*), 1:376.

39. Greenblatt, *Renaissance Self-Fashioning*, 13.

40. Sharpe, "Crown, Parliament and Locality," 84. Penry Williams in *The Tudor Regime* notes this need to govern by compliance, a cultural phenomenon whose recognition Sharpe discusses as a scholarly trend. Sharpe goes on to suggest that changes in modes of gaining compliance were among the most significant phenomena leading toward revolution in early modern England. Hospitality, I think, was frequently meant to be a traditional answer to these changes.

41. Sacks, "Search for 'Culture' in the English Renaissance," 475. In her examination of urban hospitality, Heal looks at the example of Exeter, a city governed by a powerful mercantile oligarchy. Heal suggests that confidence in the oligarchy is evident in the apparent absence of public hospitality in the city. Consent was certain; public hospitality was not needed (*Hospitality*, 338).

42. Sanford and Townsend, *The Great Governing Families of England*, 2:61.

43. Ibid.

44. Nares, *Memoirs of William Cecil*, 1:378.

45. Nichols, *Elizabeth*, 1:91.

46. Ibid., 205. According to a contemporary account, Sir Thomas Gresham actually completed a reconstruction of his house in a single night in order that Elizabeth might wake to a more pleasing hospitality. See Nichols, *Elizabeth*, 2:280–81.

47. See McClung, *The Country House in English Renaissance Poetry*, 73–77. In her introduction to *Entertainments for Elizabeth I*, Wilson comments on one such lodging: "It is notable that the Earl of Leicester is given lodgings corresponding to those of the Queen, with her favourite cousin, Hunsdon, close to him, but that the courtiers put nearest the Queen are Hatton, presumably as leading favourite, and the group of young men, Greville, Ralegh, Gorges, Coke, and &c. (this last presumably intended to allow for any new favourite who might arise"(56).

48. Quoted by Nichols, *Elizabeth*, 1:xxvii.

49. For a discussion of these intrigues, see J. B. Black, *The Reign of Elizabeth, 1558–1603* (Oxford: Clarendon, 1936).

50. Nichols, *Elizabeth*, 1:204.

51. Wotton, *The Elements of Architecture*, 82. A curious gloss on this system of values is Francis Willoughby's construction of a hall based on a typical assemblage of pageant figures that would have been found at Kenilworth. See Friedman, *House and Household in Elizabethan England*, 24.

52. Nares, *Memoirs of William Cecil*, 1:378. For an excellent discussion of this controversy, see Heal, *Hospitality*, 257–99.

53. Quoted by Heal, *Hospitality*, 257.

54. George Paule, *Life of Whitgift* (London, 1612), 77.

55. Nichols, *Elizabeth*, 1:327.

56. Quoted in Nichols, *Elizabeth*, 1:340, 342.

57. Nichols, *Elizabeth*, 1:74.

58. Nichols, *James*, 2:945.

59. Sharpe, "Crown, Parliament and Locality," 79–81.

60. Quoted by Heal in *Hospitality*, 21.

61. Quoted by Friedman, *House and Household in Elizabethan England*, 24.

62. See, for example, Nicholas Yonge, *Musica Transalpina* (London, 1588) and Thomas Morley, *Plain and Easy Introduction to Practical Music* (London, 1597). I thank Bruce Horner for bringing these materials to my attention.

63. Nichols, *James*, 2:140.

64. Ibid., 781.

65. Ibid., 945.

66. *York*, 1:451, 488, and passim.

67. See Heal, *Hospitality*, 376–88.

68. Hyde, *Gift*, 45.

69. *The Diaries of Lady Anne Clifford*, 26. Subsequent references are in text.

70. *Diary of Lady Margaret Hoby, 1599–1605*, 157.

71. Nichols, *James*, 3:444–45.

72. See Bergeron, *English Civic Pageantry 1558–1642*, 26. As I suggest in the next paragraph, the recognition of similarities between the hosting of the towns and that of the nobility is essential to a comprehensive understanding of the period's so-called micropolitics; Heal offers useful cautions about the conflation of these entities (*Hospitality*, 305–7).

73. *Norwich, 1540–1642*, 59, 60.

74. Nichols, *Elizabeth*, 1:261.

75. For a sample of this fashioning of city identity, see Bernard Garter's *The Joyful Receiving of the Queen's Most Excellent Majesty into Her Highness' City of Norwich* and Thomas Churchyard's *A Discourse of the Queen's Majesty's Entertainment in Suffolk and Norfolk.* I discuss both of these texts in Chapter 4.

  76. Quoted in Nichols, *Elizabeth*, 1:97.
  77. Nichols, *Elizabeth*, 1:97.
  78. Ibid., 281.
  79. See, for example, Nichols, *James*, 2:416; 3:414, 422–23.
  80. Cited by Timbs, *Nooks and Corners of English Life*, 249.
  81. *Chamberlains' Accounts*, in *Norwich, 1540–1642*, 98.
  82. See Friedman, *House and Household in Elizabethan England*, 22.
  83. Jameson, *The Political Unconscious*, 39.
  84. Levin, *New Readings vs. Old Plays*, 191.
  85. Greenblatt, "The Circulation of Social Energy," in *Shakespearean Negotiations*, 5.
  86. Montrose, "Gifts and Reasons," 433.

Having escaped the trap of the "King James Version," the critic may still wish to conclude with a rather neat narrative of dominance and thwarted resistance. Greenblatt's texts, which move between practices and their re-presentations, have been indicted for precisely this failing. See, for example, Terry Eagleton, "The Historian as Body-snatcher," review of *Learning to Curse: Essays in Early Modern Culture*, by Stephen Greenblatt, *TLS* 18 Jan. 1991: 7. In *Puzzling Shakespeare*, Marcus proposes "local reading" as a corrective to this tendency:

> "Local" reading operates in the space between different systems for generating meaning—between the evanescent interpretation which fascinated Renaissance audiences . . . and the broader kinds of interpretation facilitated by our own more general explanatory models. (37)

For Marcus, what we must lose in our ability to nail down solid referents and linear causalities is made up for by our own reflection on "the passion for decoding" itself.

I take Chartier's discussions of *practice, representation,* and *appropriation* to be a most salutary influence on the tendency toward reification. See his *Cultural History: Between Practices and Represen-tations*, 1–14, 35, 39–40.

87. Barroll, "A New History for Shakespeare and His Time," 441–64.

88. Sharpe, "A Commonwealth of Meanings," in *Politics and Ideas*, 9.

89. Bakhtin, "The Problem of Speech Genres," in *Speech Genres and Other Late Essays*, 60. That the people of early modern England understood something like speech genres and considered them repositories of householding is suggested by the dialogs of Claudius Hollyband and Peter Erondell, two Huguenot refugees who taught French in Elizabethan England. The teachers' dialogs, published as *The Elizabethan Home Discovered in 2 Dialogues*, are organized on the principle of speech genres, two of which are "The Receiving into the House" and "Table Talke."

90. Ironically, genre scholarship has been largely purged of dialectical thinking. Classification, the idea of genre as a "grouping of literary works," has remained the dominant tack. See, for example, Dubrow's *Genre*, 45–81, which clarifies the shapes of this traditional view. The notion of genre as "grouping" comes from Wellek and Warren's *Theory of Literature*, 241. Only in recent decades, with the influential work of Claudio Guillén, Rosalie L. Colie, Paul Hernadi, and Alastair Fowler has the desire to classify been challenged by a concern for the fluidity of generic boundaries and an interest in the *function* of generic constructs. In the hands of Tzvetan Todorov and Jonathan Culler, genre scholarship turns its attention toward the reader's expectations insofar as they derive from genre. See, for example, Guillén, "Poetics as System," 193–222; Colie, *The Resources of Kind: Genre Theory in the Renaissance*; Hernadi, *Beyond Genre: New Directions in Literary Classification*; Todorov, "Typology of Detective Fiction," in *The Poetics of Prose*; Culler, *The Pursuit of Signs*, 58, 123; and Fowler, *Kinds of Literature*, 38, 42. Quite uniformly, however, these critics make genre a purely literary concern, a matter of tradition (Fowler) and literary competence (Culler). By examining the effects of playwrights' appropriations of hospitality on genre, I hope to escape the conservative—even repressive—habits of traditional genre scholarship, to benefit from recent scholarship, and to grasp in some detail the transformative energy of generic forms.

91. Cf. Jameson's suggestion in *The Political Unconscious* that "genres are essentially literary *institutions,* or social contracts between a writer and a specific public, whose function is to specify the proper use of a particular cultural artifact" (106). See also Williams, *Marxism and Literature,* 180–85; Martines, *Society and History in English Renaissance Verse,* 14–15; Goldberg, "Shakespearean Inscriptions," in *Shakespeare and the Question of Theory,* 116–37; and Dubrow, "The Country-House Poem," 153–79.

92. Heal's work with hospitality is definitive. My debt to her research and insight is great. See the entries under her name in the Bibliography.

93. For a discussion of the classical sources of this debate, see McClung, *The Country House in English Renaissance Poetry,* 7–17. For a discussion of Old Testament sources and their relation to English literature, see Creevy, "Hospitality in the Old Testament and English Literature," 14–36. Heal discusses Old and New Testament sources in each of her articles.

94. *Grevious Groans for the Poor,* sig. C3r–C4v.

95. See *The Brewer's Plea: Or a Vindication of Strong Beer and Ale.*

96. Dalechamp, *Christian Hospitality,* 36. For supplementary reading, see also Heal's "The Archbishops of Canterbury and the Practice of Hospitality."

97. Quoted by Campbell in *The English Yeoman under Elizabeth and the Early Stuarts,* 249.

98. Geuss, *The Idea of a Critical Theory,* 13. For a discussion of mystification in relation to Elizabethan courtesy theory, see Whigham, *Ambition and Privilege,* 63–87.

99. Bristol, *Carnival and Theater,* 84.

100. *Ben Jonson,* 8:95. On "mystification" in the poem, see Raymond Williams, *The City and the Country,* 26–34.

101. Stafford, *A Compendious or Brief Examination of Certain Ordinary Complaints,* 45.

102. Tusser, *Five Hundred Points of Good Husbandry,* 67.

103. See Heal, "The Idea of Hospitality in Early Modern England," 77.

104. Harman, *A Caveat for Common Cursitors,* in *Cony-Catchers and Bawdy Baskets,* 81.

105. Lupton, *London and the Country Carbonadoed and Quartered,* 101–2.

106. Stow, *A Survey of London,* 1:89.

107. Greaves, *Society and Religion in Elizabethan England*, 588.

108. R. R., *The House-holders Helpe, For Domesticall Discipline*, 27.

109. Hollander, "Political Tourism in Cuba and Nicaragua," 28–37.

110. McClung, *The Country House in English Renaissance Poetry*, 30.

111. Heal, "The Idea of Hospitality in Early Modern England," 80.

112. Though I do not discuss his work in this chapter, Thomas Nashe and his investment in hospitality is the subject of Chapter 4. For an example of Greene's handling of the idea, see "A Quip for an Upstart Courtier" in *The Life and Complete Works in Prose and Verse of Robert Greene, M. A.*, ed. Alexander G. Grosart (London, 1881–83), 11:209. Hibbard defines the genre in "The Country-House Poem of the Seventeenth Century," 159–74. For a sample of James's poetry, see "An Elegie written by the King concerning his counsell for Ladies & gentlemen to departe the City of London according to his Majestiees Proclamation," *The Poems of James VI of Scotland*, 2:178–81.

113. Jonson, *Pleasure Reconciled to Virtue*, in *Ben Jonson: Selected Masques*, 2:81–84.

114. Walker, *A Manifest Detection of Dice-Play* in *Cony-Catchers and Bawdy Baskets*, 32.

115. See Heal, *Hospitality*, 179. See also Heal's insightful reading of James's emphases in royal proclamations in "The Crown, the Gentry, and London," 213.

116. See Gilligan, *In a Different Voice*; Chodorow, *The Reproduction of Mothering*; and Ochshorn, *The Female Experience and the Nature of the Divine*.

117. Erickson, "Patriarchal Structures in *The Winter's Tale*," 820. Cf. Ronald A. Sharp, "Gift Exchange and the Economies of Spirit in *The Merchant of Venice*," 250–65.

118. Belsey, *The Subject of Tragedy*, 150.

119. Wiesner, "Spinsters and Seamstresses," in *Rewriting the Renaissance*, 191–205. See also her extended discussion of this subject in *Working Women in Renaissance Germany* (New Brunswick: Rutgers University Press, 1986).

120. Cf. Heal's more placid summary of women's positions, *Hospitality*, 182–83. I do not wish to suggest that no woman of aristocratic birth could host on her own. Queen Elizabeth hosted. In 1614, Queen Anne hosted the wedding of Lord Roxburgh and Jane Drummon at Somerset House. A certain royal prerogative protects these hostesses. Lady Hatton, wife of Sir Edward Coke, seems to have presented a genuine problem to male authority with her hosting. On 8 November 1617, she hosted King James and others at a splendid dinner—carefully excluding her husband from participation. See Nichols, *James*, 3:444–45.

On the other hand, a particular illustration of this discursive emptying comes from the juxtaposition of a typical text on hospitality, directed to a male householder interested in improving his position in life, against Gervase Markham's clear identification of a female householder/reader in *The English Housewife* (London, 1615) to whom the author prescribes the most mundane of household chores.

121. Kahn, "The Absent Mother in *King Lear*," 33–49 and Orgel, "Prospero's Wife," 50-64, both in *Rewriting the Renaissance*.

122. Stallybrass and White, *The Politics and Poetics of Transgression*, 3.

2

Shakespeare's Romantic Comedies and the Diminution of Dominance in Courtly Hospitalities

Who among Shakespeare's contemporary readers would make hospitality a focus in reading the romantic comedies? Bright worlds of ineffable amazement, these conservative and courtly plays would seem to have only the most quotidian (and hence invisible) investment in housekeeping matters. My aim in this chapter is to put primary genres of hospitality into relief amid the plays' glittering choreographies. As a way of beginning this process, I want first to turn to Sir Philip Sidney's *Countess of Pembroke's Arcadia* for the way it prefigures Shakespearean romantic comedy while simultaneously posing initial questions, from the vantage point of the 1570s and 1580s, about the appropriation of hospitality. In moving from Sidney through Shakespeare, my task will be to clarify the ways that Shakespeare's appropriation of hospitality denies the smooth reception of the genre by a heterodox elite.

Hosting Civil Wildness and the Shaping of Reception

I believe that the particular anxiety of Shakespeare's romantic comedy begins, in part, with Sidney's trepidation over the production of a text without precedent. Like most authors, Sidney pondered the fate of his labors. An inventive, peculiarly English work of *bricolage* unrivalled in the language, Sidney's *Arcadia* (as we tend to call the author's reworking of his original text) gave its creator pause for good reason. Its allusive mix of erotic desire and political action couched in the tribulations of female succession make the book a most provocative foray into Elizabethan culture. Sidney had already attempted to manage the affairs of state more directly by advising the queen in her choice of marriage partners; and that attempt seems to have precipitated his removal from court, a tack that left him hosting at his sister's house with time to write the *Arcadia*. Ever hopeful of doing the right thing to improve his station in life, to broach the highest strata of England's ruling elite, Sidney must have worried about the work's effects on its readers as it circulated through court circles. How would the work be received? So, with the deft hand of the polished courtier, he took special care in shaping the text's reception.

Sidney's strategy involved a careful tuning of what theorists have come to call the "implied reader." As Wayne Booth suggested some time ago, an "author creates, in short, an image of himself and another image of his reader; he makes his reader, as he makes his second self, and the most successful reading is one in which the created selves, author and reader, can find complete agreement."[1] Every text offers the reader a role to assume, one that will, to a greater or lesser degree, mesh with the reader's own position in his or her culture. In more contemporary parlance, one might say that the text offers a series of subject positions to which the audience will be drawn.[2] Of course, as Wolfgang Iser has pointed out, Booth's "successful reading," that complete agreement between real and created positions, can never truly occur: "as the one can never be fully taken over by the other, there arises between the two the tension we have described."[3] Negotiating the strata of elites in early modern England in the language of romance involved careful attention to the production of this tension.

In the case of the *Arcadia,* Sidney offered copies of his "toyfull booke" and a certain authority to his brother Robert and his friend and future biographer Fulke Greville. For his part, Greville certainly laid claim to Sidney's texts. These male examples notwithstanding, Sir Philip chose to inflect his romance's implied reader by gesturing toward his sister, the Countess of Pembroke. So, if the text provokes, we may recall the author's address to his sibling:

"For indeed, for severer eyes it is not, being but a trifle, and that triflingly handled. Your dear self can best witness the manner, being done in loose sheets of paper, most of it in your presence; the rest by sheets sent unto you as fast as they were done."[4] In an age that took the circulation of manuscripts for granted, the writer reemphasizes the scattered quality of his work, its loose sheets.

The work implies a reader whose feminized "idle times" make reading possible, mere trifling far removed from the negotiations of authority in Elizabethan life. Sidney convenes a certain authority for this audience by attesting to his sister's "presence" as a "witness" of the composing. Anxiety has become a fashioned matter of audience and reception, defused by attribution to a woman's sphere of less consequence, labelled as so much housekeeping. The invocation of housekeeping absolutely supports this strategy: "Here now have you (most dear, and most worthy to be most dear lady) this idle work of mine, which, I fear, like the spider's web, will be thought fitter to be swept away than worn to any other purpose" (p. 57). Take this work of adventure and politics, Sidney says, and receive it as the typically invisible stuff of household ordering. It may be kept or swept away, but either way it will remain inside the household. The writer can enjoy a certain confidence in his strategy because the *Arcadia*'s implied audience, in the figure of the countess, has been contained as woman and reader and housekeeper.[5]

When the Countess of Pembroke published the work in 1593 as *The Countess of Pembroke's Arcadia,* she managed Sidney's inflections by making clear on the title page her authority to "augment" and "end" the text. The woman's part suddenly means more than tidying up loose ends; it may even mean a kind of subversive *jouissance,* a womanly hosting of the male entertainment.[6] In the hands of Sidney's fit reader, romance ought to be householding cheer and chore, entirely defused of political content. Seen another way, the text offers its real readers a particular role, remarking their gender, authority, and domesticity. How striking then that after his particular care in prefacing the *Arcadia* Sidney would thread his tale with hospitable practices, offering his audience provocative occasions through which they might experience tension between their real and implied roles.

The tantalizing plots of Greek romances—*Amadis de Gaula,* Sannazaro's *Arcadia,* and Montemayor's *Diana*—in front of him, his mind racing with shipwrecks, songs, monsters, contests, and shepherds, Sidney has scarcely begun *The Countess of Pembroke's Arcadia* before he turns to a scene of hospitality. Having survived amazing perils, Musidorus is rescued by shepherds from Arcadia who assume his care: "But a little way hence; and even upon the next confines there dwelleth a gentleman, by name Kalander, who vouchsafeth much favour unto us: a man who for his hospitality is so much haunted that no news stirs but comes to his ears" (p. 68). The heroes of romance are always, to a certain degree, strangers, romantically vulnerable. Sidney himself, thanks to his failed political maneuverings, conceived of the *Arcadia* during his own estrangement from court. Dependent on the hospitality of his sister, he described his own hosting during the grey October of 1580: "How idlie wee looke on our Naighbours fyres."[7] Perhaps for these reasons, Sidney wanders very little in the world of romance before establishing hospitality as the decorum of care and introduction, as a center for his entertainment. News—who's in and who's out—swirls about the hospitable lord. Hosting makes him a center of action, of possibility, for the writer. In this way, neighbors' fires animate the writer's generic options.[8]

With an interest that seems out of place in a narrative so committed to adventure and desire, Sidney lingers idly over matters of housekeeping. Discrepant perspectives emerge. In a manner anticipating pamphleteers' accounts of royal progresses, the narrator describes Arcadia approvingly: "As for the houses of the country—for many houses came under their eyes—they were all scattered, no two being one by the other, and yet not so far off as that it barred mutual succour: a show, as it were, of an accompanable solitariness and of a civil wildness" (p. 70). The Arcadian landscape conforms to the ideal image of a hospitable English countryside as recounted time again in pamphlet, poem, and proclamation. As Wotton suggested, hospitality hums in this pastoral setting as "a show" because every house may be a theater of hospitality. In this country, as at Cecil's Theobalds, hospitality proceeds in perfect proportion to degree. Thus the shepherds desire "to know something of you and of the young man you so much lament, that at least we may be the better instructed to inform Kalander, and he the better know how to proportion his entertainment" (p. 71). Like English hospitality, the Arcadian practice demands inquiry and a careful sorting of the guests. It preserves absolutely the distinctions of rank.

The narrator comments on the travellers' arrival, one not unlike Duncan and company's arrival in *Macbeth,* by approving of the household setting. The passage moves via primary genres of welcome, so much a part of English society that it seems to anticipate the phrasing of Shakespeare's tragedy with its attention to the "air" and "prospect" of hospitable dwelling, "about which they might see (with fit consideration both of the air, the prospect, and the nature of the ground) all such necessary additions to a great house as might well show Kalander knew that provision is the foundation of hospitality and thrift the fuel of magnificence" (p. 71). Ever interested in romance, Sidney takes time to carefully discover the origins of hospitality in provision, marking the connection between hospitality and the magnificence of English rule. Hospitable practice must be economical. Prudent provisioning must leaven a nobility's taste for opulence. In this proper context, an immediate and pleasant welcome comes from the servants, "not so many in number as cleanly in apparel and serviceable in behaviour, testifying even in their countenances that their master took as well care to be served as of them that did serve" (p. 71).

Sidney takes care to gloss practice with commentary before turning to Kalander's own welcome, which fulfills the most stringent requirements of the pamphleteers: "'I am no herald to inquire of men's pedigrees; it sufficeth me if I know their virtues, which (if this young man's face be not a false witness) do better apparel his mind than you have done his body'" (p. 72). In this passage hospitable ideal and practice come together. Not only does Kalander entertain the stranger without regard to degree, but he also hosts instinctively, judging the guest's worth from his face. Degree is confirmed in the hosting with the result that Kalander's household makes wildness civil, the function of hospitality in a romance world. As Myron Turner explains, "Hospitality, as seen in Kalander's behavior towards Musidorus, is humanity expressed in the ritual beauty of courtly manners. His behavior, also his simple yet elegant way of life, are part of a larger social ideal of harmony and beauty in which the shepherds, as well as their aristocratic lords, participate."[9]

Of course, harmony has its political underside. In fictionally realizing this ideal, Sidney teases out conflicts of degree, virtue, gender, and desire that prove to be the essence of Shakespeare's romantic comedy. Under the guise of elaborating this ideal, Sidney preserves, simultaneously, every rank of English hierarchy.

Lodging is finally offered to strangers of the proper rank. The participation Turner describes means being fixed summarily in aristocratic shaping.

One of the age's master rhetoricians, Sidney constructs this ideal vision as a politically charged antithesis to the dead world of Laconia, which Claius describes as

> not so poor by the barrenness of the soil (though in itself not passing fertile) as by a civil war, which being these two years within the bowels of that estate between the gentlemen and the peasants (by them named Helots) hath in this sort as it were disfigured the face of nature, and made it so unhospital as now you have found it: the towns neither of the one side nor the other willingly opening their gates to strangers, nor strangers willingly entering for fear of being mistaken. (p. 70)

In Sidney's imagination, the other side of hospitality is warfare between ranks. The estate becomes personified in representation, its bowels torn by conflict between gentlemen and peasant. Fearful "of being mistaken," no one can trust the kind of instinctive recognition practiced by Kalander.

So, on the border of civil wildness exists the disfigured face of nature where no strangers are entertained. An "unhospital" world, Sidney asserts, is made by the way its people inhabit existing hierarchies. Lest we forget, Sidney reminds us that even in a romance world the signs of hospitality reveal the true condition of communal order. And lest we dismiss Sidney's commentary as mere fictional musing, it would be well to recall that in a proclamation of 1632 Charles I attempted to enforce the same relation between hospitality and domestic security, pointing to the past when, "by their Housekeeping in those [distant] parts, the Realme was defended, and the meaner sort of the people were guided, directed and relieved."[10] What Sidney wished to represent and what Charles longed to avoid was the fact that people can always choose to undo civility. The idea deserves emphasis: matters of hospitality sustain the very hierarchies on which an early modern community is founded.

Basilius's abandonment of his household responsibilities provides the ultimate elaboration of these notions. Because of the oracle's prophecy that his daughter's marriage will lead to death, Basilius denies his hospitable responsibilities. He gives up house-keeping and retires into seclusion, a strategy thwarted by his welcoming of the disguised Pyrocles into his retreat. The balancing of civility and wildness proves difficult. The conflicting demands of thrift and magnificence complicate this juggling while the arousal of sexual desire threatens to absolutely confound all hierarchical enterprise. As we have already seen, failure means more than broken hearts; it implies the destruction of host, family, and country.

Without a doubt, Sidney's intriguing efforts as an English writer of romance exerted a powerful influence on the development of romantic comedy on the Elizabethan stage. The author's union of erotic desire and political argument practically created a language for Shakespeare's romantic comedies.[11] Sidney's example seems to demand an inquiry into the role of the household in a world of romantic desire. What do hosts and guests have to do with lovers? At the same time, Sidney's concern over the shape of his audience prompts one to seek the shape(s) of the audience implied by Shakespeare's romantic comedies. How did this implied audience fit with the real and heterodox audience watching the comedies? In what sense does Sidney's own positing of a female audience, with the power to augment and end, haunt the Shakespearean genre? Finally, perhaps most importantly, in what ways does the genre's negotiation of a reception for its hospitalities engage the very hierarchies of Elizabethan rule?

Romantic Comedy and the Possibility of Reception

If scholarship has been slow to ask such questions, it may be because the genre of romantic comedy has been particularly beset by traditional habits of classification, patterns that bear an uncanny resemblance to reified versions of England's class system. How would one go about exploring the genre's unstable mediations of aristocratic authority when, ever since Shakespeare's romantic comedies received their first modern critical attention from H. B. Charlton in 1938, scholarship has been obsessed with the ways in which the comedies form a kind of narrowly defined tale of aristocratic triumph? On the one hand, Charlton argued for—and such important critical voices as Northrop Frye, M. C. Bradbrook, and Leo Salingar have pursued—a study of the evolution or development of the genre.[12] The other dominant tradition, illustrated by the work of C. L. Barber, Ruth Nevo, William Carroll, and Alexander Leggatt, groups the plays according to a single pattern such as "love" or "transformation" or "clarification."[13] Both of these traditions succeed insofar as they describe a pristine and monological world of aristocratic desire.

Challenges to this dominant perspective are few, at times self-repudiating.[14] One of the most fascinating alternatives is Walter Cohen's view of the genre as another form "for expressing, enacting, and securing the successful adaptation of the aristocracy to social and political change."[15] Part of a much larger hypothesis, that the absolutist state "first fostered and then undermined the public theatre," Cohen's thesis concerning romantic comedy is provocative; but the conclusions tend to rest on traditional generic configurations: "Romantic comedy, firmly founded on marital love, its climactic weddings presided over by great lords, dramatizes the adaptation of the nobility to a new social configuration, an acceptance of change inextricable from a reassertion of dominance" (pp. 19, 187). Cohen's recognition that romantic comedy's capacity for closure must in some way be a product of mediation between the age's dominant orders and the theater is salutary. His Burkean emphasis on adaptation surely catches one of the primary motives behind the representation of hospitable practice during the period.

Above all, Cohen's argument inspires new questions, most powerfully by its reduction of the genre to a looked-for conclusion we never see on the Elizabethan stage: the wedding. We may wonder how a genre can be founded on marital love when it devotes almost no time to the representation of marital love. Furthermore, if romantic comedy dramatizes "adaptation to social change," how can we further explore particular comedies' relations to particular social phenomena and particular evidence of social change?[16] How can we make cultural forces in their various particularities—roles of women, economic conditions, household practices, marriage customs—exist as more than gestural analogues in our commentaries?

One way of bringing romantic comedy into more complex relation with its context is by studying the ways it first implies readers and then encourages and discourages reception in its audiences. If one believes with Cohen (as I do) that some kind of aristocratic adaptation is being negotiated in Shakespeare's romantic comedies, then the tenuousness of that adaptation ought to be remarked amid the play's drives toward closure. I suggest that we seek this instability in the possibilities of reception. A Shakespearean romantic comedy, no less than Sidney's romance narrative, offers its audience a series of implied roles. Rarely, of course, is the identification a perfect fit. Moreover, as Richard A. Burt has argued, the ideology of a dramatic work occasions an especially fraught instance of reception that Burt describes with the term "rewriting." Based on their rank and gender, audiences will fracture into separate groups and receive the work as so many tasks of rewriting.[17] This rewriting will go forward only in light of the advances and obstacles arranged by the literary text.

For the critic, disjunctions between audience and identification, conundrums in the rewriting, can be the starting point of a genuinely provocative critical practice. Rachel Brownstein's work with English fiction, Clark Hulse's analysis of *Astrophel and Stella*, Caroline Lucas's study of Elizabethan romance, and Gary Waller's work with sixteenth-century verse all suggest the possibilities of such a criticism.[18] Typically the struggles over reception call attention to themselves over time and sooner or later someone studies their various displacements.

In the case of Shakespeare's romantic comedies, however, this process has been subject to steady, disciplinary elision. Time and again, interpretations depend on unquestioned assumptions about what a real Renaissance audience could have done with the roles they were watching. The job of critical reading is here complicated by critics' parallel collapsing of these factions into an amalgam happily in tune with the conservatively drawn subject positions offered by the genre's closure. Indeed, such conflations absolutely ground every notion of triumphant aristocratic adaptation and celebration, for the critic must be able to argue that a Sidney in the audience would be capable of identifying with an Oxford on the stage.[19] Studying an age that observed hundreds of distinctions of rank, critics have assumed too easily that one aristocratic triumph is as good as the next.

I have in mind, as a partial corrective, a critical path suggested by Marianne Novy, who asks us to consider the relationship of
Kate and Petruchio in *The Taming of the Shrew* in terms of how it
could be received by "spectators who are divided among and
within themselves in their attitudes toward marriage."[20] An exception to the general tenor of criticism, Novy's approach begins to
account for our difficulty in assigning a victor to the taming plot.
With this precedent in mind, I want to make Shakespeare's romantic comedies generically accountable to a small portion of their
cultural context—hospitable practice. I want to qualify the conservative nature of these plays by pointing to the way they shaped
their own reception among a divided elite. Indeed, when
England's elites are viewed in some detail—say, in their differing
positions of rank, in their differing status as hosts and hostesses—
a serious disjunction appears between the particular genre and the
culture it seems to reflect. The *possibility of reception* (no simple
aesthetic response) will thus become the basis of critique—with a
single, but crucial, caveat. I will not claim that these points of
disjunction undo the culture's hierarchies at specific seams; that
kind of causal reasoning would be simply impossible to prove. I
claim instead to find moments of tactical and strategic (referring
back to the terminology of Michel de Certeau) contestation played
out on the threshold between play and context, moments when the
play's appropriation of hospitality disrupts the possibilities of reception amid a heterodox elite.

Would-be hostesses and practicing hosts were everywhere in
Shakespeare's audience; but they were as different as Cecil and
Sidney, the flawed Hertford and the active Gresham, the Countess
of Derby and Lady Hatton. Whereas contemporary historicist criticism frequently depends on a monological reduction of dominant
powers to the "State" or a single "aristocratic body," or "the dominant culture,"[21] a given romantic comedy would have shaped its
reception in light of a heterogeneous elite—more properly, elites—
full of conflicting aims, different means, and different relations to
hospitable practice. At the very least, the critic of the romantic
comedy's courtly world ought to take into account the way that
gender differences sever a univocal perspective. These distinctions
replicate among the following groups: the monarch or ruler, the
peerage, a hierarchy of clergy, "old families" like the Howards,
"new families" like the Wriothesleys, suspect families like the

Dudleys, a middle but further divided range of "genteel" that separated a Sidney from a Cecil *after* the Cecil became a baron,[22] a crowd of ill-defined "gentlemen" of which Shakespeare claimed membership, and a growing merchant class that intersected with the above groups.[23] Geographic differences, between the country and the city, between the north and the south, divide the groups still further. As Andrew Gurr suggests, it was just such a heterodox mix that came to view Shakespeare's plays.[24]

Since no single elite existed during the period, the possibility of conservatively rewriting one of Shakespeare's romantic comedies must necessarily break up into a series of unstable receptions. Although we know far too little about what Shakespeare's audience actually *did* with the romantic comedies, can we not imagine, for a moment, the Earl of Hertford watching *Much Ado about Nothing* and the possibility of his identifying with Claudio, Leonato, and Don Pedro? The play certainly offers a series of subject positions defined by their dominant agency, but the possibility of reception remains knotty. If the said earl shifts his reception gingerly, he may indeed register an "aristocratic triumph" at the end of the play; but he will only be able to do so by conflating all the discrepant male subject positions in a way unallowed by his own culture. On the other hand, if this earl simply watches the play, his own position must appear rather unstable. We can imagine, at the same time, an awkward moment of identification in which a woman in the position of Lady Anne Clifford's mother, attempting to align her own displaced position as mistress of the house with the powerful roles of Rosalind and Portia, leaves the theater with only a frustrated sense of woman's triumph. Although such imaginative reconstructions could hardly document actual responses, they surely guide us in gauging the potentiality of reception.

What the romantic comedies tested, England's successful householders put into practice, understanding that courtly decorum meant noble householding.[25] As we have already seen, the business of governing was interwoven with a network of noble householding. Many in Shakespeare's audience, from merchant to Elizabeth herself, could identify with the concerns of the hosts in Shakespeare's romantic comedies: Antipholus of Ephesus, the Lord in *The Taming of the Shrew,* Petruchio, Theseus, King Ferdinand, Duke Senior, Leonato, and Sir Toby. These hosts seek traditional goals: nurture (which usually means marriage for themselves or for their children) and entertainment (which means the enhancement of reputation and simple pleasure). Both of these aims fit nicely inside the traditionally marked bounds of the genre, even as they displace the aristocratic hostess.

Seen through the eyes of an aristocratic host, the practice of hospitality in these plays becomes not so much central as anxiously ubiquitous. Of romantic comedy, the host in the audience may always ask, what has happened to *my aims?* When we add the discrepant perspective of Sidney's displaced hostess as the other side of hosting that makes a romance possible, the romantic comedies fail to offer their age the same old clarification. To romantic comedy, the reader may always put a form of Orgel's question concerning *The Tempest:* where is the wife? The same question might be put to the *Arcadia:* where is Kalander's wife? In what sense, we will want to ask, does the exclusion of married hostesses in re-presentation allow for the inclusion of a feminine audience actively engaged in augmenting and editing the fictional world? Viewed in terms of the possibilities of reception, romantic comedy provokes more questions than it settles.

Epitomizing the protocols of the age, marriage in Shakespeare's romantic comedies always hinges on successful hospitality. With Cohen's thesis in mind, we might say that conservative closure always hinges on successful hospitality. *A Midsummer Night's Dream* epitomizes this patterning. Theseus announces as much for his own marriage when he commands Philostrate: "Stir up the Athenian youth to merriments, / Awake the pert and nimble spirit of mirth" (1.1.11–13). Having "woo'd thee with my sword," Theseus seeks marriage *and* communal order through hospitality. Shakespeare allows his audience to watch, in other words, the ways in which hospitality produces fantasies of rapprochement eliding the blatant exercise of male authority and sexuality. In the meantime, the royal host stirs up more than he knows, for the fairy world hosts as uninvited guests for Theseus's wedding celebration. For their part, Quince and his company enable Theseus's entertainment and wedding while Hermia and Helena, like the women depicted in Lady Anne Clifford's diary, make what they can of the situation. The pace quickens. As Bordieu's anthropological reading of such dynamics suggests, the practice of hospitality incites a scherzo of provocation upon provocation.[26]

Shakespeare's romantic comedy positively thrives on this patterning. The hospitality King Ferdinand calls "necessity" in the first act of *Love's Labour's Lost* becomes a specific strategy of courtship as the play proceeds. Ferdinand will woo "and win them too; therefore let us devise / Some entertainment for them in their tents" (4.3.367–68). Holofernes's players aim to assist and so provide a "feast of languages." Duke Senior's observance of the traditional practices of hospitality in *As You Like It* enables the love of Rosalind and Orlando. Thanks to Duke Senior's welcome, the wild forest becomes a civil space of transformation—but not without engaging the disruptive energies of sexual desire. From the first, Shakespeare played with this consequence, focussing on the moment when the roles of father and host conflict, and nurture seems not to mesh with marriage. An audience aware of the age's conventions of hosting would mark the Duke's decorous welcome in *The Two Gentlemen of Verona* with recognition and trepidation: "Welcome him then according to his worth" (2.4.80). The proper practice of Kalander, almost by definition, spells trouble for the existing structure of male authority in the household.

In a more rough-and-tumble fashion that seems to affirm male authority, Petruchio hosts his new wife in *The Taming of the Shrew*. This early play offers, I think, the best introduction to the place of hospitality in Shakespeare's romantic comedies. It suggests, moreover, the particular stakes involved in the meeting between audience and textual refraction. Here is the stuff of welcome, drawn straight from the daily hospitalities of Elizabethan life, echoing Kalander's welcome in the *Arcadia*. In Shakespeare's play, brushed coats and a fine curtsy ought to reproduce the host's authority and, in turn, produce the marriage of Petruchio's desiring. The tortured Kate simply must succumb to the full weight of patriarchal decorum, for like most powerful hosts of the day, Petruchio offers a canonical and shaping hospitality. Unlike most pamphlets of the day, however, Shakespeare takes pains to reveal the ways in which this traditional practice succeeds not because of its "rightness" but because of the tactical advantages it affords.

The playwright prepares us for this insight with the drama's induction. Never far from the host's mind, the pleasures of shaping through entertainment motivate the Lord to trick Sly: "It will be pastime passing excellent, / If it be husbanded with modesty" (i.65–66). When he awakes, Sly supposes the entertainment will be some kind of "tumbling-trick." Informed "it is more pleasing stuff," he reaches a conclusion whose sense makes a curious match with Burghley's practice: "What, household stuff?" With comic insight, Sly recognizes that a foreign world of conventional behavior has appeared around him. I want to explore Sly's experience in some detail, arguing that this "household stuff" embodies the most conservative—even repressive—tendencies of the genre as it realizes hospitality's potential for acculturation. Not surprisingly, the susceptibility of Sly to hospitable illusions presages some of the deepest tremors of Renaissance tragedy. Here the beginning of my argument, in romantic comedy, and its end, in tragedy, come together in a critical awareness of vulnerability. It has become fashionable to scrutinize the production of this vulnerability in terms of theatrical practices, an approach I will not seek to overturn so much as domesticate.[27]

When the Lord first encounters Sly, the noble does no more than any other householder of the day. He scrutinizes the sleeping man's appearance and determines what can be given him:

> O monstrous beast, how like a swine he lies!
> Grim death, how foul and loathsome is thine image!
> Sirs, I will practice on this drunken man.
> What think you, if he were conveyed to bed,
> Wrapped in sweet clothes, rings put upon his fingers,
> A most delicious banquet by his bed,
> And brave attendants near him when he wakes,
> Would not the beggar then forget himself? (i.32–39)

In the Lord's hands, Sly's shape becomes malleable. Do we have any other confirmation that Sly resembles a "monstrous beast"? In fact, the hospitable practice of the Lord will allow him to reshape the drunken sleeper. In this way, a person of some rank remakes the image of the lower orders with victuals and spectacle. If the Lord's ideas seem fantastic, we have only to recall the age's pamphlet literature, with its tales of a choice of beef prepared for all such beggars in London. In fact, the Lord's practices touch every convention of hospitable decorum. Like Burghley, he gives orders to players and then commands a servant: "Take them to the buttery / And give them friendly welcome every one. / Let them want nothing that my house affords" (i.101–03). Unlike the lord at Theobalds, this host boldly announces his plan to mold his guest. But how far can the Lord's shaping go? The host contemplates an almost Faustian power: "Would not the beggar then forget himself?" Could aristocratic hospitality actually erase and rewrite identity? The Lord's "test" seems positive in the practicing. From the perspective of the host, hospitality's "power" seems considerable.

I put the fashionable idea of power in question above because, though the term satisfies contemporary usage, it really explains little about scope or application. It seems obvious that the power the Lord contemplates is of the same "kind" as that practiced by Burghley and others in their entertainment of Elizabeth and James. At the same time, the extreme difference in class means that, in application, this "power" must be fragmented, awkward in its utility. What is being forgotten, and what is being inserted in its place? Sly first responds to this waking world with a recitation of his lineage: "Am I not Christopher Sly?" With the prodding of his "servants," Sly turns to a Baconian empiricism: "I see, I hear, I speak, / I smell sweet savors and I feel soft things" (ii.68–69). Empirical observation quickly engenders transformation, for the monstrous beggar has "turned verse."

Suddenly, more than anything else, Sly would like to "stay awake" in this world. In his feeble way, he attempts to play the part by anticipating the correct responses to this dimly understood practice. More pleasure in entertainments, Sly surmises, means household stuff, the nature of which, I suggest, appears in the first household custom the verse-speaking Sly is asked to perform: "Will't please your mightiness to wash your hands? / O how we joy to see your wit restored!" (ii.74–75). In Muchembled's terms, the restoration of Sly's wit derives here from the "constraint of bodies," a confining of bodily practices that instituted a genuine break between classes in early modern Europe: "It is certain that the popular masses reflected this change only slowly and partially, and this accentuated the gap between their mores and those of the dominant circles. The elites found all the more reason to scorn the common people: weren't humble folk dirty, smelly, ugly, vulgar, coarse, and oafish, according to the canons of the new urbanity?"[28] Sly may learn to wash his hands, but only from within the illusion. He reflects constraint slowly, distracted by the "vulgar" pursuit of his "Lady": "Madam, undress you and come now to bed" (ii.115). Sly's desires are, of course, comically constrained.

Imitating the public theaters, the Lord's entertainment offers Sly a boy dressed as a woman. Blended smoothly with a lord's hosting, contemporary theatrical practice makes plebeian life all the more oafish in its desiring.

In reshaping Sly, a lord's wit and the washing of hands come together: the power of hospitality to erase and rewrite identity is the power of acculturation, the power to impose civility's clean hands, to remake through the pleasure of household stuff. In this case, the Lord's wildness does not find so much as construct civility, a representational practice that, as Marianne Novy observes, cannot be entirely contained by the terms of the play: "As the 'real' Lord entertains us by showing that Sly can take a completely different place in the social order, the play begins to raise questions of how much that social order is a human construction whose validity is more like that of a game than that of divine or natural law."[29]

Hospitable practice constructs, but the representation of hospitable practice will necessarily reveal constructedness. What does this mean from the perspective of the host? The genteel host certainly triumphs. Taking advantage of the practice of hospitality, he has managed to fashion in one stroke civility and its antithesis. He has demonstrated a fashioning power not unlike Wolsey's and simultaneously confirmed that his creation of a monstrous Sly simply clarifies a matter of character.[30] If the play hints too boldly that what passes for "natural" is really human construction, then it also offers its elite audience the comfortable fantasy that the tools of hospitable shaping are in good hands.

The conservative nature of Shakespeare's romantic comedies may be absolutely defined by such processes of acculturation, cultural pedagogies that wait in Frye's and Barber's models like so many spider webs. Usually glossed as a theorist of theater, Theseus goes far in defining the courtly techniques of acculturation as he situates himself in the ambiguous role of host:

> The kinder we, to give them thanks for nothing.
> Our sport shall be to take what they mistake . . .
> Where I have come, great clerks have purposed
> To greet me with premeditated welcomes;
> Where I have seen them shiver and look pale,
> Make periods in the midst of sentences,

> Throttle their practised accent in their fears,
> And, in conclusion, dumbly have broke off,
> Not paying me a welcome. Trust me, sweet,
> Out of this silence yet I picked a welcome.
>   (5.1.89–90, 93–100)

Theseus the host understands his role through Theseus the (conqueror) guest. We should not be surprised, he suggests, that the lower orders attempt civil speech genres that fail in the presence of true civility. The aristocratic host keeps them in their place and treats them with kindness by taking what they mistake, by picking welcomes from what the lower orders cannot express. Consequently, Theseus's kindness, his ruler's philosophy of hosting, implies a strategy of cultural conquest. Not only does the hospitable situation isolate the lower orders, it engenders a silence out of which the culture's authorities may pluck the very capacity of speech. To be sure, this strategy hardly indicates some *unusually* evil bent on the part of the aristocracy, for it animates the whole of authoritative relations in the period. Shakespeare simply elaborates the existing image of the "unkind Theseus" alive in his source materials and familiar to his audience, linking source to contemporary cultural practice.[31]

If the lower orders become subject to civilized economy, the elites find no simple stability in the same economy. Representation of hospitable practices makes this clear. In Shakespeare's romantic comedies, distinct segments of the ruling elite are silenced and shaped in the same way. Examples abound, but the situation in *Much Ado about Nothing* epitomizes this economy. The embodiment of internecine struggle between versions of dominance, Don John offers himself as guest. Leonato responds: "Let me bid you welcome, my lord. Being reconciled to the Prince your brother, I owe you all duty" (1.1.137–38). Here the language of hosting reproduces the period's hierarchy of duty and encourages the reconciliation of conflicting political agendas. Like the guests at Cecil's Theobalds, Don John is expected to assume his position in the ruling hierarchy as he assumes his lodging; his hosting makes the other elites vulnerable. (I will have more to say about Don John as guest later in this chapter.)

In a manner recalling the Lord's handling of Sly, Don Pedro subtly constrains and shapes the erotic desires of Hero, Benedick, and Beatrice. The ruler "silences" Benedick, Beatrice, and Claudio in order to choreograph his own entertainments. In each case, he takes and redistributes what they mistake. In particular, he must refigure Beatrice; for, as Jean Howard has shown, Beatrice exists as a challenge to the male authority of the court.[32] By arranging for players, taking a part himself, and utilizing the household topography (the theater of hospitality) to confirm his illusions, Don Pedro civilizes Beatrice and the other would-be lovers. In this play, hosting gathers elites together in such a way that the very structures of dominance become malleable.

Petruchio's taming of Kate similarly depends on nothing so much as a kind of hospitable acculturation of a woman from his own class. The servants that were summoned with such care for traditional values now serve the husband's tactical interests:

> Go, rascals, go, and fetch my supper in.
> "Where is the life that late I led?"
> Where are those—? Sit down, Kate,
> And welcome. Food, food, food, food! (4.1.123–26)

Petruchio isolates his wife's uncivil behavior in a tortuous welcome that never really offers food. Like the Lord in the play's induction, he hosts the "monstrous creature" so that she, like Sly, must wonder: where is the life that late I led? Echoing Sly in the induction, Petruchio explains that Kate is, after all, his "household stuff" (3.2.227).[33]

This male version of acculturation reaches its most offensive form (for most critics of Shakespeare) in *Two Gentlemen of Verona* when Valentine offers Silvia to Proteus as an example of civil behavior correcting—by exceeding in "generosity"—the uncivil actions of his "friend." Almost as an afterthought, the playwright seeks to resolve the drama's conflict by appealing to the powerful protocols of hospitality. As a kind of jovial gloss for his prior offer, Valentine offers his band of outlaws to the Duke as "reformèd, civil, full of good" (5.4.157). The consummation of their civility will, according to the play's host (the Duke) proceed in a now-familiar register: "Dispose of them as thou know'st their deserts. / Come, let us go; we will include all jars / With triumphs, mirth, and rare solemnity" (5.4.160–62). Degree obtains in a civilizing hospitality. The outlaws are silent, eventually disposed of—not unlike the women. Welcomes are plucked. Closure comes in civilizing marriage: "Our day of marriage shall be yours: / One feast, one house, one mutual happiness" (173–74). In this finale, represented practice yields genuine political advantage as it enables the acculturation of "gentlemen / Such as the fury of ungoverned youth / Thrust from the company of awful men" (4.1.44–46). Outlaws follow the analogous submission of women. Ungoverned and splintered elites have been brought from the wild into civility.

The realization of such a civil wildness is perhaps most eloquently managed by Duke Senior in *As You Like It*. As A. Stuart Daley has demonstrated, the Forest of Arden is no idyllic tangle of foliage, but a topography resembling the deforested reality of the English landscape, a place that recognizes English cold, English hunger, and an Englishman's desire for food. As Daley shows, in this forest world hospitality is, as England's pamphlet literature suggested, an uncertain necessity. Corin complains of his master's lack of hospitality and in so doing echoes often-ignored complaints of Duke Senior: "My master is of churlish disposition / And little recks to find the way to heaven / By doing deeds of hospitality" (2.4.75–77). Acculturation seems to hold the answer, as Daley explains: "The Forest's inhabitants also represent the classical three estates of the commonwealth, thereby allowing for the play's stress on the individual's obligation to his calling or vocation, which was then esteemed to be indispensable to a person's harmonious life in society and to achievement of the common good."[34]

The recognition of this obligation occurs in the primary genres of hospitality. Duke Senior is approached by Orlando, who practically embodies Shakespeare's notion of fractious elites:

> ORLANDO: Forbear, and eat no more!
> JAQUES: Why, I have eat none yet.
> ORLANDO: Nor shalt not, till necessity be served.
> JAQUES: Of what kind should this cock come of?
> DUKE SENIOR: Art thou thus boldened, man, by thy distress,
>   Or else a rude despiser of good manners,
>   That in civility thou seem'st so empty?
>   (2.7.88–93)

The confrontation happens suddenly and so must be managed tactically. An ungoverned gentleman, Orlando couches his anger in the language of the table. He expects the wild to offer nothing of hospitality without force and so, in the language of King Ferdinand in *Love's Labour's Lost*, asserts the *necessity* of hospitality. As Shakespeare's host, Duke Senior makes clear that the issue is one of acculturation, of good manners, of civility in the wild. Like Shakespeare's other hosts, Duke Senior answers the desperation of conflicting aristocratic aims. Shakespeare meanwhile builds his scene from the speech genres of hospitable practice: "Welcome. Set down your venerable burden / And let him feed" (2.7.167–68). After the model of Kalander and the sullen Musidorus, Duke Senior assures his guest: "Welcome, fall to. I will not trouble you / As yet to question you about your fortunes. / Give us some music; and, good cousin, sing" (171–73). The liminal space that allows the play's resolution looks less like Barber's "release" than it does an ideal realization of hospitality as civil wildness with a host of aristocratic agendas intact.

Untenable Hosts

From the perspective of the host, Shakespeare's romantic comedies tantalize with experiments in household stuff, with the possibilities of acculturation in hosting. The reality that Cecil noted with "The Queen stayed" seems in Shakespeare's hands a glittering exploration of authority. Recent scholarship interested in the possibilities of subversion has qualified such a claim by pointing, in Howard's words, to the fact that "a contradiction opens within the material conditions of stage representation between what is being represented and who is doing the representing."[35] The simple act of taking "parts," of allowing members of the lower orders to reproduce the antics of the rulers, so the argument goes, may undermine the existing structures of authority. This argument makes an important contribution to our understanding of theater and culture. Nevertheless, in the case of romantic comedy, the critic may err in making this dynamic the single source of critique and resistance in the genre.

Reading *Much Ado about Nothing* with superb clarity, Howard sees, for example, a consolidation of authority in Don Pedro's theatrical manipulation: "And while the cynical Benedick can imagine his friends as deceivers, he cannot think this of the grave Leonato: 'I should think this a gull but that the white-bearded fellow speaks it. Knavery cannot, sure, hide himself in such reverence' (2.3.115–17). Age has authorizing force" (p. 179). Whose age? Don Pedro's? Obviously, not. Howard has demonstrated that the ruler hosting (much as Elizabeth did) at a noble's house *depends* on men of lower rank (white-bearded Leonato) to realize fictions. Howard admits this dependence, but her commentary grants a monological authority to Don Pedro. From the perspective of a host, however, Don Pedro's power must seem less in this example. Nevertheless, because she can assert the "material conditions of stage representation" as a constant source of subversion, Howard passes over the cracks in this version of aristocratic control.

Similarly, Louis A. Montrose wants to claim for Theseus the final triumph of a dominant order: "If Theseus finally overbears Egeus' will (4.1.178), it is because the father's obstinate claim to 'the ancient privilege of Athens' (1.1.41) threatens to obstruct the very process by which Athenian privilege and Athens itself are reproduced. Hermia and Helena are granted their desires—but those desires have themselves been shaped and directed by a social imperative."[36] The summary is convincing but not of a piece, for Montrose admits that Theseus and Egeus represent conflicting agendas, that Theseus "overbears Egeus' will." In fact, the authority of the male social imperative splits in these two men. Montrose goes on to conclude that Theseus's usurpation of the noble householder's authority only enhances the power of a ruling elite: "Athenian privilege and Athens." This account hides the real economy: *one elite's power has increased as another elite's power has been confiscated.*

A Renaissance householder could, moreover, take exception to Montrose's confident statement that the women's desires have been "shaped and directed by a social imperative." For at the end of the play, these desires have been shaped most dramatically by the fairy world—an enchanted party hosting at Theseus's court for the wedding festivities. Theseus's guests have done exactly as they pleased, shaping and directing, exchanging shapes and directions. In offering these qualifications, I certainly do not wish to adduce some level of "revolutionary" activity heretofore neglected by materialist criticism; rather I am suggesting that materialist criticism, by failing to appreciate the complicated exchange between real and implied hosts in the genre, has confirmed a "dominant authority" that could not have been received as such by Shakespeare's contemporaries.

In *Much Ado about Nothing*, Don Pedro offers hospitality for Leonato: "My dear friend Leonato hath invited you all. I tell him we shall stay here at the least a month, and he heartily prays some occasion may detain us longer" (1.1.132–35). That Shakespeare consciously, logically for his age, is beginning to weave together the uncertain languages of hospitality seems apparent in Don Pedro's tag at the end of the invitation: "I dare swear he [Leonato] is no hypocrite, but prays from his heart." Why raise the issue of truth? Leonato's response borrows from Shakespeare's most characteristic language of love's labors in the sonnets: "If you swear, my lord, you shall not be forsworn. Let me bid you welcome, my lord" (136–37). Hosting is an uncertain business played out in the terms of erotic desire: "In loving thee thou know'st I am forsworn, / But thou art twice forsworn, to me love swearing" (Sonnet 152). This complex desire recalls the forswearing hinted at by the Princess in *Love's Labour's Lost*: "I hear your Grace hath sworn out house-keeping: / 'Tis deadly sin to keep that oath, my lord, / And sin to break it" (2.1.103–5). Guests, like lovers, cradle declarations of care, picking them apart tactically for hints of hidden motives.

Hospitality and desire share the same language. From his first efforts as a playwright, Shakespeare toys with the ways welcoming awakens desire. Indeed, the very protractions demanded by aristocratic decorum stand as a minor obstacle to the immediate attraction of soon-to-be lovers and so only serve to heighten desire. From *The Comedy of Errors* to *The Winter's Tale*, Shakespeare acknowledges this pattern. Antipholus of Syracuse finds in the erring welcome of Luciana a "sweet mermaid" (3.2.45). In consonance with the experience of his dramatic forbears, Leontes finds lust in the practice of hospitality, borrowing the pamphleteer's description of ancient tradition to name infidelity. Leontes complains that his "gates" have been opened (1.2.196). Volumes have been written about the irrationality of Leontes's desire and the "absence" of violation that drives the jealousy.[37]

In fact, Leontes and his counterparts in romantic comedy could appeal to dramatic precedent. For the playwright interested in comic models, John Heywood's *John the Husband, Tyb his Wife, and Sir John the Priest* (c. 1520) dramatizes the suspicion of the husband over Tyb's "gadding" with the priest. One of England's less intelligent householders, John agrees to invite his enemy for dinner and pie:

> Shall he come hither? by Cock's soul I was a-curst
> When that I granted to that word first!
> But since I have said it, I dare not say nay,
> For then my wife and I should make a fray.[38]

Here in an early form is the Renaissance householder's double business. By following the dictates of traditional hospitality, he runs the risk of awakening desire that will undo his authority. John wants no credit for the hosting: "Wife, thou shalt have the worship / And the thanks of thy guest, that is thy gossip" (p. 74). Nevertheless, hosting proves to be the comic dissolution of John's already endangered authority. Soon he is setting the table, fetching a stool, washing cups, checking the ale. When John returns with the guest, it is he—the "host"—who must perform a laborious set of chores that make it impossible for him to consume his own food. Tyb offers the entertainment to her guest: "Welcome, mine own sweetheart, / We shall make some cheer or we depart" (p. 80). The householder's only recourse is to drive them both from the house, but hosting leaves his mind troubled with the thought that Tyb and the priest will yet do him some "villainy." Even in this early English comedy, hospitality fuels desire and offers a tactical mode of contestation. Leontes's doubts are the outcome of an old comedy.

Nowhere does Shakespeare draw this dynamic so distinctly as in *Two Gentlemen of Verona*. In the arrival of Proteus at the court of Milan, the terms of hospitality presage desiring quibbles. Valentine instructs Silvia: "Welcome, dear Proteus. Mistress, I beseech you / Confirm his welcome with some special favor" (2.4.97–98). Twice Valentine begs that Silvia "entertain" Proteus, a term that in this context would certainly suggest erotic desire to a Renaissance audience. Proteus's contemplation of the meeting sounds very much like the lover of Shakespeare's sonnets and Leonato of *Much Ado:* "To leave my Julia, shall I be forsworn; / To love fair Silvia, shall I be forsworn; / To wrong my friend, I shall be much forsworn" (2.6.1–3). From the perspective of the Renaissance host, Shakespeare's romantic comedy is developing in a most disturbing fashion. For the ancient and successful authority practiced through hospitality by men such as Cecil seems to contain its own diminution in this awakening desire.

As he wrote his romantic comedies, Shakespeare contemplated the tragic possibilities of this process. Old Capulet, in *Romeo and Juliet*, wants to host, but his hosting depends on a servant "to find those persons whose names are here writ, and [who] can never find what names the writing person hath here writ" (1.2.41–43). Like Proteus, Romeo accepts a stray invitation of hospitality only to give over his old love for a desire awakened in the entertaining. The hosts in Shakespeare's audience would have had little difficulty in sensing the perils of household stuff looming in Shakespeare's romantic comedies:

> Two households, both alike in dignity,
>   In fair Verona, where we lay our scene,
> From ancient grudge break to new mutiny,
>   Where civil blood makes civil hands unclean. (1–4)

To the extent that it prompts erotic desire, hospitality may first subvert the authority of the host and then the aristocratic order. Civil wildness, so essential to romantic comedy, always hints at the possibility of civil blood, as Verona and Sidney's Laconia attest.

I suggest, then, that romantic comedy only adapts and confirms dominant authority heterogeneously, strengthening one elite to weaken another. A kind of aristocratic authority is always confirmed in romantic comedy, but the final possibilities for authoritative action as described at the play's beginning are always less at the play's end. As hospitality inherently loosens erotic desire, the host's political authority is diminished. By way of concluding this chapter, I want to consider the ways that Shakespeare's appropriation of the idea of hospitality enacts a *diminution* of authority. My argument will focus on the fact that neither in Shakespeare's romantic comedies nor in Shakespeare's England can we locate the "independent host." Almost by definition, the host manifested his will through an elaborate system of functionaries who handled the minor offices of welcome, purveyance, the preparation of food, the planning of musical and theatrical entertainment, and so on. A host could never entirely see for himself or listen for himself. The distance between will and action was thus broken by a series of gaps. In romantic comedy, hosts consistently lose authority in these gaps. As the laws of thermodynamics tell us, something is always lost in the circulation.[39] Insofar as Shakespeare chooses to re-present this process of loss, the opportunities for rewriting the play as so much noble adaptation become awkward.

If hospitality implies a male usurpation of woman's authority in the noble household, then the appropriation of hospitality in romantic comedy, focussed as it is entirely on the aristocratic world, "frees" the aristocratic heroine from household responsibilities. In this light, it is fascinating to posit a woman, perhaps the Countess of Pembroke, as the implied audience of romantic comedy. In her handling of Sidney's manuscript, the countess asserted the woman's right to "edit" and "augment" a male narrative of desire. Her hospitality had enabled the composition in an age that made male hospitality the locus of authority. Like the Countess of Pembroke, strong women in Shakespeare's romantic comedies edit and augment male appropriations of hospitable discourse. To their audiences these characters offer subject positions that do not mesh neatly with existing patriarchal hierarchies.

An inkling of this capacity occurs at the end of *Love's Labour's Lost* when political responsibility, in the form of death, interrupts the entertainment. To borrow Berowne's word, the women have "deformed" male authority. The wooing entertainments have been edited in terms of the interests of powerful women. The proposed academy has been augmented by the women's imposition of stricter regimes. At the end of the play, the male hosts are diminished, haunted, even shaped, by the will of the female editor. A similar case occurs in *Two Gentlemen of Verona*. Julia disguises and receives the aid of a host: "Now, my young guest, methinks you're allycholly. I pray you, why is it?" (4.2.27–28). As in *Love's Labour's Lost*, the woman becomes a guest who edits the final scene. It is the disguised guest, after all, who interrupts Valentine's offer of Silvia: "Behold her that gave aim to all thy oaths, / And entertained 'em deeply in her heart" (5.4.102–03). Women in romantic comedy entertain the human obligations of male entertainment, editing the practice with humane care.

As male authority contracts, Shakespeare expands the genre from its models in Greene, Peele, and Lodge. A decidedly Shakespearean heroine appears, a liminal hostess with male mobility capable of accomplishing what the genre's male hosts cannot: Rosalind of *As You Like It*. The ruling aristocratic household has been displaced and the woman banished. When Orlando "can live no longer by thinking," Rosalind edits:

> Believe then, if you please, that I can do strange things. I have, since I was three years old, conversed with a magician, most profound in his art and yet not damnable. If you do love Rosalind so near the heart as your gesture cries it out, when your brother marries Aliena shall you marry her. (5.2.56–61)

Elizabeth's householders created pageants asking the assembled guests to believe in the magic of a woman. Rosalind produces her own mythological entertainment, a final version of erotic desire and resulting order. Marriage is yet at the end of the entertainment, but the pageant has been edited.

For Tennenhouse this final movement exists as a genuine triumph for male authority. The playwright has first shifted male power to the women:

> But this shift in power from male to female—Orsino to Olivia—is part of a circuit of exchange which relocates power in the male through the marriage ceremony which concludes all of the comedies. When the male figures—Petruchio, Theseus, Orsino, Bassanio—do come to embody patriarchal power, however, the power they embody has changed. In the transfer of this power from male to female and back again, romantic comedy transforms it. Having passed into the body of a woman, power becomes her gift to give. As such, it assumes a more humane and less violent form.[40]

With its quasi-anthropological perspective, Tennenhouse's argument is rather convincing. Having determined that power in Elizabethan culture is the subject of his analysis, he assumes a position outside the culture and describes with clarity a particular shaping of that power as forms of authority circulating through theater. But this kind of analysis excludes the specificity of subject positions from which Shakespeare's audience could view his romantic comedies; it excludes their difficulty in rewriting these ideals and practices for use in the culture.

Although from a twentieth-century perspective the evolution of a "more humane and less violent form" of power is (for many) a positive achievement, it could not have been so in the eyes of the Renaissance host. Imagine, for a moment, Lord Burghley attempting to assume a place in *As You Like It*. Imagine that he, not surprisingly, identifies with Duke Senior. Could we comfort him with the knowledge that (1) his lost authority has been reinstated in a male form, (2) his daughter has practiced a fantastic hosting far outstripping his powers to alter his own fate, (3) his old power has become more humane? I suspect that Burghley would answer: (1) reinstated but not in me! (2) my daughter has my power? (3) what is humane? This hypothetical viewing deserves qualification, of course. We may assume from an absence of comment that no one considered the genre and its editing heroines as "deeply revolutionary." But this is not the point. In his appropriation of hospitality, Shakespeare has created an implied audience that resists inhabitation. The playwright has captured the gender division and usurpation implicit in the role of host in order to posit a subject position no authority figure of the time would care to inhabit. So complete is this accomplishment that the whole history of scholarship devoted to the genre simply ignores the final position of host. Edited and augmented, this kind of closure hardly initiates civil war. It does, however, prepare the way.

From the moment that we first meet the Duke in *Two Gentlemen of Verona*, he fulfills the requirements of a perfect English host, entertaining willingly, in strict accord with degree. As we have already noted, however, his admitting of guests engenders a desire that directly undermines his authority. To say that guests make the household—and the authority of the male host—vulnerable is an understatement. Bedford puts it succinctly in *1 Henry VI*: "I have heard it said, unbidden guests/ Are often welcomest when they are gone" (2.2.55–56). The exploration of this fact in *Two Gentlemen of Verona* reveals much about the origins of this vulnerability. By definition, hosting establishes a decorum of credulity for entertainer and entertained, a convention not unlike the Romantic notion of a "willing suspension of disbelief." That the Duke succumbs to this protocol with respect to Valentine's intentions is made only more striking by his belief in the purity of Proteus's motives when the unexamined guest tells of Valentine's plans to steal Silvia.

In *Much Ado about Nothing*, Shakespeare puts the credulity of hosting at the play's center. We may recall that Leonato carefully includes Don John in his welcome at the play's beginning. In essence Don John's capacity for destruction comes from his being a guest. Shifting the scholarly focus on the play from matters of appearance and reality, Elliot Krieger has defined the work's crucial question: "what about the society of Messina both allows its inhabitants to create deception as a continual menace and at the same time leaves them unable to recognize and to forestall the deceptions with which they are confronted?"[41] One answer, partial but essential, is that this courtly world, like the one shaped by Elizabeth, realizes its aims through household entertainment, an admitting of guests into a heightened world of credulity where queens become deities and, it seems, virgins, whores.

In his own crass way, Borachio speaks the terms of this engagement. In his first appearance, he reports of entertainment: "I came yonder from a great supper. The Prince your brother is royally entertained by Leonato, and I can give you intelligence of an intended marriage" (1.3.37–39). As Wolsey or Cecil would have appreciated, royal entertainments, suppers in particular, produce useful intelligence. In Shakespeare's romantic comedies, the intelligence always hints at erotic desire. Having established the terms of his role, Borachio explains his methods with a slanting quibble: "Being entertained for a perfumer, as I was smoking a musty room, comes me the Prince and Claudio, hand in hand in sad conference" (51–53). One who gauges courtly motives and plots through entertainments may be easily "entertained" for another. Almost by definition, hospitality seems to permit this kind of play with social function and tactical opportunity. Pretending the hospitable function of sweetening a room with juniper, Borachio succeeds because of the credulity implicit in hospitable functions.[42]

Don John disrupts the courtly order to the extent that he follows his servant's lead. The formula for success comes from Sir Henry Wotton's clear understanding of the household as a theater of hospitality. Don John offers a formula for this theater that would have pleased Elizabeth's nobility as they attempted to shape and redistribute power through household productions: "If you dare not trust that you see, confess not that you know" (3.2.104–5). Though the ends are different, Don John's method of offering a hospitable construction of reality resembles nothing so much as the Earl of Hertford's 1591 entertainment of Elizabeth in which he went so far as to construct a whole mock village to house the court. Passing by the village that wasn't "really" there, Elizabeth arrived at the household to watch water deities that were not "really" there.[43] The success of Hertford's hospitality depended not on reality but on the ruler's "trust in seeing." Drizzle falls on Borachio and his plans just as it did on Hertford's fanciful plans. In the end, Don John's manipulation fails, but it succeeds in casting an entirely different light on hosting—so essential to the functioning of Elizabeth's court and of romantic comedy as inspired by Sidney. The existing order triumphs, but its vulnerability has been established. The ruling orders' pleasure in "what is not" leaves them open to manipulation.

Perhaps the best way to appreciate the nature of aristocratic triumph in Shakespeare's romantic comedies is to distinguish the triumph of an order from the triumph of the agents of that order. To the extent that the genre meshes the aristocratic order with the forces of acculturation in early modern Europe, a triumph is assured. On the other hand, to the extent that the civilizing host attempts to deploy the protocols of hospitality, he suffers diminution, the most telling instances of which arise out of the host's reliance on other powers to realize his entertainments.

The example of Theseus is fascinating in this light both for the diminution it reveals and for the consistent attempts of scholars to contain the effect. Since Charlton, it has been customary to view Theseus and Hippolyta as the normalized authority in the play.[44] We have already noted how, in his reading of the comedy, Montrose condenses the authorities of Athens into the authority of Theseus, ignoring the diminution of Egeus's authority. Such a reading depends, moreover, on the careful elision of Theseus's reliance on other powers to realize the authority he exercises. Montrose contends that Hermia "wishes the limited privilege of giving herself. Theseus appropriates the source of Hermia's fragile power: her ability to deny men access to her body. He usurps the power of virginity by imposing upon Hermia his own power to deny her the use of her body."[45] Montrose's argument demands qualification, for Theseus *wants* to "usurp" and "impose." In fact, before he gets the opportunity, Hermia has spent a night with the ruler's uninvited fairy guests. The resolution provided by the play, confirming as it does the aristocratic order, has been produced in fact by the unwarranted effects of the ruler's hosting. The order triumphs, but the agency of the ruler, like the agency of the householder Egeus, seems diminished. In what sense could one say that such representations of practices could be received as comfortable adaptations?

The most intriguing example of this process occurs in Howard's more intentionally subversive reading of *Much Ado about Nothing*. Here we return to Sidney's anxiety and find it distilled into much ado. I have already noted Howard's maintenance of an air of subversion about the play, but the claim remains little more than atmospheric as she describes the contribution of Dogberry and Verges to the play's triumph:

> The world is only righted by two lower-class figures who flounder mightily in the Queen's English, and who capture the villains virtually by instinct rather than by any rational understanding of what was overheard or said or done by anyone. Moreover, it seems that the gift of intuition is bought at the price of speech and rationality. Dogberry and Verges exist almost outside of language, and this placement denies them any real social power.[46]

In short, according to Howard, the success of the two characters keeps "alive the dream of a world where good and evil are transparent to the eye of innocence, and inferiors correct the 'mistakings' of their betters without ever threatening the essential beliefs of those betters" (p. 177). We cannot ignore that the play triumphs, embarrassingly it seems, through the agency of Dogberry and company. How to explain this fact? Howard draws from the resources of the genre in acculturation. Like Theseus, she circumscribes the agency of the lower orders on the basis of their inability to speak a civilized tongue. The fact remains, however, that Dogberry and company communicate well enough on their own terms. Speech exists. They are certainly not mad. Rationality exists. Dogberry and his crew simply lack a certain civility. To exclude their part on the basis of instinct is to suppose that instinct is a base phenomenon of the lower orders who lack reason. In fact, as we have already seen in Sidney's narrative, Kalander—the ideal aristocratic host—evaluates his potential guests on the basis of instinct. Indeed, throughout Renaissance drama, disguised nobility is recognized instinctively. Of course, the most important claim in Howard's reading is that the lower orders, by enabling a triumph of aristocratic control, do not challenge established beliefs. Again, if we distinguish between an aristocratic order and aristocratic agents, Howard's claim may be revised. The order survives, but in the processes of identification and construction, the authority of Don Pedro and Leonato is obviously diminished.

Finally, the Renaissance householder could always fall back on Sidney's assurance that such matters were little more than a spider web, "fitter to be swept away than worn to any other purpose." And, after all, was not this Shakespeare's assurance as well, when he offered Puck at the end of the play:

> Not a mouse
> Shall disturb this hallowed house.
> I am sent, with broom, before,
> To sweep the dust behind the door. (5.1.376–79)

It was only housekeeping, a civil wildness, an idle theme.

NOTES

1. Wayne C. Booth, *The Rhetoric of Fiction*, 137n. For a thoughtful elaboration of this notion, see Iser, *The Act of Reading*, 27-38.

2. The best introduction to this dissemination of subject positions is in feminist film theory. See, for example, the variety of approaches offered in *Feminism and Film Theory*, ed. Constance Penley (New York: Routledge, 1988). Also, see Silverman, *The Subject of Semiotics*.

3. Iser, *The Act of Reading*, 37. Indeed, as Iser points out, the

possibility of cultural criticism depends on this tension, for "the sacrifice of the real reader's own beliefs would mean the loss of the whole repertoire of historical norms and values, and this in turn would entail the loss of the tension which is a precondition for the processing and for the comprehension that follows it" (37).

4. Sidney, *The Countess of Pembroke's Arcadia*, 57. Subsequent references to this work will be from this edition and appear parenthetically in the text.

5. For an excellent discussion of this containment, see Waller, "The Countess of Pembroke and Gendered Reading," in *The Renaissance Englishwoman in Print*, 333. Lucas provides a fine commentary on the countess as reader of the *Arcadia* in her *Writing for Women*, 118–32.

6. Waller makes this suggestion about the countess's career with particular reference to her psalms: "The countess's 'tinkerings' in the psalms are at once evidence for her being written by the masculinist patriarchal/fratriarchal discourse of her age; yet at the same time they show the glimmerings of a 'disaffection' as she struggled to encode her own *jouissance*" (339). For a discussion of the term *jouissance* in the context of feminist theory, see Moi, *Sexual/Textual Politics*, 118–21.

7. Sidney, "To Robert Sidney," 18 Oct. 1580, *The Complete Works of Sir Philip Sidney*, 3:133. That Jonson would write his great lyric "To Penshurst" in praise of the Sidneys' hospitality seems, in this light, all the more resonant.

8. This animation seems to have extended to Jonson, whose "To Penshurst" praises the Sidneys' hospitality, in part, by echoing Sir Philip's images of the practice in the *Arcadia*. For a discussion of this connection, see Hibbard, "The Country-House Poem of the Seventeenth Century,"159n.

9. Turner, "The Disfigured Face of Nature," 123.

10. Charles I, *The Royal Proclamations of Charles I, 1625–1640*, 2:350.

11. Tennenhouse, *Power on Display*, 18–19.

12. Charlton, *Shakespearean Comedy*; Frye, *The Anatomy of Criticism*, 163–86; Bradbrook, *The Growth and Structure of Elizabethan Comedy*; and Salingar, *Shakespeare and the Traditions of Comedy*.

13. Barber, *Shakespeare's Festive Comedy*; Nevo, *Comic Transformations in Shakespeare*; Carroll, *The Metamorphoses of Shakespearean Comedy*; and Leggatt, *Shakespeare's Comedy of Love*.

14. Krieger's *A Marxist Study of Shakespeare's Comedies* prepares the reader, with its very title, for a dialectical analysis of material culture and Shakespeare. Yet when the critic approaches *A Midsummer Night's Dream*, his attention comes to rest on ideas of "the imagination." In reading *As You Like It*, Krieger studies the "Nature/Fortune opposition" (68, 72). Suddenly, Marxism looks very much like formalist explication, a limitation avoided by Terry Eagleton as he wheels more freely through a political revision of Shakespeare's writings. Describing his work as "an exercise in political semiotics, which tries to locate the relevant history in the very letter of the text," Eagleton's examination of *A Midsummer Night's Dream* and *Twelfth Night* in *William Shakespeare* (Oxford: Basil Blackwell, 1986) hinges on the play of desire in language (ix, 20, 34). The subversive energies Eagleton finds in the plays remain trapped in a literary domain uncomplicated by the plays' countless mediations.

15. Cohen, *Drama of a Nation*, 187.

16. With more attention to individual texts, Tennenhouse locates the capacity for aristocratic adaptation in the fact that Shakespeare's comic heroines never threaten to seize control of the state or its icon—the body of the aristocratic female. They can therefore provide the means of interrogating certain features of the aristocratic culture without challenging the hierarchy based on the purity of the aristocratic community (41).

17. Burt, "'Tis Writ by Me,'" 332–46.

18. Brownstein, *Becoming a Heroine*; Hulse, "Stella's Wit," in *Rewriting the Renaissance*, 273; Lucas, *Writing for Women*; and Waller, *English Poetry of the Sixteenth Century*. Another fascinating version of this argument is made by Quilligan in "The Comedy of Female Authority in *The Faerie Queene*," 156–71. Quilligan notes Spenser's isolation of Queen Elizabeth as his implied reader; she contends that the poet invoked *comedy* as a means of representing the unsettling authority of a female ruler.

Obviously the examples above share a feminist agenda. This should not imply that the approach is limited to feminist concerns. In his *Rhetoric of Motives*, Kenneth Burke anticipates many of these strategies as he lays out the terms of a sociological and anthropological criticism guided by attention to processes of *identification*.

19. Using Sidney and the Earl of Oxford and their famous dispute on the tennis court as a basis for her analysis, Quilligan probes the animosity between elites of different rank in "Sidney and His Queen," in *The Historical Renaissance,* 171–96. Quilligan's reading absolutely confounds an uncritical conflation of aristocratic positioning in Shakespeare's plays.

20.   Novy, "Patriarchy and Play in *The Taming of the Shrew,*" 279.

21.   I draw examples from several of the most influential critics working with these materials: Dollimore, "Transgression and Surveillance in *Measure for Measure,*" in *Political Shakespeare,* 73; Tennenhouse, *Power on Display,* 56–57; and Moretti, "The Great Eclipse," in *Signs Taken for Wonders,* 41-42.

22.   For documents describing the rise of these "new families," see C. H. Williams, ed., *English Historical Documents, 1485–1558,* 259–67. For a discussion of the Sidneys' and the Cecils' negotiations of marriage, see Tennenhouse, *Power on Display,* 30.

23.   Revisions of the lingering use of a monological elite can be found. See, for example, Sharpe, *Criticism and Compliment,* 10–11, 21, 27.

24.   Gurr, *Playgoing in Shakespeare's London,* 49–59.

25.   Burghley, as discussed in Chapter 1, perhaps best illustrates this relationship. See Smuts's *Court Culture and the Origins of a Royalist Tradition in Early Stuart England* for an extended argument; see also Sharpe, *Criticism and Compliment,* 16.

26.   Bordieu, *Outline of a Theory of Practice,* 12.

27.   See, for example, Egan, *Drama within Drama,* 5–7; and Garber, *Shakespeare's Ghost Writers,* 87–88.

28.   Muchembled, *Popular Culture and Elite Culture in France, 1400–1750,* 189–90.

29.   Novy, "Patriarchy and Play in *The Taming of the Shrew,*" 265. It may be worth noting that James I resisted the imposition of this civil protocol of handwashing on his own Royal Person.

30.   Although the critic may hardly reason from Sly's absence at the play's end, I think it poetically appropriate that the upshot of the Lord's hosting is the disappearance of his plebeian guest. In the practice of hospitality, the common man is little more than a marker, a cipher hardly necessary for the end of a representation. I think it generically illustrative, moreover, that the Lord's shaping of the lower orders through hospitable practice gives way so "naturally" in romantic comedy to a man's attempt at the shaping of a woman through the same practice.

31. For a discussion of this version of Theseus, see Pearson, "'Unkinde' Theseus," 276–98.

32. Howard, "Renaissance Antitheatricality and the Politics of Gender and Rank in *Much Ado about Nothing*," (hereafter referred to as "Renaissance Antitheatricality") in *Shakespeare Reproduced*, 180.

33. Lady Anne Clifford records a real, albeit milder, version of hospitable taming at the hands of her own husband in her diary, 31.

One could go so far as to say that, in his handling of source materials, Shakespeare does precisely the same thing as Petruchio, taking folktales of taming and hosting them in another class so that they forget themselves. To follow this use, see Brunvand, "The Folktale Origin of *The Taming of the Shrew*," 345–59; and Newman, "Renaissance Family Politics and Shakespeare's *The Taming of the Shrew*," 86–100.

34. Daley, "The Dispraise of the Country in *As You Like It*," 304.

35. Howard, "Renaissance Antitheatricality," in *Shakespeare Reproduced*, 183. On this institutional dynamic, see Weimann's "Towards a Literary Theory of Ideology" in *Shakespeare Reproduced*, 265–72.

36. Montrose, "*A Midsummer Night's Dream* and the Shaping Fantasies of Elizabethan Culture," in *Rewriting the Renaissance*, 72.

37. Felperin, "'Tongue-tied our queen?'" in *Shakespeare and the Question of Theory*, 3–18.

38. John Heywood, *John the Husband, Tyb his Wife, and Sir John the Priest*, 73.

39. See Serres, "The Origin of Language," in *Hermes*, 71–83.

40. Tennenhouse, *Power on Display*, 68.

41. Krieger, "Social Relations and the Social Order in *Much Ado about Nothing*," 49–61.

42. Evidence of this kind of attention to the olfactory qualities of entertainment appears in the Norwich *Chamberlains' Accounts* for 1542–1543: "Item paid for perfume for the chambyr whyche saverd sore" (*Norwich, 1540–1642*, 8).

43. Nichols, *Elizabeth*, 3:103.

44. Bonnard, "Shakespeare's Purpose in *A Midsummer Night's Dream*," 268–79.

45. Montrose, "*A Midsummer Night's Dream* and the Shaping Fantasies of Elizabethan Culture," in *Rewriting the Renaissance*, 73.

46. Howard, "Renaissance Antitheatricality" in *Shakespeare Reproduced*, 177. Contrast this position with Annabel Patterson's step toward revision in "Bottoms Up: Festive Theory in *A Midsummer Night's Dream*," in *Renaissance Papers* (Durham: Southeastern Renaissance Conference, 1988), 25–39: the play's "inarticulate message remains: a revaluation of those unpresentable members of society normally mocked as fools and burdened like asses, whose energies the social system relies on" (38).

3

Powerful Pinners and the Dispersion of Genre

Hospitality has never been the sole province of the aristocracy. In addition to his grand tales of royal, noble, and religious householding, John Stow recounted a hospitality of the neighborhood in his *Survey of London:*

> In the months of June, and July, on the vigils of festival days, and on the same festival days in the evenings after the sun setting, there were usually made bonfires in the streets, every man bestowing wood or labour towards them: the wealthier sort also before their doors near to the said bonfires, would set out tables on the vigils, furnished with sweet bread, and good drink, and on the festival days with meats and drinks plentifully, whereunto they would invite their neighbours and passengers also to sit, and be merry with them in great familiarity, praising God for his benefits bestowed on them.[1]

The meat and drink set out for all comers fulfills the age's hospitable ideal. Stow sets the scene apart. As twilight comes on, the household becomes a mere backdrop to a hospitality of the streets. Here, the whole burden of preparation has been lifted from a single host, and *every man*, as Stow points out, contributes wood or labor. Every man is host. In place of a genteel reinforcement of degree, Stow stresses that this hospitality encourages a "great familiarity." Like aristocratic hospitality, this common version depends on gifts and the everyday speech genres of invitation and welcome. Like its noble counterpart, plebeian hospitality finds a kind of apotheosis on festival days. What distinguishes this version of hospitality most from its aristocratic counterpart is the common people's experience of hosting as a communal activity, binding the individual to others.

If, as Lewis Hyde tells us, *"the gift must always move,"*[2] then plebeian hospitality in early modern England faithfully preserves the motion of ancient ways. Stow elaborates this facet by pointing out that "among neighbours that, being before at controversy, were there by the labour of others, reconciled, and made of bitter enemies, loving friends, as also for the virtue that a great fire hath to purge the infection of the air" (p. 101). In such instances, hospitality's shaping powers enable cheerful, quotidian ends. The production of this reconciled community could include, as Stow explains, elaborate spectacle, "garlands of beautiful flowers" and "lamps of glass, with oil burning in them all the night." One suspects that this sentimental picture of communal harmony has been touched up by the author, a suspicion that alters our historical sense of the traditions even as it encourages an exploration of the writer's appropriations of the idea. In Stow's words, this plebeian hospitality makes "a goodly show" (p. 101).

The present chapter proceeds from the notion that hosting by the lower orders makes a goodly show, a comedy in fact. Alongside the courtly play of romantic comedies, goodly shows of neighborly practice appeared, plays such as Thomas Dekker's *The Shoemakers' Holiday* and Thomas Heywood's *The Fair Maid of the Inn.* Drawing from the world of shoemakers and inns, playwrights replaced the copiousness of a noble's table with the copiousness of an ordinary host like Blague in *The Merry Devil of Edmonton:* "Welcome, good knight, to the George at Waltham, my free-hold, my tenements, goods & chattels. Madam, heer's a roome is the very *Homer* and *Iliads* of a lodging, it hath none of the foure elements in it; I built it out of the Center, and I drinke neere the lesse sacke. Welcome, my little wast of maiden-heads! What? I serue the good Duke of Norfolke."[3] Here were characters who served up the speech genres of welcome with savory abundance. As the play-

wright represented this copiousness according to the generic conventions of comedy, a version of plebeian life emerged that could,
in turn, become repertory for members of the lower orders in their
daily lives. It became possible to envision theatrically a situation
wherein communal relations displaced traditional hierarchies. In
these productions, plebeian figures met figures of authority on
different ideological ground. Characters cut from the same stuff as
Dogberry used their uncivil tongues to triumph as the plays'
central figures.

In what sense, this chapter asks, did the representation of
plebeian hosting take the form of a conflict between the lower
orders and the ruling elites? Need we—can we—talk of subversion in these depictions of popular culture? Initial answers to these
questions lie in a consideration of the generic contours of Renaissance comedy and the genre's paradoxical investment in simply
reflecting the social order even as it sported with the disruptive
energies of Carnival. I have chosen to focus on Robert Greene's[4]
George a Greene, the Pinner of Wakefield in this context because of its
devotion to matters of hospitality. I hope that what I suggest
concerning this unusual and little-discussed play will have
applicability for revisionary studies of other plebeian practices and
their appropriations in other neglected works. Meanwhile, in
order to avoid leaving this play in isolation, I will note its points
of contact with other plays of the period, with works as similar as
The Shoemakers' Holiday and as different as *A Midsummer Night's
Dream*. The possibility of resistance and subversion depends, it
seems, on the relative hospitality of genres.

Comic Genres and the Possibility of Resistance

D. J. Palmer neatly distills the history of comic theory into the
consensus that comedy means "a sense of triumph over whatever
is inimical to human or social good, however this ideal is defined."[5] Scholarly practice has divided Renaissance comedy according to the origin of its triumph in either satire or celebration.
In the former category, to borrow the distinction made by Dover
Wilson, the audience learns to laugh at the inimical forces. Into this
category go the plays of Jonson and Middleton.[6] In the latter
grouping, the audience laughs with the characters as the triumph

evolves into pure festivity. Shakespeare's romantic comedies and a play such as Dekker's *The Shoemaker's Holiday* exemplify the qualities of this group.[7] From this principal division, scholarship has gone on, like Polonius, to propose a flock of smaller comic genres: romantic comedy, city comedy, festive comedy, tragi-comedy, problem comedy, and so on. To a much greater extent than the study of tragedy, the study of Renaissance comedy has been determined by the multiplication and application of lesser genres. Yet for all the differences these various genres imply, the nature of comedy's "triumph" remains the same: the restitution or reinvigoration of the culture's existing hierarchy. Of course a multiplication of genres is not inherently "bad," but critics must reconsider this process: whose interests do these genres serve?

It should go without saying that the extant body of Renaissance comedies has hardly benefited from the multiplication of comic genres. Even the most cursory perusal of Terence P. Logan and Denzell S. Smith's *Survey and Bibliography of Recent Studies in English Renaissance Drama* reveals a plethora of comedies that fail to support the existing group of genres and so receive only the most cursory attention in discussions of authorship or influence. A reader stumbles across "city comedies" that meet all of the genre's conventions except that they become celebratory. Faith in division crumbles further when the reader discovers, as Geraldo U. de Sousa has done, that the quintessential city comedies of Jonson depend on a mix of romance elements.[8] So, the list of mutations, fractures, and lesions goes on. As we turn up more excluded comedies, the metaphor of the body fails. Soon, Renaissance comedy begins to resemble an outback, unexplored, full of vestiges of practices we rarely consider. Apprentices, smiths, shoemakers, and pinners populate this topography. Like the aristocracy, they bicker, look wise, look silly; certainly they entertain.

We have been taught to ignore such plays because they simply are not "as good" as the major plays prized by the genre-filled canon. We have learned, to borrow the terminology of Franco Moretti, that *Much Ado about Nothing* is an "event," whereas *George a Greene* is "banal," "predictable," "mass," and "normal."[9] Moretti, I think, offers the best theoretical case for reconsidering the way we hierarchize genres. Having failed to pay attention to this other topography, Moretti contends, we write literary history that "closely resembles the maps of Africa of a century and half ago," full of "bizarre hypotheses" and "legends." Moretti calls for "a 'slower' literary history; and a more 'discontinuous' one" (p. 16). In the particular case of Renaissance comedy, our criteria of comic genre enable a careful exclusion of plays devoted to the practices of the lower orders and to multiplicity and open-endedness.[10] Comedies that prize, for example, a neighborhood's hospitality are simply relegated to the "obscure." Above all, what established critical practice misses by ignoring these "normal" comedies is an often unpredictable mode of triumph incongruous with the culture's existing order. Dogberrys made of tougher stuff and finer wit stand side-by-side Dogberrys made of lesser stuff and lesser wit—as heroes. There may be, in the end, more reality in these heroes than in the "legends" sponsored by scholarship devoted to the world of romantic comedies.

A fascinating exception to the pattern of exclusion is Michael Bristol's reading of Strumbo in the anonymous *Locrine*. In this play, generic triumph occurs uneasily between existing genres of comedy, between satire and celebration. Strumbo's "survival is predicated on the resources of strategic misinterpretation and versatile improvisatory competence. He understands as little as possible, avoids risks and, in the end, evades the demands of authority, finds a new wife and settles down again in clownish content."[11] In this play, the plebeian character triumphs through strategies of evasion that hardly confirm the stability of the social order or the authority of the ruling powers. Misinterpretation of the kind that seems to disqualify Dogberry from hero status in Shakespeare's play becomes strategic in *Locrine*, the very basis of the lowly fellow's survival. As Bristol explains, "Despite their exaggerated idealization, the interests of the epically distanced characters—dynastic marriage and war—can generate nothing other than betrayal, revenge and despair" (p. 149). In this way, the fuzzy, transgeneric world of *Locrine* catches the bitter taste of the early portions of Shakespeare's romantic comedies and the unsavory tactics of Yellowhammer's London in *A Chaste Maid in Cheapside*.

Locrine, however, remains a play apart. Strumbo triumphs, a fact Bristol attributes to the clown's enactment of the ancient traditions of carnival as described by Bakhtin: "These texts of Carnival situate themselves exactly at the frontier between elite and popular culture, the zone where reciprocal pressure, contamination, and the diversity of speech types and discursive genres is greatest; and it is precisely in these mongrel or heteroglot texts that the repressed or excluded meanings of popular culture become most intelligible" (p. 58). Carnival may be the *tertium quid* of scholarship's binary division of comedy into satire and celebration. It encourages the discovery of genre's bases in class, professional, economic, and regional divisions. As Bakhtin suggests, the term includes pageantry, parody, curses, oaths, a whole catalog of billingsgate.[12] Carnival feels like comedy even as it encourages generic dispersion and a recovery of popular cultures. Carnival meshes with but always destabilizes comedy. We recognize, of course, that the "texts of Carnival" cannot "situate themselves" but instead appear as the Renaissance playwright assembles the speech genres of the everyday life around him. When the critic confronts a comedy that challenges existing generic boundaries, it is usually the case that the playwright has appropriated carnivalesque elements to such a degree that academic categories falter.

The crucial questions raised by Bristol's unconventional reading of comedy finally frame my own inquiry into the world of the Wakefield pinner and his capacity for antagonism toward the ruling orders. Up to this point, I have suggested only that these "other comedies" triumph in ways incongruous to the existing order. Bristol offers a variety of interlocking addendums. In the passage above, he suggests that such works make the plebeian perspective "intelligible." In the passage quoted in the introduction to this text, he argues for "the capacity of popular culture to resist penetration and control by the power structure." In his conclusion, Bristol affirms that "Carnival is not anti-authoritarian. But Carnival is a general refusal to understand any fixed and final allocation of authority" (p. 212).

In light of Bakhtin's theories and Bristol's readings, I would accept such conclusions concerning the nature of Carnival. But Bristol's argument, like the present chapter's, is never wholly about Carnival. We may cast the comedy of Strumbo as Carnival, but can we ignore the fact that no unlettered plebeian "authored" the play? Can we take an evanescent phenomenon and use it allegorically to read represented practices filtered through the age's generic conventions of comedy and more generally through the consciousness of an author who must be several removes from the clown he describes? Given these appropriations, we may question the effectiveness of such a dramatic text in producing genuine resistance.

I suggest that even though the carnivalesque can be a most rewarding antidote to the reductionist divisions of comedy into isolated genres, Bristol's example makes clear the need for several important qualifications of any study of plebeian culture and Renaissance comedy. First, it is vital that we constantly remark the processes of appropriation that have shaped any text which appears to present the pulsing life of plebeian experience. Next, in order to isolate these manipulations, the ideological shaping, implicit in the appropriation, we must consider a particular cultural phenomenon in archaeological detail.[13] How much do we know about the practice, before we consider its representations? Finally, it seems essential to determine *what can be claimed* in a given study for the antagonistic success of the appropriated plebeian culture. The argument that a given representation "refuses" or "resists" authority requires evidence of success from the culture. Are there other, perhaps even more specific, claims that could be made?

George a Greene, The Pinner of Wakefield

In light of these qualifications, I approach *George a Greene* as a comedy almost completely excluded from discussion by the profession's generic categories. The playwright, who for sake of convenience I will refer to as Robert Greene, has appropriated the idea of hospitality and, not unlike Stow, has begun to explore a fanciful history of neighborly practice.[14] In Bristol's defense, one finds in this play a perfect example of a plebeian hero who functions to refuse and resist the imposition of a fixed and final allocation of authority. But this refusal is, as I have suggested, complicated by its appropriation. A clarification of the nature and success of the Pinner's triumph and its effect on our experience of comedy as a genre will be the final aim of this chapter.

The play's plot is heteroglot and, as Moretti would have it, *normal*. In the manner of a chronicle, Greene sets the action during Edward's reign over England as James of Scotland threatens on the border. The Earl of Kendall has marshalled a serious rebellion. When Kendall's forces seek aid from Wakefield, George a Greene, the town pinner (a more prestigious form of our contemporary dog catcher), finds himself and his community implicated in the rebels' demands. In the manner of the romance, the Pinner eventually defeats Kendall and his men singlehandedly while winning his love, Bettris, in an echo of New Comedy, from her father, Grime—a course that allows time for the pageant-like defeat of Robin Hood and the vanquishing of an angry mob of armed shoemakers. In a slight subplot that suggests Greene's *James IV* and a nascent tragicomedy, James woos and threatens the married Jane a Barley as she looks down from her castle. James is defeated and brought before Edward. Everyone assembles in a courtly resolution shaped by the conventional construction of Renaissance comedies. Throughout the play, George is distinguished by his flare for the tactical, the improvised maneuver that succeeds by virtue of its superior timing.

Like the *Arcadia*, this neglected cousin depends on hospitable practice for its beginnings. The rebel Kendall opens the play and defines the work's essential structure by extending a welcome "to Bradford, martial gentlemen, / Lord *Bonfild,* and sir *Gilbert Armstrong* both, / And all my troops, even to my basest groom.[15] The other side of Bakhtin's notion of generic digestion is this play's indigestion of primary speech genres as the playwright repeatedly invokes the habitualized forms of hospitable welcome to open scenes. Time and again his characters utter an everyday formula that stands in for dramatic structure. In the tradition of Wolsey and Cecil, Kendall's welcome is meant to shape positively the course of political action. In a perfect illustration of hospitality's powers of mystification, Kendall encloses the language of revolution in a concern for the poor:

> As I am *Henry Momford,* Kendall's Earl,
> You honour me with this assent of yours;
> And here upon my sword I make protest
> For to relieve the poor or die myself. (1.1.8–11)

Like the archetypal master in the housekeeping tracts, Kendall welcomes his guests and justifies his authority by directing attention away from his actions and toward the situation of the poor. This obvious strategy asks the audience to play Venetian ambassador to King James, probing for the real agendas behind an official's hospitable concerns. Here, as motive disappears into provisioning, revolution becomes the only answer to a failed hospitality—a crux latent in Shakespeare's plays. In *King John*, for example, the King of France chooses the same tack as Kendall when he situates himself

> In warlike march these greens before your town,
> Being no further enemy to you
> Than the constraint of hospitable zeal
> In the relief of this oppressed child
> Religiously provokes. (2.1.241–46)

When we turn to Shakespeare's *King Lear*, we will want to note how, in a similar vein, both Lear and Edgar claim to be moved by hospitable zeal in an inhospitable world. Whether from the mouth of Elizabeth and James or Lear, Philip, Edgar, and Kendall, the idea of hospitality can always be appropriated for political struggles.

In its simple fashion, this play makes no attempt to hide Kendall's real agendas. This "normal" text seems to have an investment in sharing with its audience all the ways that hospitable practice can be manipulated. Purveyance, that most basic of household necessities, has become a crucial strategic aim for Kendall and his forces. One way or another, the countryside must provide the resources to carry on the rebellion. The example of Wolsey's hospitable catering for the English soldiers comes to mind as Bonfild takes note of how "our soldiers find our victuals scant. / We must make havoc of those country swains" (1.1.29–30). Kendall deputizes Mannering as purveyor, sending him with official seals to Wakefield. At issue in this scene is loyalty, victuals, and the mystification of unequal allocation on which hospitality and, in turn, hierarchical rule depends. The hospitality of the aristocracy may include the lower orders—but only through purveyance. Kendall and his men will appear as such obvious villains in this play because they awkwardly disregard the conventional patterns of mystification that obscure the hard realities of hospitable dealings. In this way, the playwright exposes patterns of exploitation and simultaneously ensures that the exposition will not be taken as subversive.

Like the people of Bristol or Wells who received the surprising word they would be playing host to Elizabeth or James, the people of Wakefield learn that they must host Kendall's forces. As we have already seen, news of such guests was hardly cause for uncomplicated rejoicing. A given town might go so far as to petition to be "spared" from the hardship of hosting.[16] The people of Wakefield would certainly petition, if they could. Nevertheless, as the leaders of the community assemble to discuss the situation, the playwright uses the language of Stow to emphasize the existence of a cohesive community. Like a guild member stepping forward in a medieval mystery play, the Pinner gives expression to this vision:

> Why, I am George a Greene,
> True Liegeman to my King,
> Who scorns that men of such esteem as these
> Should brook the braves of any traitorous squire.
> You of the bench, and you, my fellow friends,
> Neighbours, we subjects all unto the King. (1.2.91–96)

Kendall will get no victuals because Wakefield endures as a community of neighbors whose authority *as community*, to borrow Bristol's terminology, resists and refuses this imposition of an unequal allocation of social wealth. Far from being artless, George a Greene forms this communal position with a tactician's control of rhetorical figure. The final lines of the quoted material depend on *synonymia*, an ideologically loaded amplification through synonyms. The "you" and "we" of Wakefield expand from members of the bench, to fellow friends, to neighbors, to subjects of the king. So when George a Greene steps forward like a Saint George in a holiday show, a form of carnivalesque antagonism toward imposed authority is realized. Moreover, no Theseus steps in to pick a welcome from a stuttering host. The Pinner speaks a most capable language for Wakefield. But how should we register these represented accomplishments—as resistance? subversion?

The language of hosting tells all. In complete disregard of hospitality's capacity for mystification, Mannering threatens the neighbors with "thirty thousand men strong in power," "mighty puissance and his stroke" (1.2.70, 111). But what does village life have to do with these epic terms? The Pinner responds, not unlike Locrine, with misinterpretation, perhaps even a complete failure to understand the power of the aristocracy. With a panache that anticipates Kent's rough treatment of Oswald in *King Lear*, George makes Mannering eat the seals of Kendall's authority. The texts of deputization become the rude fare of hospitality. More important, Kendall knows how to interpret Mannering's feast: "Such news, Bonfild, as will make thee laugh" (1.4.211). Plebeian hosting, even in this antagonistic mood, makes a good comedy, a good show. Simultaneously, it serves a pedagogical function, teaching about the pleasures of other comic modes through the reactions of the Wakefield citizens. These neighbors respond with laughter, praise, and hospitable invitations:

> For highly hast thou honoured Wakefield town
> In cutting a proud Mannering so short.
> Come, thou shalt be my welcome guest today;
> For well thou hast deserv'd reward and favour.
> (1.2.146–49)

From this speech we learn how to value George's actions and how to discriminate between the hospitality of the aristocrat and the common folk. The Pinner has honored Wakefield in a rare, comic entertainment. Whereas the man of rank hosts in order to refashion powerful guests, the plebeian version enables a refashioning of fellow hosts. Wakefield becomes more powerful in its imagination of itself. In recompense, the Pinner receives the town's most hospitable treatment assured by faith in reciprocal care.

Again, recourse to comedies of this other tradition confirm that such scenes are hardly anomalous. In *The Shoemakers' Holiday*, Dekker opens his play by establishing, in the words of the Earl of Lincoln, the honor to be derived from hospitality originating in a community authority:

> My Lord Mayor, you have sundry times
> Feasted myself and many courtiers more;
> Seldom or never can we be so kind
> To make requital of your courtesy.[17]

From the outset of Dekker's play, this other hospitality has been stressed *not against but as an alternative to aristocratic hospitality*. For all of its simplicity, this play digests speech genres by foregrounding (with an almost pedagogical desire to make clear) their origins in different classes and different ideological agendas. As Palmer points out in his introduction to the play, Lincoln's words achieve a considerable irony as the drama progresses, for both Lincoln and Lord Mayor Otley offer hospitality only for social advantage (p. xiv).

By establishing the ideal in the first words of the play and then undermining the sincerity of its adherents, Dekker sets the stage for Simon Eyre's fantastic hospitality. More eloquent than George a Greene, Eyre blusters in the same language of communal care, nurturing one of England's future soldiers, as he sends Ralph off to war: "Hold thee, Ralph, here's five sixpences for thee: fight for the honour of the Gentle Craft, for the gentlemen shoemakers, the courageous cordwainers, the flower of Saint Martin's, the mad knaves of Bedlam, Fleet Street, Tower Street and Whitechapel!" (1.1.216–20). With a love for vowels and consonants and an enduring love of every detail of his community, Eyre undertakes a powerful shaping of an alternative version of authority. Like George a Greene, Eyre envisions a government deriving from the topography of the community, from Fleet Street to Tower Street, enlivened by his own mad hosting.

In Sir Thomas Smith's *De Republica Anglorum* (1583), the author's careful hierarchy of English authority specifically locates "Shoomakers" in the group of artisans who "have no voice nor authority in our commonwealth," yet Smith admits that in a given community, for lack of greater authorities, these men may assume positions of power.[18] In their respective plays, George and Eyre take advantage of the world as delineated by the hierarchically minded Smith. These plays hint that much can be gained though the system remain intact.

It would, of course, be a mistake to confuse these two characters with the pinners and shoemakers who populated early modern England. In considering George's powerful practice of hospitality, we are really locating a playwright's desire to generically dramatize an entertaining social triumph, to catch a "type" in the act of winning. In these terms, how can we value the aggressive, jovial, and alternative versions of power offered by George and Eyre? Surely, even for variety's sake, no Renaissance play-wright would imagine pinners and shoemakers displacing impor-tant aristocrats on the public stage. Therefore, to understand the Pinner's triumph, I propose that we abandon, for a moment, the often-used models of "containment-subversion," "resistance," and "popular revolt." In each of these models, power is conceived of in the market sense of scarcity. The lower orders revolt to take the power back. The lower orders resist a prior allocation of power at the hands of aristocracy. The lower orders exercise a power, unaware that it has been granted them by the elites, only to be quashed at the proper moment.

As an alternative to these current descriptions, I suggest that playwrights such as Greene and Dekker are instead positing a comic triumph based on two key assumptions: (1) that power is infinite and there for the making and (2) that power need not be over someone or some thing in order to be power. In their appropriations of hospitality, George and Eyre need take nothing away from the existing hierarchy in order to unify and strength-en their communities. George remains subject to the king, even as he energizes his fellows with the title of "neighbors." Eyre does the same. While I cannot claim that real pinners and shoemakers achieved some permanent displacement of aristocratic authority by virtue of these plays, I would argue that playwrights such as Greene and Dekker make genuine forays into their culture by appropriating hospitality in order to imagine power otherwise. One way of appreciating the novelty of such creations is by contrasting the Pinner's domestic confrontations with those created by Shakespeare.

Anticipating Shakespeare's fatherly hosts in the romantic comedies, Grime struggles with the same impossible interlacing of politics, hospitality, and erotic desire. Rather than view Grime as a source of Shakespeare's dramatic construction, I prefer to exam-ine how his actions enter into dialog with actions of Shakespeare's comic fathers and so contribute to the shape of comedy in the pe-riod. Grime explains his behavior to his guests in the familiar terms of pamphlet literature: "Your welcome was but duty, gen-tle Lord: / For wherefore have we given us our wealth, / But to make our betters welcome when they come?" (1.4.180–82). As we have already seen, hospitality confirms class position; it exists as civil manners covering unequal allocation. In a more subtle play,

Grime's statement would be allowed to stand, only to be undermined, eventually, by the course of events. Here, Grime has an
immediate aside: "O, this goes hard when traitors must be flattered! / But life is sweet, and I cannot withstand it: / God, (I
hope,) will revenge the quarrel of my King" (1.4.183–85). Although
Grime hardly seems to undergo a trial of conscience and violence,
his quandary anticipates the Jacobean stage's tremulous household caught in layers of intrigue and mixed allegiance.

In the familiar context of Shakespeare's comedies, Grime's
example controverts the actions of the famous fatherly hosts, a
pattern too little assimilated by feminist criticism which takes
Shakespeare as the sole model for Renaissance practice. Like
Shakespeare's fathers, Grime is well aware of desire: "I say, Sir
Gilbert, looking on my daughter, / I curse the hour that ere I got
the girl; / For, Sir, she may have many wealthy suitors" (1.4.187–
89). Grime announces this fact knowing, like the Duke in *Two Gentlemen of Verona*, that his current guests could betray him. For her
part, Bettris wants only George a Greene. As in Shakespeare's
comedies, the authority of the host teeters in the presence of conflicting desires. But in this play, the woman's desire takes nothing
away from her father—nor from the aristocracy. Instead, it simply
preserves the worth of the lower orders:

> I care not for earl, nor yet for knight,
> Nor baron that is so bold;
> For George a Greene, the merry pinner,
> He hath my heart in hold. (1.4.234–237)

Such a version of desire would surely leave Shakespeare's aristocracy comically nonplussed, for the Pinner truly begins to take the
place of a noble lover. Indeed, later in the play George contemplates love in a manner not unworthy of the general rabble of
Orsinos and Claudios:

> The sweet content of men that live in love
> Breeds fretting humors in a restless mind;
> And fancy being checked by fortune's spite,
> Grows too impatient in her sweet desires;
> Sweet to those men whom love leads on to bliss,
> But sour to me who hap is still amiss. (2.3.350–55)

In George's meditation, the comedy of the lower orders reaches up to embrace the comedy of its betters. Scholarship's neat catalog of isolated genres dissolves in the wash of "sweet desires."

Generic conventions in the Renaissance are far more restless than we often credit them with being, a fact brilliantly illustrated by Bettris's predicament over George's "fretting humors." Like Shakespeare's Hermia, Bettris receives the "fatherly" response of anger—not from her father, Grime, but from the noble guest: "Shut up thy daughter, bridle her affects; / Let me not miss her when I make return; / Therefore look to her, as to thy life, good Grime" (1.4.241–43). Seen in dialog with Shakespeare's plays, the scene resonates in unfamiliar ways. While much necessary and illuminating scholarship has focussed on the psychological inter-action of Shakespeare's fathers and daughters, Greene's play sug-gests how the New Comedy's father figures could be emptied and made (as Dickens would say) to do the police in several voices. It seems, then, that patriarchal oppression has untold roots in do-mestic practice: Shakespeare's fatherly hosts may promise such violence because hosting in the aristocracy is a more volatile and dangerous activity than in the lower orders. What appears as a decidedly male attribute must be constantly reviewed for its par-ticular admixture of biases tied to both gender and rank.

Perhaps for this reason, when Renaissance comedy depicts the arrival of strangers in courtly situations, otherness is always neatly contained. In romantic comedies, for example, discrepant aware-ness assures the audience that a stranger such as Viola means no harm. In these plays, Edward Topsell's demand that the house-hold not "forsake strangers" is enacted with the magical rewards of Baucis and Philemon.[19] In practice, as we have already seen, even in household ordinances, the English consciousness never accepted strangers, a fact confirmed by the whole of English comedy during the period.[20] Focussed as it is on the idea of hos-pitality as practiced by the lower orders, *George a Greene* bristles with this more realistic version of English perception. Strangers mean trouble. The forces inimical to social well-being arrive as a (military) host whose erotic and political desires only serve to reinvigorate the identity of the community.

In this way, King James's appearance to open the play's second act simply provides further elaboration of the challenge facing the Pinner of Wakefield. An alien presence, James arrives and scrambles the speech genres of civil welcome. The King wants to sue like a valiant lover, but Sir John's son tells James to first "knock at this gate" (2.1.272). (This is hardly James I's welcome at Theobalds as described by Savile.) By invoking the gate, the son shapes James in the image of the beggar. Jane goes on to point out the inhospitality of the stranger's demands, based as they are on his "host of men . . . witness of his Scottish lust" (306–7). As we have already seen, ideas of the host merge easily with the hankerings of the military host. Literary and nonliterary models collide as James, like Ralph Roister Doister before him, threatens to "raze thy castle to the very ground," only to be rebuffed comically by Jane's more powerful housekeeping: "I fear thee not, King James: do thy worst. / This castle is too strong for thee to scale; / Besides, tomorrow will sir John come home" (316–18). As a proper aristocratic lady, Jane refuses to play hostess even as James threatens the life of her son:

> I'll draw thee on with sharp and deep extremes;
> For, by my father's soul, this brat of thine
> Shall perish here before thine eyes,
> Unless thou open the gate, and let me in. (320–23)

Jane's evaluation of the confrontation works better as critical commentary than it does as dialog: "O deep extremes." Like the romantic comedies that it anticipates, *George a Greene* depends here on the tragicomic extremes occasioned when the arrival of guests (invited or not) engenders erotic and political desire. A contemporary reader would no doubt prefer a careful teasing out of these extremes. None is forthcoming. But whether or not the playwright achieves a successful aesthetic effect for a twentieth-century reader, the play surely produced considerable entertainment value for the householders in the Renaissance audience when James departs for battle only to be brought back to the castle gate as a prisoner. Jane commands with a bawdy quibble: "Bring in King James with you as a guest; / For all this broil was 'cause he could not enter" (2.2.348–49). This "broil" has amounted to a mere handful of lines, a kind of palette for blending erotic desire and military conquest in hospitable terms sharper than those of the play's main action.

Triumph is, finally, the vital business of *George a Greene*, particularly insofar as it occurs in the topography of village life and resonates with its language. As a prologue to the arrival of more strangers and the emergence of plebeian authority in the play, the Pinner's man Jenkin narrates his own comic triumph in love: "Though I say it that should not say it, there are few fellows in our parish so nettled with love, as I have been of late" (2.3.360–62). Jenkin goes on to explain how he was threatened by his rival, Clim the sow-gelder, in the midst of a tête-à-tête in the local wheat close. No romance code at work in this tale, the clown capitulated and accepted the job of holding the sow-gelder's horse, to protect it from a "cold in his feet." Jenkin placed his cloak under the horse's "feet" while Clim and Madge disappeared into the ditch. Still, Jenkin conquers: "But mark how I served him. Madge & he was no sooner gone down into the ditch, but I plucked out my knife, cut four holes in my cloak, and made his horse stand on the bare ground" (2.3.397–400). In the daily life of a village, lovers escape not into Arden but into a wheat close, a parodic reflection that calls to mind the plebeian structures of life that support the glittering world of romantic comedy. No Orlando, Jenkin does manage to assert his experience as being worthy to stand on its own. Ruling powers may appropriate the wheat, but they cannot in this play take the wheat close and its own languages of victory.

In anticipation of Dull, Dogberry, and the Watch, Jenkin apprehends violators of the community's laws and reports his interrogation of the strangers. That the strangers turn out to be horses does not discourage Jenkin:

> My masters, said I, it is no laughing matter; for, if my master take you here, you go as round as a top to the pound. Another untoward jade, hearing me threaten him to the pound and to tell you of them, cast up both his heels and let such a monstrous great fart, that was as much as in his language to say, A fart for the pound and a fart for George a Greene! Now I, hearing this, put on my cap, blew my horn, called them all jades, and came to tell you. (2.3.413–24)

Lowly Jenkin interprets "horse" with an uncanny inflection of carnivalesque rebellion; yet he understands that "they, being gentlemen's horses, may stand on their reputation, and will not obey me" (430–31). Jenkin's language lesson and his curious triumph in love thus prepare the way for a serious confrontation between authorities when he discovers Kendall and his men, the owners of the horses.

Although capable of verse, George confronts the rebels in the prose of the community: "I know not your degrees, but more you cannot be unless you be kings. Why wrong you us of Wakefield with your horses? I am the pinner, and before you pass, you shall make good the trespass they have done" (2.3.444–47). George takes issue not with the owners' violation of some abstract code of honor but with a trespass against the community of Wakefield.[21] Goaded by the gentlemen's taunts, George declares his most radical version of communal authority: "Now, by my father's soul, were good King Edward's horses in the corn, they shall amend the scathe, or kiss the pound; much more yours, sir, whatsoere you be" (2.3.464–66). The pinfold reigns in its place. If they transgress, kings tumble before local authority. Rather than allow such a sensitive statement to gain its full impact, the playwright quickly covers this claim with Kendall's more decidedly rebellious assertion: "Before a month be full expired, [we] will be King Edward's betters in the land" (2.3.468–69). George may now step to Edward's defense, strike Kendall, and simultaneously cue the rebels' ambush. A virtual prisoner, George weaves a timely bit of hospitality: "vouchsafe a piece of beef at my poor house; you shall have wafer cakes your fill, a piece of beef hung up since Martilmas" (2.3.536–39). Two feats have been accomplished. Inside the play world, hospitality has become a military tactic, a way to divide enemy forces and alter unfavorable odds. In terms of the play's ideological reception, the invitation to beef and cakes has provided closure for the scene even as it leads the audience further away from the Pinner's own radical statement of communal authority—a position which remains obdurate as a wheat close at the play's conclusion.

Claiming Resistance Differently at the End of the Show

George a Greene fails in the fourth act, at least according to all standards of unity usually conjured up in discussions of comic genre. Pre-empting the play's conclusion, the playwright sweeps Bettris into George's arms and concludes George's defeat of Kendall in a handful of lines. Compositional habits associated with comedy—the move toward closure in marriage or revelation, the reintegration of outsiders—give way to a carnivalesque *bricolage* of popular confrontations. George faces Robin Hood, a band of angry shoemakers, and King Edward "mumming" his way through the countryside. In place of resolutions prized so highly by critics interested in romantic comedy or city comedy, the Pinner hosts these theatrical entrances, shifting boundaries normally used to divide elite and popular culture, stage and culture, representational and nonrepresentational theater.

The plebeian revel and critical doubt conjured by this alternative generic path find satirical summation in the demands of the Citizen and the doubts of the Boy in Francis Beaumont's *The Knight of the Burning Pestle* (1607):

> CITIZEN: Let Rafe come out on May Day in the
> morning, and speak upon a conduit with
> all his scarfs about him, and his feathers
> and his rings and his knacks.
> BOY: Why, sir, you do not think of our plot.
> What will become of that, then?

On its own stage, *The Knight of the Burning Pestle* was meant to jest with this "common" desire for multiple entrances of the plebeian. Although largely uncharted, this "May Day" tradition of copious representation, frequently inflected by the hosting of the lower orders, surrounds the Pinner. For example, in the fashion of *George a Greene* and Beaumont's Citizen, George Peele's *The Old Wives Tale* depends on the arrival of strangers. Clunch discovers the lost Antic, Frolic, and Fantastic and introduces himself in the manner of the Pinner: "Why, I am Clunch the smith. What are you? What make you in my territories at this time of the night?"[23] Like George a Greene, the Citizen, and Simon Eyre, Clunch takes the stage as part of a professional community.

Such characters assume a comic pride in their profession, generating a buoyancy that makes them excellent entertainers of guests. To outsiders, they appear silly. To their community, they offer identity. Frolic thus answers Clunch in the effective language of the day: "Unless your hospitality do relieve us, we are like to wander with a sorrowful heigh-ho, among the owlets and hobgoblins of the forest" (41–43). Peele seems to have no difficulty in imagining the lower orders' appropriation of hospitality. Clunch responds: "It seems to me you have lost your way in the wood. In consideration whereof, if you will go with Clunch to his cottage, you shall have house-room and a good fire to sit by, although we have no bedding to put you in" (48–52). The speech genres echo precisely those of the ruling powers, with the clear distinction in means made evident in the bedding. "For your further entertainment," Clunch begins, and then as the dog barks, he explains: "Hark! this is Ball my dog, that bids you all welcome in his own language. Come, take heed for stumbling on the threshold. Open the door, Madge; take in guests" (54, 56–58). In the same position as Sidney several years earlier, Peele ponders a fantastic narrative of curses, conjuring, transformed daughters, and a knight. Like Sidney, Peele begins his work with a careful evocation of hospitality's decorums, the only difference being that here we watch plebeian hosts prepare the entertainment.

Would the Countess of Pembroke have identified with Madge? Certainly not. How ironic, then, that the Smith's wife has the opportunity to exercise freely the authority of hostess. Madge offers: "Welcome, Clunch, and good fellows all, that come with my good man. For my good man's sake, come on, sit down. Here is a piece of cheese and a pudding of my own making" (59–62). Unlike Tyb in John Heywood's earlier play, Madge entertains for "my good man's sake," anticipating the pure motives of Hermione in *The Winter's Tale*. And here we approach the unfamiliar terrain of *George a Greene*'s carnivalesque composition. What the guests want and what Madge provides as hostess is "a merry winter's tale [that] would drive away the time trimly" (86). Years before Shakespeare penned his romance, Peele envisioned a plebeian hosting, a hostess capable of editing and augmenting old tales of romance, and an accretive dramatic action in harmony with the Pinner's play. Free to play the hostess in her own right, Madge assumes the position of storyteller herself. Her power, akin to that of the Pinner, is evidenced when her characters actually appear. She exclaims: "Gods me bones! who comes here?" (131–32). The contrast with Sly and the Lord is obvious. In *The Old Wives Tale*, the person of low rank hosts and conjures her own fantastic entertainment. As in *George a Greene*, the dramatic narrative succumbs to the comings and goings of folk characters. Madge's example is fanciful and entertaining, but also speculative. What if the lower orders, the play gently muses, can exercise their own versions of household imagination?

This same alternative course of dramatic construction energizes *The Shoemakers' Holiday* when Eyre arrives as a guest at Otley's house. Otley offers the conventional greeting: "Trust me, you are as welcome to Old Ford / As I myself" (3.3.1–2). Host and guest go on to quibble over the hospitality: "Would our bad cheer were worth the thanks you give" (4). Eyre replies, properly: "Good cheer, my Lord Mayor, fine cheer; a fine house, fine walls, all fine and neat" (5–6). Palmer rightly points out that while Otley hosts only for "social prestige," Eyre quickly asserts himself as the real host.[24] Of course, as we have seen, hosting in order to improve one's position is the essence of hospitality. In this scene, Eyre's more plebeian version simply encompasses Otley's subdued entertainment: "O my Lord Mayor, a crew of good fellows that for love to your honour are come hither with a morris-dance. Come in, my Mesopotamians, cheerily!" (51–53). The strict sequence of dramatic action expands hospitably, as it does in *George a Greene*, to admit a tableau of merry shoemakers. Closure disperses in proportion to Eyre's success in hosting "for the honour of shoemakers."

With these examples in mind, the conclusion of *George a Greene* ought to appear in a different light, for the playwright follows this other comic tradition and turns the work's dramatic action over to the pageantry of local hosting. The effect of this choice is nothing less than the dispersion of patterns of closure that would seem to define canonical comic genre in the period. In embracing the strategies of pageant and carnival along with the remnants of a ballad tradition, the playwright makes the genre hospitable to plebeian positions of authority. In place of comedy's clarification and reintegration, the audience finds something like *a retooling of culture*. At the end of *The Old Wives Tale*, for example, the playwright offers an energized storytelling back to the lower orders. At the end of *The Shoemakers' Holiday*, the playwright returns a justified repertoire of celebration to the shoemakers. As *George a Greene* comes to a close, the playwright opts for dispersion through the ever-popular signs of Robin Hood and shoemakers. Finally, this appropriation of popular culture in *George a Greene* turns out to be most fortuitous for this chapter's inquiry into the generic possibilities of representational resistance because Robin Hood and shoemaker culture have become touchstones in the scholarly debate over plebeian practices and their representations.

Who was Robin Hood? In the simplest sense, Robin Hood was a bundle of conflicting ideas about justice, the poor, friendship, romance, and housekeeping. What was the responsibility of the rich to the poor? Could the hospitality of the household be reborn in a forest? What would a plebeian hero be like? Uniformly, Robin Hood existed as *local hero*, a version of power tied to a specific English setting.[25] Robin Hood was always somebody's neighbor. *The Jolly Pinder of Wakefield*, a ballad dating from about 1557, tells of a confrontation between George a Greene and Robin Hood; no doubt it suggested one of the play's tableaux. In this ballad tradition, more specifically, Robin was a neighborly yeoman, proud of "base" origins and committed to the enforcement of hospitality.[26] On the other hand, in versions such as Anthony Munday's *The Downfall of Robert, Earl of Huntingdon* (1597–98), the yeoman becomes an aristocratic householder betrayed by his guests during a banquet.[27] In this account, Robin Hood retails the difficulties of the aristocratic host. Contradictions multiply, but the desire to appropriate the hero for the interests of a particular rank remains constant. Far from being a simple vessel of popular culture, Robin Hood was a site of contest for the culture's imagination of itself.[28]

George a Greene depicts this old struggle. When the Pinner fights and defeats Robin Hood in the play, the power of the ordinary host and his community is valorized.[29] The playwright's handling of this ballad matter makes this clear. In *The Jolly Pinder*, Robin Hood is so impressed by George's victory that he asks the Pinner to join his band, an offer the Pinner considers in light of his other responsibilities. In Greene's version, Robin makes the same offer, but the Pinner affirms the value of his plebeian life:

> Let me live and die a yeoman still:
> So was my father, so must live his son.
> For 'tis more credit to men of base degree,
> To do great deeds, than men of dignity. (1352–55)

George admits no desire to alter his rank, only the right to claim great deeds for "men of base degree." As he does throughout the play, George demonstrates his worth with hospitality:

> Welcome, sweet Robin; welcome, maid Marian;
> And welcome you my friends.
> Will you to my poor house;
> You shall have wafer cakes your fill.
> A piece of beef hung up since Martlemas.
> (4.4.997–1001)

Like Madge and Simon Eyre, George welcomes these pageant characters into his now-familiar hospitality; conquest and entertainment combine in George's hospitality. The idea of Robin Hood in all its nuance, both yeoman and noble, has been transformed into a guest of this vision.

Shoemakers present a similar opportunity to the author of *George a Greene*. Peter Burke has described the existence of a "shoemaker culture" throughout early modern Europe. In France, Germany, Portugal, and England, shoemakers were consistently interested in shaping a mythological identity while entering and shaping the vanguard of political movements. From Thomas Deloney in England to Jakob Boehme in Lusatia to Luis Dias of Portugal, shoemakers gained fame as heterodox thinkers.[30]

The representational gain to be had by appropriating this culture can be seen in *The Shoemakers' Holiday*. On one hand, as David Scott Kastan has pointed out, the play "is a realistic portrait only of Elizabethan middle-class dreams—a fantasy of class fulfillment that would ease the tensions and contradictions created by the nascent capitalism of the late sixteenth-century."[31] To the extent that the play markets dreams, it will be successful. On the other hand, it goes without saying that fantasy can be used in many ways. Simon Eyre may rise to the rank of lord mayor. He may thrive on the shady side of emergent capitalism. But he takes most delight in entertaining in order to heighten the authority and

worth of the Gentle Craft and bring it into relation with the
Crown: "Let your fellow prentices want no cheer; let wine be plen-
tiful as beer, and beer as water! Hang these penny-pinching fathers, that cram wealth in innocent lambskins! Rip, knaves,
avaunt, look to my guests" (5.4.8–12). Above all, shoemakers, and
Simon Eyre in particular, represent what can be made out of existing hierarchies by a common host. Linked as it is to a whole culture of shoemaker practice, this fantasy may offer something other
than false consciousness.

So, when shoemakers halt the disguised King James and King
Edward in *George a Greene,* demanding that the men lower their
staffs or do battle, the monarchy has encountered one of the age's
most powerful plebeian factions. The point of conflict seems consistent with the play's action. "My friend," the shoemaker says, "I
see thou art a stranger here." Above all, the shoemakers intend to
assert the authority of their locality against any imposition from
the outside. Like Jane and George, the shoemakers voice the belief
that no stranger will enter their community with his staff raised.
The disguised monarchs capitulate, preparing for the contest between the shoemakers and George a Greene a few minutes later.
George defeats them all. Here we watch nothing so much as a local battle, a contest between versions of local authority.[32] The
Pinner's triumphs lead the audience toward imagining versions of
a plebeian power tied to a particular place. The playwright returns
the idea of shoemakers to his audience, resonating with active resistance and a sense of their own locale.

While it would be a mistake, I think, to suggest that the playwright's construction of these heterogeneous conflicts and
plebeian triumphs constitutes a revolutionary action in his society,
I would argue for a recognition of this imagining as significant
because it appears in a language familiar to the lower orders. If
fantasy, the play offers its ideals in the language of artisans and in
the terms of localities. As Buchanan Sharp has demonstrated, artisans of the period viewed themselves as cohesive groups capable of taking concerted action—in their own region—against the
existing hierarchy of authority.[33] As J. S. Morrill argued some time
ago, the common person in early modern England might well
have declared his loyalty to county first.[34]

My argument then is about a representation of a pinner in
Wakefield and how this literary artifact might assist common folk

already prepared to imagine other forms of authority. I would not claim that these groups imagined an overturning of the existing order nor that the popular theater provided them with plans for such an undertaking. I suggest, simply, that the lower orders could take action against social inequities and enhance their own quality of life (two not necessarily related processes) because they were able to view themselves as neighbors stronger because of their common locale. When a Renaissance playwright imagines the many triumphs of a pinner, he posits and elaborates a form of power quite in touch with the real artisans working in England. Like the aristocracy, artisans negotiate a complex identification with theatrical texts.

Obviously, such an acquisition by the lower orders, though it ensures no rebellion, will seem to threaten existing patterns of dominance. As such plays gained popularity, a steady murmur of "disclosure" appeared in and around the theater, commentaries aimed at revealing the failure of entertainment among the lower orders. Thomas Harman's *A Caveat For Common Cursitors* epitomizes the strategies guiding this backlash. The pamphlet "documents" the funeral of a gentleman whose hospitality had earned him great respect in Kent. Harman reports an old man's story:

> At his burial there was such a number of beggars, besides poor householders dwelling thereabouts, that uneath they might lie or stand about the house. Then was there prepared for them a great and a large barn, and a great fat ox sod out in frumenty for them, with bread and drink abundantly to furnish out the premises; and every person had twopence, for such was the dole. When night approached, the poor householders repaired home to their houses: the other wayfaring bold beggars remained all night in the barn; and the same barn being searched with light in the night by this old man (and then young), with others they told seven score persons of men, every of them having his woman, except it were two women that lay alone together for some especial cause. Thus having their makes to make merry withal, the burial was turned to boozing and belly-cheer, mourning to mirth, fasting to feasting, prayer to pastime and pressing of paps, and lamenting to lechery. (pp. 84–85)

When plebeians take hold of hospitality, they overturn all, reversing every positive value the practice aims to maintain in an alliterative welter of "pastime and pressing." Even sexual preference submits to revision. Harman's technique is obvious: he establishes a dramatic situation full of traditional expectations and then proceeds to accumulate plebeian debasements.

Perhaps the most famous example of this strategy in the theater is Beaumont's *The Knight of the Burning Pestle*. This most forward-looking play in terms of theatrical technique neatly deflates the idea of plebeian knights and the tastes of the common folk. Like Harman, the dramatist works with a play-within-a-play, establishing a series of occasions that test commoners' tastes. What can they make of genteel entertainment? Naturally, they fail. In their failing, Beaumont suggests that such action will hardly make a "proper play"; the struggle for men of rank as well as for playwrights is how to check heterological impulses in a single order.[35] A more subtle form of debasement comes in Beaumont and Fletcher's *The Beggar's Bush* (1612–14), a play that begins by positing a plebeian householder whose authority derives from his excellent hosting. The play's romance denouement reveals, however, that the plebeian host is really of noble blood. Jonson's *The New Inn* (1629) makes similar claims for a "gentleman" of no particular standing, only to conclude with the revelation of his nobility. In such plays, either through satire or "demystification," the powerful host of the lower orders turns out to be an eccentric, or a theatrical trick.

In more blatant fashion, Henry Porter's *Two Angry Women of Abington* (1599) presents a simple hospitality between two couples. The women fall to bickering, unable to sustain the simplest of civilities. One husband upbraids his wife:

> Well, wife, you know it is no honest part
> To entertain such guests with jests and wrongs.
> What will the neighboring country vulgar say
> When as they hear that you fell out at dinner?
> Forsooth, they'll call it a pot quarrel straight.[36]

Comedies of this kind slowly encircle the dramas of pinners and shoemakers, adding their voices to those of writers like Harman, suggesting that stories of ordinary hospitalities make weak plays about silly folk who grasp little more than "belly-cheer" and "pot quarrels." That we can point to this process of containment suggests that a play like *George a Greene* was engaged in a genuine competition for the "rights" to hospitality and the imagination of plebeian power. Genre theory, with its capacity for exclusion and elision, has simply buried the evidence of this competition. Indeed, from the history of criticism, we must conclude that such plays have lost most of the contests.

More than anything else, scholarship struggles with the dispersion of its generic forms. In the age of Bakhtin, we are fast compiling a language of popular *bricolage* that will raise Carnival to the status of genre, something like a theorized version of Menippean satire. Perhaps we have already done so. Whether such a genre can remain true to the paradoxes of dispersion remains to be seen, for we may not be prepared to confront the way these other comedies end. At the end of *George a Greene*, like the noble householders who entertained Elizabeth, the hero presides over a pageant's rush of entrances and exits, having stepped momentarily into the place of Cecil. King Edward concludes: "Now George a Greene / I'll to thy house" (1374–75).[37] For a brief moment, the compositional strategies of pageant and carnival serve the lower orders as a Theobalds or a Kenilworth, opening up vast spaces for the recombination of myth, class, authority, and genre. *George a Greene* anticipates Sir Francis Bacon's complaint that "there is no vulgar but all statesmen."[38] Prestation, marked by George's cakes and beef, succeeds otherwise. Other comedies mean other powers.

NOTES

1. Stow, *A Survey of London*, 1:101. Heal discusses contemporary comment on "Hospitality among the Populace" in *Hospitality*, 376-88.
2. Hyde, "Some Food We Could Not Eat," 35.
3. *The Merry Devil of Edmonton*, 1.2.1–7.
4. Though Robert Greene's editors usually include the play in Greene's oeuvre, evidence for his authorship is less than certain. On the probability of Greene's authorship, see Charles A. Pennel, "The Authenticity of the *George a Greene* Title-page Inscriptions," *Journal of English and Germanic Philology* 64 (1965): 668-76;

and Pennel's "Robert Greene and 'King or Kaiser,'" *English Language Notes* 3 (1965): 24–26.

5. D. J. Palmer, *Comedy*, 9.

6. See, for example, Brian Gibbons, *Jacobean City Comedy* (London: Rupert Hart-Davis, 1968). Gibbons helps to create the genre of city comedy: city comedies "exclude material appropriate to romance, fairy tale, sentimental legend or patriotic chronicle" (24).

7. See, for example, Barber's creation of a distinct kind of celebratory comedy in the opening pages of *Shakespeare's Festive Comedy*.

8. Geraldo U. de Sousa, "Romance in the Satiric Comedies of Ben Jonson and Thomas Middleton, 1603–1614," (Ph.D. diss., University of Kansas, 1982), 32. See also David M. Bergeron, "'Lend me your dwarf': Romance in *Volpone*," *Medieval and Renaissance Drama* 3 (1986): 99-113; and W. Nicholas Knight, "Sex and Law Language in Middleton's *Michaelmas Term*," in *"Accompaninge the Players": Essays Celebrating Thomas Middleton, 1580–1980*, ed. Kenneth Friedenreich (New York: AMS, 1983), 89–108. Knight points out that Shakespeare "uses exactly the same judicial and legal vocabulary [as city comedy] with equal precision and competence" (90). Jonsonian scholarship of the 1980s often concerned itself with the breaking down of rigid assumptions about the generic shapes of comedy. See, for example, Anne Barton, *Ben Jonson, Dramatist* (Cambridge: Cambridge University Press, 1984) and Alexander Leggatt, *Ben Jonson: His Vision and His Art* (London: Methuen, 1981).

9. Moretti, "The Soul and the Harpy" in *Signs Taken for Wonders*, 15.

10. These latter are the terms used by Viviana Comesoli as she reclaims Dekker and Middleton's *The Roaring Girl* in "Playmaking, Domestic Conduct, and the Multiple Plot in *The Roaring Girl*," *Studies in English Literature* 27 (1987): 252.

11. Bristol, *Carnival and Theater*, 148.

12. Bakhtin, *Rabelais and His World*, 5.

13. On the nuances, barely explored in the present study, of an archaeological method, see Michel Foucault's *The Archaeology of Knowledge*, trans. A. S. (London: Tavistock, 1972).

14. In *Tudor Drama and Politics* (Cambridge: Harvard University Press, 1968), David Bevington does summarize the play's action and points to Greene's exaggeration (224–27).

15. Robert Greene, *The Plays and Poems of Robert Greene,* 2:1.1.1–3. Subsequent references to this work will be from this edition and appear parenthetically in the text.

16. Nichols, *James,* 3:97.

17. Dekker, *The Shoemakers' Holiday,* 1.1.1–2. Subsequent references to this work will be from this New Mermaids edition and appear parenthetically in the text.

18. Smith, *De Republica Anglorum,* 76–77.

19. Topsell, *The Householder,* 172.

20. See Heal, "The Idea of Hospitality in Early Modern England," 77.

21. In his enforcement of popular law, a role given to Robin Hood in plebeian culture, George anticipates functionally the entrance of the more famous hero. For a discussion of this function, see Stallybrass, "'Drunk with the Cup of Liberty,'" in *The Violence of Representation,* 51.

22. Beaumont, *The Knight of the Burning Pestle,* Interlude, 4.8–12.

23. Peele, *The Old Wives Tale,* ll. 34–36.

24. Palmer, Introduction, *The Shoemakers' Holiday,* xiv.

25. See Dobson and Taylor, *Rymes of Robyn Hood,* 17. Stokes, in "Robin Hood and the Churchwardens in Yeovil," 1–25, demonstrates how, in the local Whitsun ale, Robin Hood was an important parishioner in charge of collections and entertainments. Clearly, the role dramatized by Greene has real value for the Renaissance audience.

26. Dobson and Taylor, *Rymes of Robyn Hood,* 33.

27. Munday, *The Downfall of Robert, Earl of Huntingdon,* in *The Huntingdon Plays.* As an experiment in understanding the "uses" of Robin Hood in the production of authority, compare Munday's appropriation of the outlaw in his civic pageant of 1615 *Metropolis Coronata, The Triumphs of Ancient Drapery in Pageants and Entertainments of Anthony Munday,* ed. David M. Bergeron (New York: Garland, 1985), ll. 310–413.

28. For an excellent theoretical summary of this contest, see Stallybrass, "'Drunk with the Cup of Liberty,'" 69–73.

29. My view of this moment obviously diverges from that of Stallybrass, who argues that the play's representation of the Pinner is entirely complicit with existing hierarchies, a "staunch upholder of 'good orders'": "Not surprisingly, Robin Hood is introduced into the play only as a device to demonstrate George's strength and as a loyal subject of the king" ("'Drunk with the Cup of Liberty,'" 66).

30. Peter Burke, *Popular Culture in Early Modern Europe,* 38–39.

31. Kastan, "Workshop and/as Playhouse," 325.

32. For the theatrical tastes of the day, such contests were considered excellent entertainment. One thinks, for example, of the conjuring contests in *Friar Bacon and Friar Bungay, John a Kent and John a Cumber,* and *Doctor Faustus.* Audiences in Renaissance England seem to have relished, to return to the terms of D. J. Palmer's definition of comedy, the clear-cut triumph provided by a contest.

33. Buchanan Sharp, *In Contempt of All Authority.* See also Donald R. Kelley, "Ideas of Resistance before Elizabeth," in *The Historical Renaissance: New Essays on Tudor and Stuart Literature and Culture,* ed. Heather Dubrow and Richard Strier (Chicago: University of Chicago Press, 1988), 48–78; David E. Underdown, *Revel, Riot, and Rebellion: Popular Politics and Culture in England, 1603–1660* (Oxford: Clarendon Press, 1985); and Keith Wrightson, "Aspects of Social Differentiation in Rural England," *Journal of Peasant Studies* 5 (1977–78): 33–47.

34. Morrill, *The Revolt of the Provinces.* See also Sharpe, "Crown, Parliament and Locality," in *Politics and Ideas in Early Stuart England,* 87.

35. Samuelson discusses this conservative and aesthetic task in "The Order in Beaumont's *Knight of the Burning Pestle,*" 302–18. That pinners and their kind may triumph even in the midst of such containment is implied by Miller's "Dramatic Form and Dramatic Imagination in Beaumont's *Knight of the Burning Pestle,* 67–84. Miller chooses Rafe as the real victor of the play's colliding orders.

36. Porter, *The Two Angry Women of Abington,* ll. 175–79.

37. Two of George's hospitable kindred are Hobs the tanner, who hosts King Edward, in Thomas Heywood's *King Edward IV, Part I* and Hobson the haberdasher, who hosts Queen Elizabeth, in Heywood's *If You Know Not Me, You Know Nobody.*

In their depiction of pinners and haberdashers as hosts of royalty, these plays reflect, I think, a concomitant heightening of local identity and national awareness during the period.

    38.   Quoted by Sharpe, "Crown, Parliament and Locality," in *Politics and Ideas in Early Stuart England,* 87.

CHAPTER

4

———

Pageantry, Hosts, and Parasites

No dramatic genre welcomes, entertains, and dismisses so well as pageantry. Grand banquet tables fill halls and arbors with cold herons, sliced beef, pasty of hot venison, roast mutton, quails, partridge, and mince pies. Mythological figures, Diana or Sylvanus or Ceres, grace the ordered consumption. Under Elizabeth and James, careers were won and lost spectacularly, and the tokens of success and defeat were pageants. At the same time, no dramatic genre presents the critic with more subtle—and less studied— complications of mediation; for pageantry, by its very univocal name, tends to elude the critic.[1] Lord mayor's shows, royal entries, progresses, household entertainments—all qualify the term in different ways. A collaborative (perhaps scripted) performance, pageantry fades in an instant and we struggle to reconstruct its manners. At the time of the performance, moreover, in ways quite foreign to the public theaters, the pageant has been a*imed* at a particular shaping, occasioned by a particular hospitality. Pageants, in performance, are practices, strategic and tactical, complicated by their mirroring of the real political negotiations taking place during the hospitalities. Were this the sum of its negotiations, pageantry would be complex enough to warrant increased attention. But after performance, the pageant experience is typically converted into an authorized text that *claims* to simply report the entertainment. In making such a claim, these texts mystify their own part in a secondary shaping of everyone and everything included in the original performance. Scholarship has yet to recognize these kinds of secondary shapings, phenomena that will become the focus of the present chapter.[2]

With its complex leaps and detours between hospitable practices and the representation of these practices, pageantry takes its place at the heart of this study. My aim is to explain how Elizabethan and Jacobean pageants represent hospitable practices differently than other dramatic genres: because of the way pageants foreground their own social functions in representations,[3] opportunities for *parasitic representations* abound. Said another way, pageant texts offer up—to anyone who can read—the aims of their own staging among the elites. Whereas the evanescent performance was neatly contained by the noble's estate, the queen's palace, or the city's good management, the pageant text generically admits anyone into the interstices of political and social negotiations. Although the table has been set for guests, parasites may take advantage of the host in this textual form. Indeed, it becomes possible for any writer to appropriate authorized representations of pageantry in hospitality. Conventions may be troped on, parodied, or utterly reinvented.

I have chosen two of the most provocative examples of this phenomenon for discussion: Will Kemp's *Nine Days Wonder* and Thomas Nashe's *Summer's Last Will and Testament*. An out-of-work clown and a starving writer, Kemp and Nashe feed on generic pageant forms by drawing out primary genres of hospitality for criticism and innovation. Kemp takes the progress pageant and substitutes clown for king. Nashe takes the household interlude and makes language the basis of hospitable practice.

Progresses and Pamphleteers

In late summer of 1578, Queen Elizabeth visited the town of Norwich while on progress. Knowledge of the cultural practices that combined to animate such a progress may come to the historian from a variety of sources: letters, annals, diaries, city records, and household account books. Yet the Norwich entertainment is special because shortly after the queen's visit two authorized pamphlet accounts appeared. Thomas Churchyard, one of the age's marginal but industrious talents, offered *The Entertainment of the Queen's Majesty into Suffolk and Norfolk*, and Bernard Garter compiled *The Joyful Receiving of the Queen's Most Excellent Majesty into Her Highness' City of Norwich*. Both men had produced scripts for performance during the monarch's visit. More than simple compilations of these scripts, the progress pamphlets report reception then slip into moralizing, architectural description and sundry kinds of cultural commentary. Years later, on April 29, 1604, King James was moving from feast to feast in progress toward London, stopping unexpectedly at Godmanchester to receive gifts. From Berwick to Cambridge, the new monarch collected sacks of gold, prize horses, a standing cup of gold, falcons, and poetry. Like Elizabeth's progress into Suffolk and Norfolk, James's progress is significant for the fact that it was converted into a pamphlet, *The True Narration of the Entertainment of His Royal Majesty*. Like Churchyard's pamphlet, *The True Narration* interleaves commentaries on contemporary society with straightforward "recording" of entertainments.

In practice, the progress was codified through custom. In his *English Civic Pageantry*, David Bergeron defines the aims of the progress in the following terms: (1) the improvement of health and sanitation (a comfortable escape from the plague), (2) a lowering of court expenses, and (3) an opportunity for the monarch to see and be seen. Of great interest to the scholar of plebeian culture is the way this desire "to see and be seen" includes ordinary citizens who enter the progress event, altering its shape and legitimating the sovereign presence.[4] As an aesthetic form, the progress, according to Bergeron, conforms to the following pattern: (1) meeting of monarch outside city gates for escort, (2) presentation of gifts, (3) oration, (4) pageantry, (5) household feasting, and (6) formal departure (p. 10). For the most part, critics have concerned themselves with pageantry in the narrow sense of dramatic spectacle, rarely mentioning these other elements. Taking Churchyard's pamphlet and *The True Narration* as illustrative, I would conclude Bergeron's list with a seventh element: the transformation of progress experience into pamphlet form. In fact, I contend that such pamphlets exist as a distinct generic accretion, a small but identifiable tendency to assimilate hospitable speech genres at a particular intersection of theatrical, textual, and royal forces.[5]

One of the most important characteristics of this transformation is the authors' assertions of hospitable practices as the
informing structure of pageant experience and their pamphlet
texts as simple reproductions of that experience. Indeed, Churchyard claims that only a successful hospitality would have occasioned the production of a text: "For in very deed, if the dutiful
usage of Suffolk and Norfolk had not surmounted in greatness
and goodness any five shires in England, for hospitality, bravery,
and frank dealing, I had not made mention of these causes, nor
written so large a discourse of their behaviors, and bountiful manner of duties" (p. 179). In his consistent concern with hospitality,
Churchyard promises to record carefully "who bestowed some entertainment."[6] With the tone of an empiricist, he mystifies his own
reshaping of events as so much news: "And because I saw most of
it, or heard it so credibly rehearsed as I know it to be true, I mean
to make it a mirror and shining glass, that all the whole land may
look into, or use it for an example in all places (where the Prince
commeth) to our posteritie hereafter for ever."[7]

In a similar fashion, the narrator of James's progress asserts
"long travail" and "diligence" in gathering information about "his
Majesty's receiving and royal entertainment" (p. 13). Above all, he
will record the "munificent bounty" of the households which entertained the king with "plenty of delights and delicates" (p. 13).
In every case, we learn the names of those who welcome, those
who entertain, and those who receive the reward of knighthood.
Every host gets proper credit for his hospitality. We learn, for example, of Robert Carey's practices: "The House being plentifully
furnished for his [King James's] entertainment," the king returned
after hunting "with a good appetite." James, we understand, "was
most royally feasted and banqueted that night" (p. 25). Expanding
the form beyond Churchyard's and Garter's reckonings, the author elaborates special moments of hospitality, as when Mistress
Genison, by virtue of being a widow, plays hostess. The widow
receives the author's praise: James "was so bountifully entertained
that it gave his Excellence very high contentment" (p. 28).[8] Not
surprisingly, Cecil's hospitality merits special attention: "it was
indeed exceeding all the rest in any place of England before. But-
teries, pantries, and cellars [being] always held open in great abundance, for all comers" (p. 32). As the phrase "for all comers"
suggests, the speech genres of hospitality fill out the account.

Cecil has realized a splendid ideal worthy of Stow's chronicle of golden times long past, the promise of care for all classes. In a similar, though less expansive fashion, the author surrounds his descriptions of the pattern described by Bergeron with a diligent listing of all such hospitalities. Commentary frames performances, feasts, and travel; it even distributes unlooked-for welcomes. The Earl of Shrewsbury provides woodsmen clad in green to surprise the king and lead him in hunting as a prologue to such a "superfluity of things [offered by the household], that still every entertainment seemed to exceed others. In this place, besides the abundance of all provision[s] and delicacie[s], there was most excellent soul-ravishing music; wherewith His Highness was not a little delighted" (p. 34). In the progress narrative, the description of hospitalities (a kind of *auxesis*) builds to climax after climax, each entertainment seeming to exceed all others, but this grand display depends entirely on the construction of the writer who has filtered and condensed otherwise heterogeneous materials.

Hosts multiply. We learn of the hospitalities of the Earl of Rutland, Sir John Harrington, Sir Anthony Mildmay, Oliver Cromwell (uncle to England's future leader), Sir Henry Cock, and of course Robert Cecil (William's son) at Theobalds. At this noble house, Cecil's hosting moves the author to a figure: "To speak of Sir Robert's cost to entertain him [James] were but to imitate geographers that set a little o for a mighty province" (p. 45). In a sense, the author *is* a kind of geographer. As Churchyard does for Suffolk and Norfolk, this writer maps his own vision of hospitable practices tied to particular localities, the result being a kind of cartography of civil obedience.[9]

Unlike the playwright who produces a text for performance, the author of the progress narrative asserts that his text will do business in the culture, recording the culture's practices of hospitality and the rewards of royal power. For centuries, of course, the real issue had been precisely this matter of obedience. The practice of the progress brought royal spectacle through villages that might otherwise forget about royal authority; and as accounts from the reigns of Elizabeth and James show, the progressing monarch was no frozen icon. In the movement from house to house, the royal guest could be investigator, judge, and jury. *Hospitality made the monarch's subjects vulnerable,* a historical fact of English rule that turns out to be crucial to the composition of Elizabethan and Jacobean tragedy (see Chapter 5).

When Elizabeth arrived at Lord Montague's Cowdray in 1591, the host was deeply concerned with how Elizabeth would take his not-so-covert Catholicism. In hosting, Montague opened himself up to investigation; he could hardly have done otherwise. Not surprisingly, the entire entertainment hinges on a demonstration of Montague's loyalty. Any other course might well have occasioned the dismal fate of Edward Rookwood, whose hospitality Elizabeth sought during her 1578 progress. Unfortunately for Rookwood, the queen found a Papist for a host. We learn of the incident through a letter from Topcliffe to the Earl of Shrewsbury in which the writer signifies the failing of the Papist in terms of hospitality, his "unmeet" and "bad" house.[10] We learn that Cecil soon summoned the host. This seems to be a brilliant instance of tactical maneuvering under the auspices of hospitality as Cecil demanded an account of (what seems to have been public knowledge of) Rookwood's papistry. The interview went poorly and the host was forced to trade the great hall for the local jail. Under the pretence (more tactics) of searching for missing plate from the queen's retinue, servants discovered "an image of our Lady" which Elizabeth ceremoniously condemned to flames. Rookwood was eventually deprived of his household. In the hands of these guests, the material and the moral are succinct: hospitality enables stern rule.[11]

What such accounts teach is that progresses were dangerous; entertainment, trenchers, and fairies could have grim consequences in practice. But this strategic recognition is finally less interesting than the problem such knowledge posed for the authors who would transform progress pageants' strategies and tactics into prose for public consumption. In the hands of Churchyard, the transformation is extraordinary. The pamphleteer condenses his material radically, a rhetorical move that only heightens the single similarity between letter and pamphlet. Both writers make hospitality the structure of interaction. Churchyard writes: "On Sunday, the 10th, the Queen was entertained at Euston Hall, near Thetford, by Mr. Rookwood who was afterwards but ill requited for his hospitality."[12] Obviously, a fiery account of Elizabeth's actions would have sent a message to Churchyard's readers about the queen's wrath, but perhaps too many details would have been provoking to a heterogeneous public, many of whom could adduce the facts on their own. Churchyard's conservative rendering suggests, I think, a generic tendency. Although the practice of hospitality must tactically and strategically reinforce Elizabethan and Jacobean rule, representation must constantly economize knowledge of that practice.

When a cutpurse with "a good store of coin found about him" was taken among the king's followers during James's 1604 progress, the author of *The True Narration* was faced with a similar configuration of practices. In this instance, hospitality revealed a criminal element in the monarch's subjects. Like Elizabeth, James took advantage of the progress to demonstrate his authority. The new monarch, "hearing of this nimming gallant, directed a warrant presently to the Recorder of Newark, to have him hanged: which was accordingly executed" (p. 35). Other prisoners were summarily released. In practice, this dispensation of "justice" would have been noted by some, ignored by others, and misrepresented by still others. Steven Mullaney has clarified the stakes of this practice by pointing to Sir John Harrington's complaint that "our ne Kynge hathe hangede one man before he was tryede; 'tis strangely done: now if the wynde blowethe thus, why may not a man be tryed before he hathe offended[?]"[13] Mullaney observes that

> the omission of the well-established English custom of a trial somewhat marred the royal countenance James sought to project, but it is not merely the violation of juridical process that troubles Harrington. James' intrusive display of sovereign authority suggests a monarch who does not recognize limits to his power or his domain, who might pass judgment as readily on his subjects' thoughts and intentions as on their deeds—a view to which the royally licensed account unwittingly but ominously gave credence.[14]

If spectacle mystifies the unequal allocation of power, James's naked practice awkwardly disrupts the intended effect. Only a secondary, ominous shaping can amend the progress; the pamphleteer turns the incident into an emblem. Details are selected, others discarded. The whole evolves into a clear moral: "which fault, if they [cutpurses] amend not, heaven suddenly send the rest [the same fate]!" (p. 35). A transgressor from the lower orders, the cutpurse can be dealt with simply. Unlike Rookwood, the cutpurse can never even *appear* to challenge the monarch's cherished doctrines. He is a citation, a convenient manifestation of the unruly subject who must be curbed. In sum, the representational economy of pageantry demands such politic choices.

When an author produces a pamphlet account of a progress, the textualization of the events nearly always reinforces the ideological shaping of the various hospitalities. Power is redistributed, and the process is confirmed in writing for the literate public. In this way, the monarch engages the beneficial dynamics of live performance—oral patterns of popular culture, improvisation—with the assurance of an authored version that will make hospitality's sometimes volatile ideological shaping accountable. No mere descriptive text, the progress narrative appropriates community life and submits it to narrative. In turn, a submission to narrative produces imaginary resolutions of real contradictions between class, economic, and political interests.[15]

Were this the whole story, we should simply add a new chapter to the monological history of dominant authority in early modern England; but the very textualization on which these narratives depend ultimately makes them vulnerable to imitation and parody. Whereas characters like Dogberry stammer and stumble on Shakespeare's stage, forever separated from the patterns of aristocratic entertainment, a real-life clown may actually take up the pen and enter the world of elites after that world has been given over to print culture. Narrative techniques may be borrowed and adapted for other purposes.

Progresses and Parasites

In 1599, William Kemp, Shakespeare's famous clown known for his creation of Dogberry, was out of work. And so, like his monarch, he went on progress to Norwich. In 1600, he published *Kemp's Nine Days Wonder,* a small pamphlet that purports to give a *true* description of the clown's morris dance from London to Norwich. In his dedication, Kemp claims to seek only favor and the opportunity of providing a true account of his morris: "Some swear, in a Trenchmore I have trod a good way to win the world: many say many things that were never thought. But, in a word, your poor servant offers the truth of his progress and profit to your honourable view."[16]

Without a trace of humility, Kemp adopts a royal genre, assuming the position of both monarch and pamphleteer. Like a monarch, Kemp progresses. Elizabeth goes to Norwich; Kemp goes to Norwich. Like Churchyard, Kemp writes a text that provides only the Truth. (The clown's strategies seem to prefigure much in the new century. In 1616, the same year that James published his *Works*, Ben Jonson produced his own *Works*. Texts allow writers to borrow from kings.) To what extent is Kemp's pamphlet an intervention—perhaps enabled by generic accretion—in the genre's ideological assumptions? Far from raising intractable questions of a traditional influence study, my inquiry leads to a questioning of plebeian responses to dominant authorities: in what sense is the clown's progress narrative, because Kemp authors it himself, a parasitic feeding on royal authority and royal strategies of ideological shaping? As Hamlet might explain, "Your fat king and your lean beggar is but variable service, two dishes, but to one table—that's the end" (4.3.23–25).

Kemp's narrative exists as an eighteen-leaf version of a live event (weeks in duration, counting Kemp's pauses between each of the nine days of dancing) that appears weeks after the happening. Details have been carefully selected and recombined. At Ilford, Kemp narrates, "I again rested, and was by the people of the town and country there-about very, very well welcomed, being offered carowses in the great spoon, one whole draught being at that time to have drawn my little wit dry" (pp. 4–5). The "great spoon" held about a quart, according to Dyce. Its excess gives concrete form to Kemp's "very, very well." Like the author of *The True Narration*, Kemp takes care to note his host communities: "If I should deny that I was welcome at Braintree, I should slander an honest crew of kind men, among whom I fared well, slept well, and was every way well used" (p. 9). Though Kemp will confer no knighthoods, he notes the names of his important hosts: "This Wednesday morning I tript it to Sudbury; whether came to see a very kind gentleman, Master Foskew . . . who, giving me good counsel . . . besides his liberal entertainment, departed, leaving me much indebted to his love" (p. 9).

Like his predecessors, Kemp records the gifts offered as part of the entertainment: "The noble gentleman, Sir Edwin Rich, gave me entertainment in such bountiful and liberal sort, during my continuance there Saturday and Sunday, that I want fit words to express the least part of his worthy usage of my unworthiness; and to conclude liberally as he had begun and continued, at my departure on Monday his worship gave me five pound" (p. 12). James got sacks of gold, Kemp five pounds. The differences are clear, the similarities more interesting.

Like all progress narratives, *Kemp's Nine Days Wonder* claims to report a certain experimentation. The author looks out into the English countryside, off toward the English cities and towns, and prepares to test the hospitality of the land. Will Ilford come up to Braintree? Will Norwich rival London? What the royal gests propose, the progress narrative seems to summarize after the fact. Long before demographics became a mathematical practice, the progress narrative probed contemporary society in the name of hospitality. The results, both for monarch and clown, were predictably ideal. The rhetorical illusion of experiment remained, for both clown and monarch, quite useful.

It is therefore fascinating to watch Kemp, like the authors of royal pamphlets, shape his materials in order to achieve his ends. In practice, the progress would be defined by its *copiousness* (hundreds of wagons in the royal party, hundreds of followers imitating Kemp), whereas the textualized version has been subjected to an immense *distillation*. Kemp distills these disparate voices into "kind peoples" (p. 3) and "multitudes" (p. 4). *The True Narration* depends on the same strategy (see pp. 22, 28, 43, 47). In a most curious turn of events, the author justifies textual distillation because of the way heterodox humanity undermines hospitality. People push and shove. Kemp is soon "stealing away from those numbers of people that followed me" (p. 6). The author of *The True Narration* follows Kemp's lead by noting how "common people" raised such an ongoing shout of "welcome" that the official oration could not proceed until "they were, in a manner, entreated to be silent" (p. 22). The same author describes how at Stamford Hill the "multitudes" "even hazarded to the danger of death. But as uncivil as they were among themselves; all the way, as His Majesty passed [they welcomed him] with shouts, and cries, and casting up of hats (of which many never returned into the owners' hands)" (p. 47). Years later, during a more difficult time, James angrily reproved his magistrates for allowing "the vulgar" to insult the visiting Spanish ambassador during a procession.[17]

In pamphlet form, the monarch can have it both ways—
adoring subjects and barbarous hordes. The contradictions inherent in this objectification need not be addressed. How ironic that
the needs of monarch and plebeian clown converge in this agenda: the vulgar must be distilled. It may be that textualization is
inherently inimical to differentiated humanity, that great quanti-
ties of diverging voices, by threatening the possibility of cohesion,
must be generically flattened. When progress becomes narrative,
regardless of the author's class, it taps these strategies and peddles
familiar patterns of obedience.

Kemp's innovative exploitation of *focalization*, a narrative
strategy aimed at shaping the audience's attention, certainly
seems to expand the possibilities of distillation beyond the
accomplishments of the other pamphleteers.[18] In the performance
of a progress, people crowd each other, pressing for good vantage
points that last a minute. Orations are lost in the noisy shuffle.
Welcomes go astray. In the progress narrative, this quality of
performance disappears. The text offers an undisturbed view
of the proceedings, pausing over "important" characters and
events, hurrying on to catch up with "significant" figures. Kemp's
narrative posits a vital focalizer, a textual vantage point from
which the reader observes while sharing jokes and personal
biases. In Kemp's hands, focalization heightens the reader's
experience of an ideal hospitality. When he arrives at Rockland,
Kemp comes to an inn

> where the host was a very boon companion, I desir'd
> to see him; but in no case he would be spoken with till
> he had shifted himself from his working day's suit.
> Being armed at all points, from the cap to the codpiece,
> his black shoes shining and made straight with copper
> buckles of the best, his garters in the fashion, and ev-
> ery garment fitting corremsquandam (to use his own
> word), he enters the hall, with his bonnet in his hand,
> began to cry out: "O Kemp, dear Master Kemp! you
> are even as welcome as—as—as—," and so stammer-
> ing he began to study for a fit comparison, and I thank
> him, at last he fitted me; for saith he, "thou art even as
> welcome as the Queen's best greyhound." (pp. 12–13)

The focalizing Kemp directs us toward the welcome, purifying the scene of distractions. We notice the copper buckles and their quality. We are told what to think of the host's special preparations. Focalization makes it possible for the clown to catch "corremsquandam" as the host's "own word." And the reader can laugh over the host's corruption of speech genres when he offers what Kemp terms a "dogged yet well-meaning salutation." Kemp the author practices what Greenblatt terms *recording*, the acquisition of alien voices and alien interpretations.[19] As Greenblatt suggests, recording serves the interests of dominant authorities; it enables control. Like Theseus in *A Midsummer Night's Dream*, Kemp explains that "I took his [the host's] good meaning" (p. 13). Hospitality thus focalized enables a more subtle (we might say novelistic) appropriation of the lower orders' social customs and so engenders an authority over them.

Kemp's narration of his arrival in Norwich completes this process of intervention and pre-emption as he details every element of the progress (as defined by Bergeron). A "multitude" meets him at the city gates; the mayor and other officials send for him. The officials offer household entertainments: "They not only very courteously offered to bear mine own charges and my followers', but very bountifully performed it at the common charges: the Mayor and many of the Aldermen often times besides invited us privately to their several houses" (p. 16). When all is properly arranged so the full dramatic effect can be achieved, Kemp returns to the city gates and dances. Like a monarch, he receives a welcoming oration. Thomas Gilbert provides an acrostic:

W   With hart, and hand, among the rest,
E   Especially you welcome are:
L   Long looked for as welcome guest,
C   Come now at last you be from far.
O   Of most within the city shore,
M   Many good wishes you have had.
E   Each one did pray you might endure,
W   With courage good the match you made.
I   Intend they did with gladsome hearts,
L   Like your well willers, you to meet:
K   Know you also they'll do their parts,
E   Either in field or house to greet
M   More you than any with you came,
P   Procured thereto with trump and fame. (p. 16)

Like the monarch, Kemp receives a gift: five pounds from the mayor and forty shillings a year for life.

At the end of Kemp's progress, a text ensures realization of the pamphlet ideals, and it is James's curious fortune to follow the successes of a clown. The historian interested in Tudor and Stuart rule would no doubt collate the texts of Elizabeth's and James's progresses and find in them a continuous tale of early modern spectacle and rule, but the clown's "normal" text inserts a curious sense of déjà vu into this transmission of royal authority. Seams appear. James encounters a "cutpurse"—after Kemp has documented his own meeting with a cutpurse in Burntwood on his way to Norwich (p. 6). The "hospitable widow" who entertains James (p. 28) has her precedent in the clown's pamphlet (p. 11). And James's injury and hospitable care (p. 39) have been presaged by Kemp's own bodily discomforts (p. 5). In a most unauthorized fashion, precedent favors the clown.

Genre becomes a feast and agendas turn awry as Kemp alters the course of moral commentary. Colin MacCabe has rightly defined the clown's innovation as the creation of a "transitional form" emerging "between carnival and commerce,"[20] the force of which can be seen in the narrative's minor apotheosis in praise of the mayor of Norwich as "a man worthy of a singular and impartial admiration, if our critic humorous minds could as prodigally conceive as he deserves, for his chaste life, liberality, and temperance in possessing worldly benefits. He lives unmarried, and childless; never purchased house nor land, the house he dwells in this year being but hired: he lives upon merchandise, being a merchant venturer" (p. 18).

Whereas the progress narrative tends generically toward a celebration of the traditional English community's obedience, Kemp's text retails the image of an enlightened merchant who thrives through "projection," succeeding through absences. Lacking wife, child, and house, the merchant prospers by offering a kind of liberality promised by the old tradition of hospitality. Kemp catches himself: "But, wit, whither wilt thou? What hath morris tripping Will to do with that?" (p. 18). Kemp's rhetorical surprise is betrayed by his clear purpose: "I cannot choose but commend sacred liberality, which makes poor wretches partakers of all comfortable benefits" (p. 18). Indeed, Kemp's mediation between carnival and commerce stands out when contrasted with the more typical praise of merchants offered by Thomas Heywood in his lord mayor's pageant *Londini Emporia, or Londons Mercatura* (1633), in which the author praises merchants for founding cities and connecting foreign lands.[21] The merchant deserves honor for his heroic accomplishments. In Kemp's text, the merchant deserves praise for his purely relational life; the image has parasitical possibilities as the author envisions hosts who allow everyone to feed laterally on everything else.

Like a joint stock company, Kemp has himself "put out some money" on his efforts (p. 19). Whereas the exact nature of these investments is unclear, the publication of the text confirms his accomplishments in much the same way that Thomas Harriot's authoring of *A Brief and True Report of the New Found Land of Virginia* (1588) was meant to confirm the successes of the joint stock company's colonial efforts. Just as the joint stock company, in the person of men like Kemp's celebrated mayor, sought strange worlds for investment, Kemp seeks out those peoples nurtured far (in geographic terms and class terms) from court. This alien world, merely alluded to by Churchyard, is gathered up in the clown's pamphlet, recorded in speech genres, and brought back for sale in the London markets.

No mere document of reportage, the *Nine Days Wonder* represents a kind of strategic narrativizing by a writer of low rank. I would term it a document of parasitic colonization and argue that the conversion of performance and extraliterary materials into narrative functions here as a ploy—what the French call *la perruque*, a borrowing of *official* time, materials, and codes to carry out the worker's own projects. The factory worker in Paris who uses the company's lathe to make a table for himself during company time practices *la perruque*.[22] And this is Kemp's practice as well, as he borrows royal materials, the recreational speech genres of monarchs, in order to supplement his own income. In this instance, the digestions of genre actually warrant a kind of unauthorized feeding on royal forms. The clown represents hospitable practice, I conclude, in order to set new tables for feeding amid the old hierarchies of English society. As Touchstone explains in *As You Like It*, "It is meat and drink to me to see a clown" (5.1.10).

It seems necessary that we reckon the theoretical implications of Kemp's task. Theories of Carnival and popular culture have been strangely silent on such matters, consistently aiming for notions of subversion at work in larger performance materials.

Perhaps we have been concerned with the victories of the elites for so long that we have failed to theorize the localized, concrete victories of ordinary folk? Kemp's text, filled as it is with carnivalesque energies, achieves a much more certain, more everyday, victory than subversion. Like a good parasite, and here Michel Serres offers the most extended treatment of such an odd idea,[23] Kemp has found food and income. In our desire to uphold Carnival (and the lower orders), we may wish to glorify such energies; but, as a matter of fact, these strategies were always parasitic with respect to every surrounding ritual, custom, and speech genre. People get by with what they can lay their hands on. I would not wish, consequently, to condemn Kemp's simple triumph by recollecting the fact that his recording and marketing of "alien culture" denies him the role of caretaker for the lower orders. As the parasite digests (genre's fundamental process) the primary genres of those nurtured far from court, the age hardly prepares Kemp to consider the moral implications of his acts. We who stumble on his pamphlet can only be impressed (perhaps provoked) by a lowly clown who, for a moment, presents the image of having made something out of borrowed spectacle, out of *la perruque*.

Thomas Nashe, Pageantry, Paronomasia

At the table of the great, Thomas Nashe was William Kemp's equal—a shadow, peering over the shoulders of the more fortunate, hoping to feed when the right opportunity presented itself. Both men took advantage of prevailing prose forms to reach the great hall's table. But whereas Kemp's progress pamphlet finds resolution in an isolated poaching, Nashe's *Summer's Last Will and Testament* offers innovation. Nashe refashions hospitality such that it becomes a matter of words, a matter of paronomasia. Before turning to Nashe's experimentation with the subgenre of household pageantry, I want to suggest the contours of the writer's career, the ways in which his own dogged pursuit of a position at the table anticipates his hospitable theorizing in a minor genre.

Nashe has been turned away from the gates of scholarship on many occasions, typically because of the way he blithely skips from scene to scene in search of what Hibbard calls "the immediate, local effect."[24] No general intention, according to Hibbard, governs the construction of a particular text. The requirements of print culture dictate smooth transitions. To C. S. Lewis the result comes "very close to being, in another way, 'pure' literature: literature which is, as nearly as possible, without a subject. In a certain sense of the verb 'say', if asked what Nashe 'says', we should have to reply, Nothing."[25] This quality causes Hibbard, though defending Nashe from Lewis's "sweeping" claim, to conclude that Nashe "is and always has been, a minor writer."[26] Crewe, in his poststructuralist look at Nashe, simply accepts this view as "the Nashian problem," a chance to revel in Renaissance indeterminacy.[27] In his more comprehensive study of the writer, Stephen Hilliard admits that Nashe's works "reveal the contradictions of Elizabethan society," but qualifies this statement by pointing out that these same "works do not show a very developed understanding of the social and economic conditions of their production."[28]

To scrutinize one of Nashe's texts with the eye of a literary critic, influenced as we all are by the habits of close reading, is to confront words as detritus, spawnings, collisions, fancies, debasements, and emergences. Hilliard's conclusion poses the most difficult question for the present chapter: how is it possible for such a jostling composition to *understand anything?* And only Lorna Hutson has offered an answer to this question that catches the writer's active relationship to language and distinct cultural domains. For Hutson, Nashe has a clear aim: the pursuit of "his own 'festive' notion of reading as a recreative purgation of received images and ideas."[29] Unlike earlier analyses, Hutson's revision prepares us to trace more particular negotiations.

I suggest that Nashe's works often hinge on the period's central concern with hospitality, an investment engendering a text less interested in univocal intention and subject (a set of literary values) than in gathering (entertainment's root sense of collecting and holding together) the disparate voices of the culture so that they might speak to the allocation of the community's resources, food for the hungry, shelter for the poet. A saturation of material culture born by the speech genres of the street is finally more important than literary coherence. Collocation overwhelms cohesion. Nashe's texts seek out the noisy orality one may yet find at auctions. Sentences stand up and bark when the timing is right, intervening on the smooth development of topic and the careful statement of opposing views.

From the time he came to London in 1588 until his death in 1601(?), Nashe wrote of his own marginal inhabitation of London, looking for hospitality. In his pamphlets, he complains, collects, first rants and then narrates. Gradually, Nashe evolves into the most neglected of guests, an image that has captured the imaginations of generations of critics.[30] Perhaps the secret of this authorial success lies in Nashe's basing his writerly identity in hospitable complaint. The hospitality we ignore in other genres becomes Nashe's "life" in *Pierce Penniless* (1592): "Nay, I would be ashamed of it if *Opus* and *Usus* were not knocking at my door twenty times a week when I am not within; the more is the pity, that such a frank gentleman as I, should want."[31] Nashe always valued his frankness, his own term for his audible style. His eyes fixed on the successes of Greene and Marlowe, Nashe starved as he sought a patron and host: "But all in vain, I sat up late, and rose early, contended with the cold, and conversed with scarcity; for all my labours turned to loss, my vulgar muse was despised & neglected, my pains not regarded, or slightly rewarded, and I my self (in prime of my best wit) laid open to poverty" (1:157).

The writer struggles for success in the literary canon, his efforts made impossible by the present age's disregard of hospitality. Nashe sketches the scene in the following manner: "Famine, Lent, and desolation, sit in onion-skinned jackets before the door of his endurance, as a *Chorus* in The Tragedy of Hospitality, to tell hunger and poverty there's no relief for them there: and in the inner part of this ugly habitation stands greediness, prepared to devour all that enter" (1:166). In response, he cultivates a vulgar (James's term for the noisy lot that insulted the Spanish ambassador) muse fascinated with the language of the streets, everyday habits, and the odd application of learning.

The experience of scarcity, a condition always unsettling to canonical literature, dominates his life. Against our contemporary tendency to exclude the author from critical discussions, Nashe asserts his own fashioned life of want, becoming for us the archetypal Elizabethan as he becomes increasingly obsessed with the inescapability of this single great tragedy. For Nashe, the pamphleteer's complaint over hospitality is naturally fused with the predicament of the Elizabethan writer. Habitation founds writing; writing, habitation. In *Lenten Stuff* (1599), written in exile after nearly being imprisoned for his collaboration on the scandalous play *The Isle of Dogs*, Nashe elaborates this connection by identifying with Homer: "That good old blind bibber of *Helicon*, I wot well, came a begging to one of the chief cities of Greece, & promised them vast corpulent volumes of immortality, if they would bestow upon him but a slender outbrother's annuity of mutton & broth, and a pallet to sleep on; and with derision they rejected him" (3:155).

Such is Nashe's "autobiographical" tale of woe, a seductive fabulation of his own authority. In a strategy not so different from Kemp's placing himself at the center of the progress narrative, Nashe has inserted himself into the pamphlet world of hospitable commentary. In contrast to Jonson, who embraced the evolving author function as the legitimation of his talents and the basis of Horatian control, Nashe seems to invoke authorial presence in order to link hospitable practice and literary production. Like a writerly cutpurse, he swipes the author function and stuffs it with everyday life.

For Nashe, frustration occasioned invention. What he could not transact on the London streets or at the gates of the nobility, he began to invent in torrents of prose. If volumes could not be exchanged for hospitality, then volumes might reinvent hospitality. His method deserves attention. In *Pierce Penniless*, he laments, for example, that the scarce wheat which once fed the hungry now goes to the vain production of starch for dressing lawn ruffs. Deftly, the author directs our attention to a particular instance of a communal allocation of resources. Next, he probes the existence of this allocation in words, suggesting that "the lawn of licentiousness hath consumed all the wheat of hospitality" (1:181). Hutson's is surely one of the first accounts of Nashe to appreciate the kind of strategy at work in this passage in the context of Elizabethan complaint over manufacturing. Nevertheless, as she juxtaposes the passage to Philip Stubbes's *Anatomy of Abuses* (perhaps the most famous complaint text of the period), Hutson sees in Nashe's work only a parody of Stubbes's simplifications (pp. 25–27). To make her point, Hutson looks at Stubbes's heavy-handed identification of starch as an "idol" tied to sin and pride. I suggest that, by recognizing Nashe's more sophisticated awareness of language, one need not reduce Nashe's own complaint to mere parody. For in its own obscure fashion, Nashe's figure exposes the feint by which society swallows the very possibility of hospitality. Since the wearer of lawn ruffs might easily

mince that "fashion has nothing to do with hospitality and allocation," Nashe anatomizes these relationships by showing the vulnerability of the administrative expression. He displaces the
abstract "fashion" with the concrete "wheat" that might feed the
hungry. Whereas Stubbes rails at pride and simply renames starch,
Nashe breaks open the language of communal rationalization.
Perhaps the result still parodies the sin-quenching prose of
Stubbes, but it also foregrounds the productiveness of language in
the allocation of communal wealth.

  Nashe is Kemp's sophisticated brother, for his aural technique
owes something of its existence to England's traditions of clowning and characters such as the Vice. Speaking the language of the
everyday, the clown traditionally encourages confusion in literary
assertions of abstract value that would otherwise seem quite
tenable to the dominant elements of a culture. Weimann points out
that this "confusion, however, is a contradiction, and reveals a
broader context in which one element (often the more abstract) is
undermined by a more concrete concept."[32] The theoretical
implications of such a mode of reading and writing are vast and
relatively unexplored in literary scholarship. In a sense, the undermining of the abstract by the concrete as practiced by Nashe is a
Renaissance version of what we now call dialectical materialism.
For Nashe, this mode of analysis works because Elizabethan culture is radically homonymous. The vulgar muse will always hear
life's concrete necessities in abstract statements.[33] The inhospitable posture can always be heard differently. Nashe's writing
simply elaborates his hearing. The play of *paronomasia* may enable the recomposition of hospitality.

  As the preceding discussion suggests, Nashe's tactics intro-
duce a fascinating complexity into the generic shape of the household pageant. In her *Pageantry on the Shakespearean Stage,* Alice V.
Griffin defines the genre by its (1) small audience, (2) use of the
ample space of the estate, (3) evolution of sometimes brilliant
welcoming lyrics, (4) presentation of gifts, (5) dependence on the
affective presence of the sovereign, and (6) receptivity to experimentation.[34] Above all, as Bergeron points out, speech is the
crucial element, animating the whole and making possible
experimentation. Speech ensures that the audience can share the
experience. Speech ensures a sense of spontaneity, a feeling that
the woods and streams have truly just recognized a monarch in

their midst. In the evolution of this genre, Wotton's notion of the household as a theater of hospitality was fully realized. At Harefield in 1602, for example, Time welcomes Elizabeth on the final progress of her reign: "The Guest that we are to entertain doth fill all places with her divine virtues, as the sun fills the world with the light of his beams."[35] The pageant character's speech recognizes Elizabeth as both audience and guest, an observer of literary performance and domestic obligation.

In this union of literary and household practices, the host could exercise an immense and, if Dana B. Polan is correct, *negative* control over the production of ideology in the culture. Polan describes spectacle's functioning: "While much criticism of the ideological function of art has concentrated on what such art shows (for example, studies of positive and negative images of women), the politics of fiction may reside as much in what such fiction does not say as in what it does show. Spectacle offers an imagistic surface of the world as a strategy of containment against any depth of involvement with that world."[36]

On a larger scale and of much greater duration than the masque, the household pageant realizes just such an "imagistic surface." When Elizabeth arrived at Elvetham on 20 September 1591 and met a Poet clad in green and laurel, she seems to have had no desire to poke the pretty figure and test its "depth." As the Poet spoke, six Virgins appeared to move obstacles out of the queen's path. Representing the Graces and Hours, the Virgins wore gowns of taffeta and flowers. Discussing the surface, Bergeron remarks: "It is a scene worthy of a Botticelli."[37] The fact of unequal allocation of social wealth disappears amid copious visions of dryads and fairies enraptured by the sight of the Queen of England. This conservative effect achieves an apotheosis in the textualization of the pageant performances. The surfaces are frozen, and what is lost in spectacle is more than made up for by legitimation of royal authority.

When Nashe tried his hand at the genre in the early 1590s, the household pageant had reached a kind of apotheosis, ripe for parody and ironic innovation. In the Wanstead entertainment of 1578, Sidney had introduced an element of satire into his *Lady of May*, but for the most part the dynamic of spectacle was alive and well. In his own iconoclastic fashion, Nashe came to the genre prepared to *hear* the speeches of this refined form, ready to follow the performative qualities of language. The pamphleteer's pageant thus reads like a glossary of aural figures: *antanaclasis*, the homonymic pun; *antonomasia*, a descriptive phrase for a proper name or a proper name for quality associated with it; *asteismus*, a facetious or mocking answer that plays on a word; a noisy version of *euphemismus*, a circumlocution used to palliate something unpleasant. Unlike the world of Elvetham, Nashe's Croydon has its share of unpleasantries. Whereas the progress narrative calmly appropriates the community's speech genres in order to polish them for kings, Nashe uses the pageant text to force primary genres of welcome and care against each other, the process being finally more productive than Hutson's notion of purgation.

Summer's Last Will and Testament *and Harvest Ears*

Written during the most productive period in the author's life and probably performed for Archbishop Whitgift and his household at Croydon Palace, *Summer's Last Will and Testament* (1592) explores the possibilities of "hearing culture"—with a grace unique in Nashe's works.[38] From scene to scene he brings together court, street, rural culture, the old order and the new, in conver-sation. As the voices multiply, Nashe seeks (to borrow a term from Bakhtin) a *heterological* solution, a coming together of primary genres: disparate social speech types, social dialects, professional jargons, generic and geographic languages, languages of generations and age groups, tendentious languages, languages of the authorities, of various circles and of passing fashions, languages of households, and languages of literary circles.[39] If genre typically forms through a digestion of such materials, then Nashe's mode of composition may amount to a kind of gorging. What mirth we find emerges, in C. L. Barber's words, from "housekeeping."[40] The embodiment of Greek poetry, Homer wanders from city to city like a stranger crossing the Elizabethan countryside, looking for hospitality that will support his writing. Or so it seems to Nashe. Since hospitality fails in its obligation of charity, the poet may exchange a few corpulent volumes for his scraps at the gate. And Homer, Nashe tells us, "was a grand jury man in respect of me."

Will Summers, "a Goose, or a Ghost at least" of the famous court fool who had died in 1560, introduces the show with "summer" at its center, but this summer smells of paranomasia. Summer means, in the first place, Will Summers—the fool—who comes out ruffled, "for what with turmoil of getting my fool's apparel, and care of being perfect, I am sure I have not yet supped tonight" (3–5). From the first lines of the pageant, Nashe departs from generic convention and directs his audience's attention toward a broad hospitality that functions in turmoil. In the brilliant household pageants of Elizabeth's reign, such as Elvetham and Cowdray of 1591, Elizabeth met mythical figures, porters, and anglers. Never did she meet a figure like Will Summers, complaining of his costume and the problems of performance. At Croydon, the pageant will begin before the monarch arrives. Summers must, he complains, "speak to you in the person of the idiot our playmaker," upon whom he will be revenged by sitting "as a *Chorus* and [flouting] the *Actors* and him at the end of every scene" (21–22, 91–92). By his very name, the character is situated in England's rich history of clowning and allowed to chew on the show's central idea of "summer." The clown is *antanaclasis* brought to life. Instantly, Nashe introduces a complicating meta-perspective into the show's surface, violating the genre's typical avoidance of depth, making the traditional household pageant teeter between literature and domestic practice. Will Summers's presence makes the show aware of itself as pageant, balanced precariously between distinct registers of rank and faction.

At the same time, Summer means the mythical deity who, Summers explains, "must call his officers to account, yield his throne to Autumn, make Winter his executor, with tittle tattle Tom boy" (82–84). Clown and monarch grow out of the sound of the same word. The audience will hear conversations between the monarch and his subjects, who enter the playing space to answer for their behavior. In the typical pageant, the monarch listens to praise; here the audience watches a monarch seek and fail to find exchanges governed by *comprobatio*. In Summer, the old monarch, we see an imperfect reflection of Elizabeth, whose own entertainments were marked by the notion "of gathering in the powers reigning in the countryside" so that they might yield to Her Majesty.[41] The fading summer reflects England's summer under

Elizabeth, and those who watch want to know what comes after. We learn that Summer has been "Looking each hour to yield my life and throne,"

> But that *Eliza*, England's beauteous Queen,
> On whom all seasons prosperously attend,
> Forbade the execution of my fate,
> Until her joyful progress was expir'd. (131, 133–36)

Indeed, Elizabeth was on progress at the time, enjoying the hospitality of her subjects. With his insertion of "the monarch" into this work of aural resemblances, Nashe has begun to digest the entire course of Elizabethan pageantry in a fashion far more sophisticated than that available to Kemp. As Helen Cooper explains, the genre changed in response to Elizabeth's desire to participate in the performance.[42] Toying with this royal desire, Nashe takes the queen's usual subject position and turns it into a mere literary role, harmoniously scripted with echoes of Eliza. Royal agency has been subsumed by the sound of pageantry.

Finally, the show invokes the dismal and torrid summer of 1592. As Hibbard so aptly observes, the pageant achieves "an unwonted depth and poignancy from the proximity of the plague-ridden city. To Nashe and those for whom he wrote, life itself appeared as a brief holiday from the terror of death. His play is pervaded by a sense of mutability, subdued to a pitch at which it does not conflict with the general lightness of tone, yet ever present as a kind of ground bass."[43] Summers foregrounds this effect blatantly: "Forsooth, because the plague reigns in most places in this latter end of summer, Summer must come in sick" (80–82).

Identities collapse and multiply as Nashe exploits the genre's capacity for aural effects. As he did for his own identity in the pamphlets, Nashe takes the position of the monarch and infuses it with communal concerns. Ontology becomes contrapuntal. In a few lines, Nashe has made the pageant digest topical reference, myth, class hierarchy, and monarchy. Vertumnus summons Ver (spring) before the monarch, whose song Summers finds "a pretty thing, if it be for nothing but to go a begging with" (175–76). Summers observes from the streets of the 1590s. He turns out to be right. For Ver has spent all "on good fellows" and now delights in justifying his extravagances with a stream of commonplaces calculated to echo Summer's own impotent capacity to hold on to his possessions: "This world is transitory; it was made of nothing, and it must to nothing: wherefore, if we will do the will of our high creator (whose will it is that it pass to nothing), we must help to consume it to nothing" (256–59). In repetition, "nothing" achieves its own silly logic. As a model, Ver offers Geta, the Roman Emperor, who consumed a meal two miles long (270). For his vain argumentation Ver receives from his monarch the season of Lent. In Nashe's world, extravagance that feeds only itself must yield to "woe and want" (157).

This first exchange establishes the conversational mechanism for the rest of the show. With his final moments, the monarch repeatedly attempts to locate proper service. Generic expectation dictates lyric *comprobatio* as when the Poet addresses Elizabeth at Elvetham: "Thy presence frees each thing that liv'd in doubt."[44] But Ver is free already. Instead of compliment, he offers aggressive engagement. In Nashe's show, words matter most, and a monarch may wait in vain:

> SUMMER: Believe me, *Ver*, but thou art pleasant bent;
> This humor should import a harmless mind:
> Know'st thou the reason why I sent for thee?
> VER: No, faith, nor care not whether I do or no.
> If you will dance a galliard, so it is: if not,
> Falangtado, falangtado. (177–82)

Ver provokes Summer by refusing, from the very beginning, to acknowledge his lord's authority. "Falangtado," nonsense that it is, disrupts the conversation because it gives Summer nothing. In order for hospitality to exist, entertainer and entertained must be willing to cooperate in a language that makes possible exchange and transformation—above all, a return to the concrete. Particularly for a Renaissance audience aware of the conventions of household pageantry, Ver's carelessness must have been genuinely funny.

On the other hand, Summer's simple desire for a good conversation, not so different from Lear's at the end of Shakespeare's play, achieves a gentle poignancy: "Nay, stay a while, we must confer and talk" (184). In conversation, an old host should be able to find solace. In the dialogue *Civil and Uncivil Life* (1579), a text more household than literary, the spokesman for the old ways defends traditional hospitality because of its reciprocity, its mixing of guests and hosts. As entertainer, the host can expect his guests to "entertain their master with table talk, be it his pleasure to speak either of hawks, or hounds, fishing or fowling, sowing or grassing, ditching or hedging, the dearth or cheapness of grain, or any such matters, whereof gentlemen commonly speak in the country."[45] Here is hospitality's *raison d'état,* its essential condition for political practice apparent in More's dinner at Cardinal Wolsey's household. Country and courtly hospitality come together in function. The traditional practice ought ultimately to ensure the host's conversation and solace, a term "applied to that recreation considered necessary to a monarch who otherwise might become dull and demoralized and, through his or her own ill health, in turn bring sickness to the body politic of which the monarch was the head."[46] In Nashe's pageant, solace comes with difficulty.

Nashe's obvious delight in fashioning sounds takes a more cultivated form with the appearance of Sol, who by his very presence, as a representative from both myth and 1592, reminds his audience of the dry Thames and London's suffering population. Summer inquires of his servant, "Canst thou produce, to prove my gift well plac'd? / Some service or some profit I expect" (459–60). Sol describes his service with all the humility he can muster: "T'is a credit for your excellence, / To have so great a subject as I am" (465–66). Naturally, Sol's excellence comes in pretty words. His being rests, he says, in "eloquence," a value wholeheartedly embraced by the dominant elements of Elizabethan society as indicative of genuine civility.[47] But the smooth surface of eloquence makes no room for the poor souls it neglects in steaming London. Literary values fail utterly in light of household practice. Summer judges: "He that sees all things oft sees not himself" (542). In this way, Sol is not so different from Ver. Both servants ensconce themselves in a burgeoning literary language in order to avoid the world. By contrast, Summer answers with simple, hospitable poignancy: "Where was thy care" (552).

At this point, Will Summers intervenes. Between the language of the monarch and the language of courtly pleasure, the vulgar muse knows an earthy digression concerning a notary named Histiaeus who, wishing to communicate with his friend Aristagoras, shaved a servant's head (pretending to treat his illness) and wrote a message on the bald pate. Aristagoras had only, Will tells us, to shave his servant upon arrival to recover the message. So, the clown concludes that Sol may be one who "writes under hair": "If I wist there were any such knavery, or Peter Bales *Brachigraphy*, under Sol's bushy hair, I would have a barber, my host of the Murrion's Head, to be his interpreter" (611–14). With a kind of alehouse precision, Summers makes Sol's bushy costume and bushy verse concrete. No communication, no exchange is taking place between monarch and servant.

Nashe wittily elaborates this moral with the entrance of Orion, whose pack of dogs comes howling into the performance space. In contrast to Ver and Sol, Orion answers his ruler: "'Tis I, dread Lord, that humbly will obey" (639). Autumn interrupts to complain of the barbarous curs, attributing venom, infection, and plague to the beasts. Orion's defense reshapes the terms of service by first reckoning dogs' relation to words:

> To come to speech, they have it questionless,
> Although we understand them not so well:
> They bark as good old Saxon as may be,
> And that in more variety than we. (675–78)

As Clunch's barking Ball suggests in *The Old Wives Tale*, dog eloquence comically transcends human eloquence with its pure Saxon roots. More important, dogs "set upon the enemies" and serve faithfully their friends. Orion deftly cites the example of Ulysses's dog Argus who, when the master's hospitality was abused and all had forgotten him, offered the warrior his only welcome. The satire is both funny and explicit.

Harvest enters this space *"with a scythe on his neck, & all his reapers with sickles, and a great black bowl with a posset in it born before him: they come in singing"* (SD). As before, Summer seeks a good conversation about what he (Summer) possesses: "What plenty hast thou heaped into our Barns? / I hope thou hast sped well, thou art so blithe" (813–14). Unlike his predecessors, Harvest's answer is unequivocal and hospitable: "Sped well or ill, sir,

I drink to you on the same. / Is your throat clear to help us to sing
hooky hooky?" (815–16). Without concern for potential recompense,
Harvest obeys the customs of hospitality by seeking participation
and cooperation in the entertainment. We are no doubt meant
to compare Harvest's genuine invitation with Ver's careless offer
to dance.

Autumn, scholar that he is, takes issue with Harvest's answer.
Winter will later cast some doubt on Autumn's (and the genre's)
anatomizing motives in a discussion of communal allocation,
claiming that such scholars exist as "drunken parasites, / Term'd
poets, which, for a meal's meat or two, / Would promise monarch's immortality" (1268–70). In Nashe's pageant world, everyone
clamors for a chance to feed. Harvest enters an arena of competition where he must argue a case. He begins by clarifying his
opponent's motives: "Answer? why, friend, I am no tapster, to say
anon, anon, sir" (822–23). With Harvest's assistance, one thinks of
Hal (in *1 Henry 4*), confusing the luckless tapster so that Francis's
"tale to me may be nothing but 'Anon!'" (2.4.29–30). Autumn
would toy with the hospitable fellow, but Harvest maintains his
authority: after all, he has responded to his monarch with more
than "hooky hooky."

Summer proceeds to "arraign" Harvest on charges of hoarding; but as Hibbard has shown, the servant is a more complex
character. Embodying the harvest-home feast, he is also

> the yeoman farmer, as the age liked to imagine him.
> Summer, on hearsay, accuses him of the crime that
> delinquent members of his class were generally sus-
> pected of practising, hoarding of grain and unchari-
> tableness. His answer, given in a down-to-earth prose
> that is admirably sustained, amounts to a complete
> self-vindication and equates him with the virtue of lib-
> erality, and the much admired practice of housekeep-
> ing, or hospitality.[48]

In the figure of Harvest, Nashe gathers a whole cart of hospitable
practices, their supposed abuses and their obvious ideals. In put-
ting this overdetermined re-presentation on trial, Nashe
nurtures the possibility of provocative innovation: from Harvest,
we finally learn how to converse differently—from the hungry

margins of Elizabethan England. Nashe seems to suggest that a
"down-to-earth prose" best explains the often subtle, typically
chaotic possibilities of speech. "I keep good hospitality," he says.

Harvest not only vindicates himself, he elaborates hospitality's
possibility in paranomasia. To this end, Harvest suggests that we
"hear" the conversation of his age differently: "And yet I give no
alms, but devour all? They say, when a man cannot hear well, you
hear with your harvest ears: but if you heard with your harvest
ears, that is, with the ears of corn which my alms-cart scatters, they
would tell you that I am the very poor man's box of pity, that there
are more holes of liberality open in harvest's heart then in a sieve,
or a dust-box" (877–83). The technique Nashe tests in pamphlets
receives full elaboration here as cultural hermeneutics. People hear
a unitary language that denies the abundance inherent in both
words and fields. As a corrective, Harvest suggests that we might
hear differently were we to hear a generous allocation of material
substance in the *words within words* of everyday conversation,
a hearing that playfully exchanges terms from the heterological
flow of speech genres sustaining the culture. Such a hearing substitutes the yeoman's ears, the concrete produce of the fields, for
the abstract expression which by itself would simply reinforce a
particular dominant interest.

We ought to pause here to reckon the import of Harvest's brief
triumph. Hutson, for example, finds Harvest "blithe" and his
speech a "mockery" (p. 164). Nashe's work purges, but, according
to Hutson, it "lacks the integrity to persuade" and "in breaking up
separate formulations [as Harvest does] it refuses to ensure provision of memorable meaning for future use by the reader" (p. 123).
This view, tied as it is to a sense of Nashe responding to contex-
tual constraints, surpasses the traditionally negative approach of
Lewis, Nicholl, and Crewe—even as it remains burdened by
Nashe's handling of language. For Hutson, the show does little
more than hand down the old moral language. Such a verdict
discounts, among other things, the monarch's approval. Summer
tells Harvest, "Thou doest me the best service of them all" (921).
More than old commonplaces, Harvest embodies England's material resources, their production and allocation. The complaints he
engenders have their basis less in myth than in the everyday
life of most Elizabethans, who devoted much energy to matters of
corn, hunger, and hoarding.

Certainly, many writers in the 1590s represented either literary myth or household allocation. But Nashe's particular accomplishment lies in his suspension of disparate worlds through the character of Harvest. From this position, Harvest seems to suggest that an excess of language (the Nashian problem) will enable a parallel reallocation of language *and* material resources, thus fulfilling the ancient requirement of hospitality. The idea is fresh, radical in both its own day and our own. Even Summers must grudgingly concur that "this stripling *Harvest* hath done reasonably well," musing that this "bundle of straw" might well be carried "to my chamber door, and laid at the threshold as a wisp, or a piece of mat, to wipe my shoes on every time I come up dirty" (951–52, 958–61). The clown speaks more prophetically than he knows, for the kind of sophisticated perception Harvest suggests is, then and now, more "wisp" than revolution. Contemporary literary theory struggles to recover what Nashe heard centuries ago.[49]

Winter, Christmas, and Back-winter follow Harvest and minimize his triumph as they claim succession to Summer. In Nashe's hands, celebration becomes ironic comedy. Christmas arrives in silence. In Nashe's garrulous world, silence demands scrutiny. Summer wants to know why Christmas has come without "some music, or some song? / A merry carol would have grac'd thee well; / Thy ancestors have us'd it heretofore."[50] In his turn, Christmas refuses to play his part in the tradition of entertainment: "I / may say to you, there is many an old god that is now grown / out of fashion. So is the god of hospitality" (1633–34). Against all expectations, Christmas brings to the world recalcitrant silence and a denial of traditional hospitality. With the motto *Liberalitas liberalitate perit,* Christmas frames the coming reign in a perverse household ordinance. The doors are barred:

> Not a porter that brings a man a letter, but will have his penny. I am afraid to keep past one or two servants, lest, hungry knaves, they should rob me: and those I keep, I warrant I do not pamper up too lusty; I keep them under with red herring and poor John all year long. I have dammed up all my chimneys for fear (though I burn nothing but small coal) my house should be set on fire with the smoke. (1705–12)

The show reaches closure in the closure of the household. A year earlier, when Elizabeth had visited Cowdray, a Porter welcomed her by explaining that he had been awake for years waiting for "the most fortunate of all creatures" to arrive.[51] Christmas fears such porters, and Summer will never see their like. In Nashe's show, the iconography of hospitality is inverted by its traditional supporter: "So, say I keep hospitality, and bid me a whole fair of beggars to dinner every day, what with making legs, when they thank me at their going away and settling their wallets handsomely on their backs, they would shake as many lice on the ground as were able to undermine my house, and undo me utterly" (1653–58).

Hospitality is kept, Christmas admits, "but once in a dozen year, when there is a great rot of sheep, and I know not what to do with them, I keep open-house for all the beggars, in some of my out-yards; marry, they must bring bread with them, I am no baker" (1713–16). The spectacle slips, and Christmas dismisses ancient custom: "This latter world, that sees but with her spectacles, hath spied a pad in those sports more than they could" (1628–29). With perfect irony, Christmas undermines the generic form of his pageant existence. His speeches sound against Harvest's innovation. Whereas Harvest opens up cultural practices by hearing words within words, Christmas collapses the possibilities of hospitality through a play on "spectacles." The term is reduced through *asteismus* to spectacles for poor vision. Even as it recreates hospitality, Nashe's paranomasia exposes how the old hospitality can be set at naught.

Summer chides the miserable host: "Amend thy manners, breathe thy rusty gold: Bounty will win thee love when thou art old" (1731–32). Precedent suggests that this should be the moral of the pageant. The surface of spectacle should find ripeness in the nurture of a mortal monarch. In Elizabeth's entertainment at Norwich in 1578, Apollo responded to the queen's bounty with an affirmation of her immortality: "You cannot die, Loue here hath made your lease."[52] At the Elvetham entertainment, the queen found a proper conclusion that moved her to reciprocity: "And here ended the second day's pastime, to the so great liking of her Majesty, that her gracious approbation thereof, was to the actors more than a double reward; and yet with all, her Highness bestowed a largesse upon them the next day after, before she de-

parted."⁵³ By contrast, Summer's entertainment at the hands of his
own servants undermines custom; it certainly falls short of Elizabeth's experience. Having received so little, the mythical monarch
will bestow nothing on his servants: "A bad account: worse servants no man hath" (1143). His situation reflects the age: *"Totidem
domi hostes habemus, quot servos"* (1146) (As many enemies have we
at home as servants). The possibility of profound tragedy, the
world of *King Lear*, is at hand.

And what of Will Summers? The Epilogue informs the clown
that he "hath mard the play." Summers answers, *"Barbarus hic ego
sum, quia non intelligor ulli"* (1954) (I am a barbarian here, for no
one understands me). Like Nashe, like Dogberry and his company,
Summers's presence has asserted the barbarism of many speech
types amid genteel language. To those keepers of the literary canon, the resulting polyphony rankles even as it did during Nashe's
day, for a canon must necessarily unify and centralize the verbal-
ideological world through the gradual evolution of a unitary language. Bakhtin has written most persuasively of this process:

> The victory of one reigning language (dialect) over the
> others, the supplanting of languages, their enslave-
> ment, the process of illuminating them with the True
> Word, the incorporation of barbarians and lower social
> strata into a unitary language of culture and truth, the
> canonization of ideological systems determined the
> content and power of the category of 'unitary lan-
> guage' in linguistic and stylistic thought, and deter-
> mined its creative, style-shaping role in the majority of
> the poetic genres that coalesced in the channel formed
> by those same centripetal forces of verbal-ideological
> life.⁵⁴

Like Nashe, Will Summers has refused to be absorbed into such a
language because centripetal forces offer few avenues for rapprochement between classes, between unequal allocations of resources, between speech genres. In this light, it is fascinating to
consider that while little has been written about Nashe's show, a
steady stream of scholarship engages the famous lyric "Adieu,
Farewell Earth's Bliss." The poem offers what Nashe and the show
do not: a unitary poetic language.

Neither this essay nor a great black bowl with a posset and essays will bring Nashe to the hearth of the literary canon, but this was never the point. The very textuality of Nashe's work, insofar as it encourages close reading, will always frustrate literary values predicated on textual tensions. Whatever success Nashe has in imagining another form of hospitality can only achieve its full effect in a reader warmed for speech. Making such a claim, I do not intend to "prefer" speech over writing in the guise of some kind of ontological assertion. Jacques Derrida has suggested the pitfalls of such a practice; at the same time, one must remember that grammatology is finally *about* philosophical inquiry; it skirts ontology. Nashe does far less business with philosophy than he does with literary conventions and the material world of Elizabethan London. The hearing Nashe proposes is about community and human relationships—vulgar, everyday stuff smelling of poulters' stalls. If the speech Nashe hears has value *as speech*, it may have something to do with what William Gass attempts to recall:

> There is, unquestionably, an inner speech, a speech which represents our consciousness as it goes babbling on, and this internal talk cannot be replaced by writing. We may not be able to find our way past the last word to reach a wordless realm, as Plato desires us to do, but if we fail, we shall very likely find ourselves left with the spoken word as the only medium of real thought, although a few diagrams or mental pictures may sometimes supplement it, and machines make easy many wearisome computations.[55]

Pageants have long been out of favor, perhaps since the death of Elizabeth. If Polan is right about the functioning of spectacle, it may be that the modern world's hunger for the medium (initiated by Inigo Jones and Ben Jonson) quickly outstripped anything a pageant text could offer. Certainly the mellifluous rattling of internal talk, exposed to the world as Nashe's self and yet flush with the stuff of hospitable complaint, corn and ale, has never found a large audience. When the sounds of words alter the digestion of daily habits and enable a questioning of boundaries between self and culture, theater becomes dangerous and authors (as Nashe did) disappear.

NOTES

1. Only the masque, thanks to the advocacy of Stephen Orgel, has received the kind of attention pageantry deserves. David Bergeron has argued eloquently in a number of publications for more serious attention to this form. See, for example, his *English Civic Pageantry 1558–1642*, 2; and more recently, his *Introduction to Pageantry in the Shakespearean Theater* (Athens: University of Georgia Press, 1985), 1–16. Another important exception to the general neglect of pageantry is Anglo's *Spectacle, Pageantry, and Early Tudor Policy*, which offers a much-needed contextualization of the genre. Strong's *Art and Power* is the most recent and comprehensive contribution to this field.

2. I discuss this phenomenon as "textualization" in "William Kemp's *Nine Daies Wonder* and the Transmission of Performance Culture," *Journal of Dramatic Theory and Criticism* 5.2 (1991): 33–47. See also Elsky, *Authorizing Words*.

3. This is the point gracefully made by Montrose in "Gifts and Reasons" when he argues that in Peele's pageant "acts of gift-giving and relationships of power within the fiction reproduce basic characteristics of the social world in which the play is written and performed" (433).

4. Bergeron, *English Civic Pageantry, 1558-1642*, 9.

5. See, for example, Robert Laneham, *A Letter: Wherein, part of the Entertainment unto the Queen's Majesty at Kenilworth Castle, in Warwickshire, in this Summer's Progress* (London, 1575). It would be possible to include a number of pageant texts, such as those edited by Jean Wilson, in this collection, since the boundary between pageant text and progress narrative is quite fuzzy. Claudio Guillén's famous pronouncement that two texts constitute a genre may be to the point in this instance. I would, in fact, qualify the pattern as a generic accretion, a temporary deposit on the margins of larger generic forces. That such accretions do recur in the history of literature is confirmed, perhaps, by the "progress narratives" of Defoe, Steinbeck, and, more recently, William Least Heat Moon's popular *Blue Highways: A Journey into America* (Boston: Little, Brown, 1982).

6. Churchyard, *A Discourse of the Queen's Majesty's Entertainment in Suffolk and Norfolk*, in Nichols, *Elizabeth*, 2:214.

7. Ibid., 179.

8. For a discussion of widows and hospitable practice, see Heal, *Hospitality*, 178, 180–2.

9. It should not, then, be surprising that Churchyard appends to his account verses in honor of "travelling bodies" and colonial voyages.

10. Nichols, *Elizabeth*, 2:216.

11. For a fascinating discussion of this incident in terms of "competing images of womanly rule," see Marcus's *Puzzling Shakespeare*, 83–87.

12. Nichols, *Elizabeth*, 1:129.

13. Quoted by Mullaney, *The Place of the Stage*, 105.

14. Mullaney, *The Place of the Stage*, 105.

15. Jameson, *Political Unconscious*, 77.

16. Kemp, *Kemp's Nine Days Wonder*, 1. Subsequent references to this work will appear parenthetically in the text. Kemp's appropriation of the term "progress" is not unique. See, for example, *A Merry Progress to London to See Fashions* (London, 1620). In a more startling usage, the unpopular Spanish ambassador Gondomar made his own "progress" through England in 1620 (Nichols, *James*, 3:617).

17. Nichols, *James*, 3:661.

18. For a discussion of the term in the context of narratology, see Genette, *Narrative Discourse*, 189–94.

19. Greenblatt, "Invisible Bullets," in *Shakespearean Negotiations*, 35.

20. MacCabe, "Abusing Self and Others," 10. I thank Steven Mullaney for bringing this essay to my attention.

21. Thomas Heywood, *Londini Emporia*, in *Thomas Heywood's Pageants*, 56.

22. Certeau, *The Practice of Everyday Life*, 24–28.

23. Serres, *The Parasite*.

24. Hibbard, *Thomas Nashe*, 147.

25. Lewis, *English Literature in the Sixteenth Century*, 416.

26. Hibbard, *Thomas Nashe*, 64.

27. Crewe, *Unredeemed Rhetoric*, 1.

28. Hilliard, *The Singularity of Thomas Nashe*, 3.

29. Hutson, *Thomas Nashe in Context*, 120.

30. His constructed image of the poor guest has been most seductive, encouraging generations of critics to mistake posture for fact. Hutson has emphasized the constructedness of Nashe's life (2–3).

31. Nashe, *The Works of Thomas Nashe*, 1:161.

32. Weimann, *Shakespeare and the Popular Tradition*, 135.

33. In "Sidney and His Queen," in *The Historical Renaissance,* Quilligan reminds us "that we must also attempt to hear the *social* resonance of wordplay as well. The simultaneity of meaning in a pun might provide a social as well as a verbal or poetic strategy" (184).

A classic introduction to this intellectual context of dialectical thinking can be found in Henri Lefebvre's *Dialectical Materialism*, trans. John Sturrock (London: Jonathan Cape, 1968), 21–45.

34. Griffin, *Pageantry on the Shakespearean Stage*, 79.

35. Nichols, *Elizabeth*, 3:589.

36. Polan, "'Above All Else to Make You See,'" in *Postmodernism and Politics*, 63. Cf. Strong's discussion of spectacle in pageantry in *Art and Power*, 42–62.

37. Bergeron, *English Civic Pageantry*, 58.

38. It is tempting to assume that the show was indeed performed for the archbishop. See, for example, Charles Nicholl, *A Cup of News: The Life of Thomas Nashe* (London: Routledge & Kegan Paul, 1984), 135–41. But we have no record of the show's performance. Indeed, we have little record of commentary on the show. Other than passing treatment by critics such as Hibbard and Hilliard, interested in the whole of Nashe's career, I find but a single article devoted to the show: Elizabeth Cook, "'Death proves them all but toyes,' Nashe's Unidealising Show," in *The Court Masque*, ed. David Lindley (Manchester: Manchester University Press), 17–32. Cook's lively discussion compares Nashe's use of figures from myth, allegory, and history to contemporary playwright Caryl Churchill's use of a similar technique in *Top Girls*. Cook contends that this technique coupled with Nashe's control of a variety of idioms makes it possible for the playwright to suspend real and ideal in an almost Brechtian fashion. The origins of this effect in England's popular theater are discussed at length in Weimann's *Shakespeare and the Popular Tradition*.

39. Bakhtin, "Discourse in the Novel," in *The Dialogic Imagination*, 262–63.

40. Barber, *Shakespeare's Festive Comedy*, 62.

41. Ibid., 32.

42. Cooper, "Location and Meaning in Masque, Morality, and Royal Entertainment," in *The Court Masque*, 140.

43. Hibbard, *Thomas Nashe*, 90.

44. *The Honorable Entertainment Given to the Queen's Majesty in Progress, at Elvetham in Hampshire, by the Right Hon'ble the Earl of Hertford, 1591,* in Wilson, *Entertainments for Elizabeth I,* 105.

45. *Civil and Uncivil Life* (London, 1579), 38.

46. Barroll, "A New History for Shakespeare and His Time," 457.

47. For a provocative discussion of the place of eloquence in Renaissance England, see Richard Lanham, *The Motives of Eloquence* (New Haven: Yale University Press, 1976).

48. Hibbard, *Thomas Nashe,* 98. Cook points to Harvest's "ontological status" as being derived from allegory.

49. Cf. Harvest's attempt at accommodation with the declaration of Geoffrey H. Hartman (inspired by *King Lear*) in *Saving the Text* (Baltimore: Johns Hopkins University Press, 1981), 128: "Reading is, or can be, an active kind of hearing. We really do 'look with ears' when we read a book of some complexity." In this book, Hartman offers a sophisticated project of interpretation quite akin to Harvest's. Hartman's ears, however, listen to literature.

Another way of appreciating Nashe's innovation here is to compare his work to that of John Lyly, the age's recognized master of eloquent innovation. Indeed, in "Nashe, Lyly and *Summer's Last Will and Testament*," *Philological Quarterly* 48 (1969): 1–11, Michael Best notes how Nashe seems to play with Lyly's favorite strategies in the show; Best then argues that Nashe has actually revised an old Lyly play. Whether or not one accepts Best's elaborate argument for textual transmission, his account of Nashe's toying with Lyly's styles is useful. As a comparison with Lyly's *Gallathea* will show, Nashe's pageant is always more interested in the material culture carried in language and in the way language undermines language.

50. Summer's expectation finds the force of royal proclamation during the reign of Charles I. See *The Royal Proclamations of Charles I, 1625–1640,* 2:295. In the aforementioned proclamation, Charles ordered his nobility out of London and back to the country for Christmas: "the Winter time being a time when the Countrey hath most need of their [nobles'] Residence and keeping amongst their Neighbours."

51. Wilson, *Entertainments for Elizabeth I,* 88.

52. *Norwich, 1540–1642,* 274.

53. Wilson, *Entertainments for Elizabeth I,* 113.

54. Bakhtin, "Discourse in the Novel," in *The Dialogic Imagination*, 271.
55. William Gass, *Habitations of the Word*, 264.

5

Hosting Vulnerabilities in Renaissance Tragedy

Perhaps better than any other age, the Renaissance tended, and tended to, structures of vulnerability. In brilliant detail, people of the time contemplated the manifold ways in which body, mind, and soul were susceptible to traducing, seducing, inducing, and negating. Wolsey's famous condition—being *naked to mine enemies*—speaks volumes. My concern in this chapter is with the evocation of vulnerability in Renaissance tragedy. I suggest that when Renaissance playwrights wanted to imagine entrapment and the poignant nuances of vulnerability, they represented practices of hospitality.

Stated in such a barefaced manner, the notion startles, for from Hrothgar to Stow the invocation of hospitality seems practically synonymous with a rhetoric of household nurture. Nothing in the steaming bowls of posset or the high-minded ideals of pamphleteers could anticipate the Macbeths' hosting of Duncan. On the other hand, every element of these traditional practices, even in the most stable of traditional communities, is a blinder, a feint leading guest and host into potentially volatile bonds of trust. In an age of nascent capitalism, where the place of the commodity must necessarily conflict with the exchange of the gift, hospitable occasions seem especially tremulous.[1] In the pages that follow, I want to call attention to the way that *King Lear* draws on these perilous constructions. Diverting from time to time to consider examples from other Renaissance tragedies, I trace in this great tragedy a violent pre-emption of the pamphlet debate over the condition of hospitable practice in early modern England.

One of the best places to gather these precarious ideals is in those representations, discussed in previous chapters, of hospitalities offered to England's reigning monarch. Whether they represent Theobalds or Norwich, such texts consistently claim to simply report what has in fact been fashioned. Instead of a "record," we find a series of objectifications and mystifications, ideals in the service of various dominant interests. Under Elizabeth and James, these pamphlets were produced with the monarch's authorization. Unlike Lear, these real rulers controlled the manufacture of ideals in their kingdoms. These monarchs endorsed a perfect vision of royal hospitality, one that, in Henry Roberts's description of King Christian's entertainment, "shall never be razed out of memory so long as the world shall have any being."[2]

In these pageant texts, hospitality is a magnificent and timeless fantasy of care bestowed upon a loved and loving monarch, an ideal quite in harmony with the texts of *Beowulf* and Stow. *Ellipsis* and *condensation* govern the presentation of material. The difficulties of travel disappear. The governments' problems disappear. Moments of discrete hospitality sublimate into grand gestures of loving care. *Comprobatio,* the eloquent compliment to one's judges or listeners, dictates the conversation, and there is always conversation for the ruler. Were a king to possess the mind of a child filled with the passion of a titan (as Wilson Knight suggests of Lear),[3] he might read these pamphlet visions and long to settle in them forever. Like Nashe's monarch Summer in *Summer's Last Will and Testament,* a ruler might pine for the ideal reciprocity of good conversation. We know that Elizabeth became only more demanding of such entertainment as she grew old and infirm; duplications and refractions of her desire ripple through early modern England. In turning from pamphlet ideal to its fetishistic appropriation in *King Lear,* I suggest that we have isolated a distinctly *royal* fantasy: the monarch as guest.

In doing so, we approach some of the most nagging questions raised by the age's greatest tragedies. In particular, we confront Shakespeare's *King Lear:* how can we contextualize the desires that have inspired the monarch's improbable division of his kingdom, his wish to give up rule, and his treatment of his daughters? What does he expect from his daughters, from the countryside? Wilson Knight focussed attention on this question: "The images he creates of his three daughters' love are quite false, sentimentalized: he understands the nature of his children, and, demanding an unreal and impossible love from all three, is disillusioned by each in turn" (p. 177). The critic's terms are specific and helpful: Lear endorses a false image of his daughters and suffers for it. According to Wilson Knight, Lear forms a false image of love. In a most persuasive essay, Coppélia Kahn argues that Lear hopes to find a mother in his daughters.[4] Kahn's case depends on close reading and a synthetic version of psychoanalytic theory. By virtue of its assertion that some kind of fantasy governs Lear's consciousness, the essay neatly qualifies Wilson Knight's argument and goes far in explaining the opacity of Lear's actions. Indeed, might we not suppose that the condition of being vulnerable in Renaissance tragedy frequently obtains from a character's clinging to some fantasy born of psychological, political, and social pressures?[5]

I endorse the mechanics of these explanations and offer the ideal hospitality of the pamphlets as an important but previously unconsidered source of Lear's fantasies, intentionally mixing psychological desire with cultural practice. A reigning monarch such as Elizabeth might eagerly await the summer months in order to be a guest once more, while a childish monarch might desire to be a guest always. Only by giving up his kingdom and dividing it among his daughters could Lear multiply himself as guest on a constant progress. What the aristocracy took away from women through the appropriation of hosting, Lear longs to reinstate as an eternal guest of his daughters. In his wishing, the monarch fiddles with the very mechanisms of civility that support the hierarchical ordering of society in early modern England. His actions halt at hospitable cruxes and seem irrational pauses. His ranting leaps from pamphlets and seems wild and insane. His blindness comes from a fixation on ideals that enchanted Elizabeth and James.

Dialogized Ideals of Civil Life

When the author of the pamphlet *Civil and Uncivil Life* approached his gentlemanly readers in 1586, he did so with a wary care, a concern for hospitable ideals that must surprise the contemporary mind unfamiliar with the age's investment in such quotidian matters. In the phrase that has become a commonplace in my discussion, caught on the lips of Sidney, Sly, and Nashe, this pamphlet ought to be mere "household stuff," yet its anxiety heralds much for readers of *King Lear*. In argument, the pamphlet resembles many others in the ongoing discourse on hospitality: "Wherein is discoursed, what order of life, best beseemeth a Gentleman, (as well, for education, as the course of his whole life) to make him a person fit for the public service of his Prince and Country" (p. 1). In fact, the pamphlet exists as one of the age's most iconoclastic statements on the subject of hospitality. A speaker named Vincent elaborates the pamphleteers' traditional endorsement of a country hospitality, but a speaker named Vallentine reverses every one of Vincent's traditional positions. As these two characters reason the need, their conversation indexes the terrors latent in the fetishism of hospitable practice. If King Lear's motivation stems in part from a dream of royal hosting, then *Civil and Uncivil Life* points to the dark side of what can be made of pamphlet ideals, a contrapuntal text in touch with Shakespeare's tragic vision.

Like *King Lear*, pamphlets were often given over to a cataloging of ontological interrogatives, after the fashion of Lear himself: "Who am I, sir?" Like Lear, these authors angled for the simplest of answers. In their own way, they typically claimed to "sort out" subject positions for their readers, to clarify the behavior of the *complete* gardener, angler, falconer, and so on.[6] They offered ideal *functions* with ideal answers. In the process of clarification, the *complete* person created by the pamphlets was of course filled with gaps, contradictions, and a potential for absurdity—a fact Jonson grasped at the beginning of his dramatic career. *Civil and Uncivil Life* is no different; indeed, it follows Jonson's lead and aims to construct "a person fit for the public service"—with all the age's contradictions in place.

Like *King Lear*, this pamphlet entertains the idea of a bad beginning. Though the topic appears to be the tame matter of polite debate, the author imagines an angry response: "For some I have seen so passionate in opinion as cannot see or hear patiently any thing that contenteth not their own eye, or squareth not even with the rule of their own minds" (p. 5). We have no way of knowing the referents of this passage, but these men who are too passionate, fixed on the vision of their own eyes and trapped by the rule of their own minds, have obviously made an impression on the author, who now seems intent on anticipating his culture's blindness and temerity. To question the basis of civil and uncivil life is to challenge seeing and hearing, patience and content, even the rule of the mind.

In order to make concrete the obdurate nature of his audience, the author elaborates a hypothetical problem of inhabitation: "For, do we not find that the savage nations, are as loath to alter their soil as are we that inhabit a most civil country?" (p. 5). This truncated ethnography points to the heart of Lear's decisions: what would inspire a man to give up his place? The genuine test of human blindness comes in the relation (civilized or not) of man to his soil and his capacity for altering that relation. At one extreme, the author asks: "Would a civil man be pleased, to abandon his being, to abide among the savage? or that would leave the study of good letters, to take pleasure in those toys, which ignorant men delight in? surely no" (pp. 5–6). Opinions and customs may differ, but no *civil* man would abandon his place for life among the savages or the pleasure of toys—unless, as in the case of Edgar, such a life proved his only means of survival; unless, as in Lear's debacle, such a course seemed the best way of attaining one's greatest fantasy.

As a way of containing harsh reactions to his speculations, the author glances beyond the opposition of civil and uncivil toward the primal human instinct against altering one's terrain. In confronting the age's ideals of habitation, one must be especially careful about finding fault: "Since then, for so many reasons you find difference in the opinions of men: and that no counsel, wit, or will, can persuade them to one mind: my meaning is not, that though in this dialogue according to mine own fancy, I prefer the town habitation, yet thereby to find fault with any, that either because his reason so persuadeth, or his own mind so delighteth, will drive out his days in the country" (p. 6). Having conjured a faint image of rash men who might take extreme exception to contrary ideas, the author reassures us that he will be concerned only with matters of habitation, the final end being to determine the proper course for the completion of one's days, a matter of fancy. Of course we know, with the author, that habitation touches the deepest chords of one's being, that to change habitation is to change the bases of one's mind, to toy with vulnerability. How difficult, the pamphlet teaches, to yoke fancy and habitation, delight and difference, counsel and fault!

In what could be a most compelling gloss to Shakespeare's play, the author attempts to anticipate any future conflict arising from his text: "It shall therefore please me, that every man please himself, using the liberty and will of his own mind: and though it be far diverse from mine, yet I know not why his opinion should trouble me, or mine offend him: so long as the direction of either, be still in our own powers" (p. 6). By the end of the author's epistle, we can easily imagine Lear's growing fury over his habitation: "Does any here know me?" *Civil and Uncivil Life* exists as a murmuring preface to the monarch's specific question. It clarifies not "who is Lear" but a more historically fascinating question: who is it that can tell in the context of household practices? The pamphlet primes the contemporary reader for such moments of represented hospitalities when psychic pain and cultural fantasy come together in a crucible of vulnerability.

In the pamphlet, the author hesitates—perhaps because he intends a most unconventional answer to this kind of questioning. Out of hesitation, the old ideal emerges as Vincent recites the traditional terms to Vallentine: "You know the use and ancient custom of this realm of England was, that all noble men and gentlemen, (not called to attendance in our Prince's service) did continually inhabit the countries, continuing there, from age to age, and from ancestor, to ancestor, a continual house, and hospitality, which got them great love among their neighbors" (p. 12). By living according to the dictates of this model, one may expect great love. Who could deny the force of a "continual house"? Consistent with pamphlet conventions, Vincent confidently challenges Vallentine: "But I see, that gentlemen begin to take another course, & falling from use of their ancestors, do now either altogether (or very much) leave to dwell in their country houses, inhabiting cities and great towns, which manner of living I cannot allow" (pp. 12–13). Were the dialogue to maintain this position throughout, it would join the dominant chorus of pamphlet complaint. But Vallentine answers in a most anomalous fashion that the traditional model is "neither good for the commonwealth, neither for the gentles that do use it" (p. 13). *King Lear* is haunted by this assertion, the idea that devotion to the old forms that supported hospitality may cripple a society.[7]

Vincent's defense should be Lear's defense. Vincent fleshes out his hospitable ideal with men of service:

> If you knew, what honour or worship these [men who choose to serve the householder] can do, to a noble-man in his country house, you would rather give a good servingman forty pounds wages, then want his service some one day: I mean, either when you have store of strangers (for so we call our guests), or else when you are from home: For in your absence, he can-not only see things in good order, but also entertain them, first in the hall, next in your parlour . . . some heirs, (I speak plainly in this place) be so simple, as their servingmen, by their counsel, in providing, for-seeing, entertaining, and sparing, do maintain their honours and worships. (p. 39)

Ideals require hospitable service, Vincent explains. Service redress-es the householder's absence, making proper entertainment pos-sible. Strangers find lodging and comfort in this continual house. In Vincent's terms, we are learning how to "furnish" ancient cus-tom: "Were it for the worship of a gentleman, having good land and revenues to keep no more servants, then (as they do in cities) those that for their necessary uses they must needs employ? If we gentlemen should so do, how should we furnish our halls? how should we be ready for quarrellers? or how should our wives be waited on when they ride abroad?" (p. 35). The vision is complete.

But this pamphlet depends on reversals that come neatly. Like Goneril and Regan, Vallentine sees nothing in these virtues. The traditional host, he claims, entertains "needless men," "lubberly monks and fat-headed friars," tall fellows who "devoureth all" (pp. 35–40). Vallentine's opinions may sound practical to a con-temporary sensibility, but to a Renaissance mind, this is the stuff of timely revolution. How extraordinary, then, that Vincent con-cedes without hesitation:

> I must confess it true that our charge is great, and some of them are also proud and evil-natured people, as were it not for their parents' sakes (who be our good friends or tenants) we would many times discharge our houses of them: But partly for those respects, and

partly for fear, being out of service, they should fall into offence of law, we keep them, though to our great charge and discontent: for well you know, it were great pity to see a tall fellow to climb a gibbet. (p. 40)

In pamphlet form the redaction of hospitality is swift and complete. Whereas in *Two Gentlemen of Verona* the ungoverned tall fellows are integrated into civil society through the Duke's hospitality, Vincent recognizes that they are best discharged from the household. One cannot climb a gibbet and be civil. No host(ess) can entertain needless men and not become vulnerable. A modern civility and the old ways of hospitality do not mesh.

King Lear *and the Perilous Claim: "I Am Your Host"*

Coleridge complained that the opening of *Lear* was most improbable.[8] In a slightly different vein, A. C. Bradley criticized the *apparent* absurdity of the play's beginning, suggesting that "it must be pronounced dramatically faulty in so far as it discloses the true position of affairs only to an attention more alert than can be expected in a theatrical audience or has been found in many critics of the play."[9] In fact, a Renaissance audience could not have failed to connect the play's opening descent into vulnerability to the age's discourse of hospitality and civil householding. Lear's first word is "Attend." His subsequent speeches complain, demand, and rant after service, a desire studied in superb detail by Jonas A. Barish and Marshall Waingrow, and by Richard Strier.[10] We have come to refer to Lear's "division of his kingdom" when, in fact, the conflict expanding out of Lear's complaints is qualified repeatedly by household terms popularized in the pamphlet literature: the civil and uncivil speeches of daughters, the father's chiding and punishment, welcomes, the number and difficulties of guests, the turning away of family and strangers from the gate, the love that ought to come from a life of hospitality. A king, Lear must have seemed, simultaneously, a crusty old householder to savvy Elizabethans. With his entire being, he fetishizes the tried ideal articulated by Vincent, only to recognize, in absurd horror, that it cannot be inhabited.

From his earliest attempts at tragedy, Shakespeare concerned himself with the plight of the aging host. In *Romeo and Juliet,* Capulet's hosting is bound up with his aging:

> Welcome, gentlemen! Ladies that have their toes
> Unplagued with corns will walk a bout with you.
> Ah ha, my mistresses! which of you all
> Will now deny to dance? She that makes dainty,
> She I'll swear hath corns. Am I come near ye now?
> Welcome gentlemen! I have seen the day
> That I have worn a visor and could tell
> A whispering tale in a fair lady's ear,
> Such as would please. 'Tis gone, 'tis gone, 'tis gone!
> You are welcome, gentlemen! (1.5.16–25)

With high spirits, the old man's invocation of hospitality's customary forms—*You are welcome, gentlemen!*—turns into a childlike fascination with his own aging, with the dance he may yet seek and the whispering that is past. The old host longs to uphold the ancient responsibilities and so prolongs his speech. In its attenuation, this hospitable sentence resonates with the contradictions of contemporary practice embodied by Tybalt.

In the crooked fashion of coincidence, the old man's hosting has made the household vulnerable. What the old ideal inspires, it cannot contain. Representative of a younger generation, Tybalt scowls: "It fits when such a villain is a guest. / I'll not endure him" (1.5.75–76). But Capulet has already announced his responsibilities: "I would not for the wealth of all this town / Here in my house do him disparagement" (1.5.69–70). With an old man's sense of rank, Capulet answers Tybalt's renewed protests:

> What, goodman boy! I say he shall. Go to!
> Am I the master here, or you? Go to!
> You'll not endure him, God shall mend my soul!
> You'll make a mutiny among my guests! (1.5.76–80)

In nascent form, Capulet's anger looks toward Lear's rage at his daughters, at the failure of hospitable ideals, at the impotence of his age, his inability to command observance of the old ways among his family. Capulet complains in pamphlet terms about functions: boy, master, guests. Where are the ideals that ought to shape these roles? Rendered vulnerable through his attachment to these ideals, the host fails to measure the severity of the long and bloody feud amid his hosting. The pieces of hospitable discourse stand out here as moral sentences and cultural ideals, tragic in their sway over an old householder's mind.

The Life of Timon of Athens derives from this same blind observance and frustrated rage. Like a photographic negative of *King Lear*, the play presents a shadowy outline of the ideal host in an uncivil world. Whereas Lear wishes to be a guest, Timon enacts the simpler fantasy of being the ideal host, presuming that he can count on his guests for nurture should the occasion arise. What Duke Senior achieves with his offer of hospitality to Orlando in *As You Like It*, Timon attempts with Apemantus, who responds: "You shall not make me welcome; / I come to have thee thrust me out of doors" (1.2.24–25). Lear's expulsion parallels the sentiment of this churlish guest. Hospitality cannot be enforced. Nevertheless, Timon orders: "Go, let him have a table by himself; for he does neither affect company nor is he fit for't indeed" (1.2.29–30). Against the most irritating resistance, the host blindly proceeds with hospitable practice so that when Timon's resources fail and his former guests turn him away, a Stranger may offer moral commentary that might have come from a pamphlet:

> Why, this is the world's soul, and just of the same piece
> Is every flatterer's spirit. Who can call him
> His friend that dips in the same dish? . . .
> And yet—O, see the monstrousness of man
> When he looks out in an ungrateful shape!—
> He does deny him [Timon], in respect of his,
> What charitable men afford to beggars. (3.2.63-65, 71–74)

This most pamphlet-like of plays, with its types and moralizing, its hasty discoveries, comes down to this: hospitality, dipping in the same dish, hardly confirms friendship. Hosting will make men less than beggars. In his introduction to the play, Charlton Hinman notes that Timon's "transformation, though striking, has not been accompanied by an increase in self-knowledge."[11] In fact, the genuine tragedy of the play may rest in this: that a Renaissance audience could watch the drama and find it simply "correct," a pamphlet well-acted.

Unlike his predecessors in Shakespeare's canon, Lear responds to the failure of his initial vision by conjuring up another version. Here is excessive attachment not simply to daughters but to a cultural ideal of care. Lear invests everything in a perpetual progress and determines "by monthly course, / With reservation of an hundred knights, / By you to be sustained, shall our abode / Make with you by due turn" (1.1.132–35). Since he cannot find the peace of Cordelia's "nursery," Lear elaborates a plan that sounds very much like Elizabeth's gests. Surely the essence of royal prerogative in the Renaissance lay in the monarch's selection, often whimsical, typically changeable, of households to be honored with the royal guest.

Surrounding Shakespeare's fictional monarch were countless examples of exceptional hospitality for England's monarchs. We cannot appreciate Lear's decisions without drawing attention to their context of royal hospitality. We learn from *Pecks Desiderata Curiosa*, for example, of Cecil's hospitality: "His Lordship's extraordinary charge in entertaining of the Queen was greater to him than to any of her subjects. But his love to his Sovereign, and joy to entertain her and her train, was so great, that he thought no trouble, care, or cost, too much, but all too little, so it were bountifully performed to her Majesty's recreation, and the contentment of her train."[12] In Shakespeare's world, being *King Lear* meant having the expectation of such treatment. Frequent demands, great cost, a difficult train—such were the welcome burdens (so the discourse went) of royal service. *Love* of the sovereign, according to the prevailing discourse, manifests itself through lodging, food, and other entertainments. In other words, the ideal makes a certain sense. The desire to trade everything for that ideal makes tragedy.

In this way, Lear's actions build in a more probable manner, recalling the situation of Summer in Nashe's show: "Tell me, my daughters" (48); "Our eldest-born, speak first" (54); "What says our second daughter" (67); "Speak" (86); "speak again" (90); "Mend your speech a little" (94); "But goes thy heart with this?" (105). Here is perhaps the definitive form—not of irascible old age—but of the great hall's logic of conversation. Like Summer in Nashe's show, Lear expects a public conversation for solace, whether it be of hedging or grain or love. He expects *comprobatio*, the kind of balanced rhetorical compliment offered by the other daughters, a mode of address codified in print by the pamphlet literature. Lear gets nothing and his resulting rage seems tuned to the household terms of his fantasy. In Shakespeare's sources, Cordelia is not banished for her silence. When the playwright undertakes the dramatization of this most extreme course, he marks his own innovation in the language of hospitality:

> And as a stranger to my heart and me
> Hold thee from this for ever. The barbarous Scythian,
> Or he that makes his generation messes
> To gorge his appetite, shall to my bosom
> Be as well neighboured, pitied, and relieved,
> As thou my sometime daughter. (115–20)

Here for the English mind, is the ultimate distancing: the child becomes the stranger. For Lear, Cordelia's behavior strikes at the very essence of traditional, ceremonial civility.[13] The barbarous Scythian could well be expected to eat his guests, but Lear will *neighbor, pity,* and *relieve* (all terms of hospitality) the Scythian "As thou my sometime daughter." In seeking to magnify the monarch's distress, Shakespeare accumulates the terms of hospitality. As Lear later puts it, he has "stranger'd [her] with our oath." As far as the monarch is concerned, his own civil view—threatened by Cordelia's example and confirmed by most of the age's hospitable literature—has triumphed.

This first scene finds closure in withdrawl, in the enforcement of absence guaranteed to threaten a household. Lear will depart. Cordelia will go. In breaking his tie with Kent, Lear exacerbates the problem by striking at the roots of the ideal outlined by Vincent. Indeed, Vincent could almost plead with Lear: "For in your absence, he cannot only see things in good order, but also entertainment, first in the hall, next in your parlour." Ironically, Kent can only accomplish these ends by assuming a beggarly position in the culture. He attempts to maintain his monarch's household in the traditional manner and so confronts Oswald in 2.2 with a neat reversal of hospitality's decorums:

> OSW.: Good dawning to thee, friend. Art of this house?
> KENT: Ay.
> OSW.: Where may we set our horses?
> KENT: I' th' mire.
> OSW.: Prithee, if thou lov'st me, tell me.
> KENT: I love thee not.
> OSW.: Why then, I care not for thee.
> KENT: If I had thee in Lipsbury Pinfold, I would make thee
> care for me. (2.2.1–9)

In nearly every performance of the play, this moment stands out. Typically it calls for a bit of laughable stage business. The audience tenses. Quite obviously, Oswald's arrival represents an obdurate moment of hospitality. Stabling and provisioning for beasts always accompany the arrival of guests. A good host will naturally have seen to such basic requirements. Taking a page out of George a Greene's book, Kent confounds such expectations by spurning the guest and offering a pinfold for care. A Renaissance audience would no doubt feel the ground of everyday beliefs shift under its feet. Having invoked traditional practices, ideas of the proper servant and the decorous welcome, the playwright slips easily into pamphlet composition as Kent begins to rant, defining Oswald as "A Knave, a rascal, an eater of broken meats" (2.2.13). The audience applauds and the tragedy gathers itself into a detached denouement. In Lear's absence, Kent has entertained in a way that vitalizes the Theater of Hospitality.[14]

Like Kent, Edgar must seem to join the lower orders to save his life and protect the interests of the household. He announces his course in the language of hospitable complaint:

> I will preserve myself; and am bethought
> To take the basest and most poorest shape
> That ever penury, in contempt of man,
> Brought near to beast. . . .
> The country gives me proof and precedent
> Of Bedlam beggars, who, with roaring voices,
> Strike in their numb'd and mortified bare arms
> Pins, wooden pricks, nails, springs of rosemary;
> And with this horrible object, from low farms,

Poor pelting villages, sheepcotes, and mills,
Sometimes with lunatic bans, sometime with prayers,
Enforce their charity. (2.3.6–9, 13–20)

In the terms of the day, Edgar *thrusts himself out-a-doors*. His is the most desperate version of an aim we have considered in some detail: the enforcement of hospitality. During Shakespeare's lifetime, both Elizabeth and James tried to enforce hospitality. In his childish way, Lear seeks the same end. Michael Goldman rightly suggests that Edgar is the kind of beggar "that sticks his stump in your face" in order to make his point.[15] If beggars can "enforce" hospitality in any limited fashion, they do so by asserting their individual suffering against the illusions of the dominant order. Frequently, as Harman suggests in *A Caveat for Common Cursitors*, they feign, playing on the language of hospitality.[16]

By the play's fourth scene, Lear realizes a version of his fond hopes—he has become the guest. From this point forward, the play can be seen as a fraught progress between fragile households—Goneril's, Regan's, Gloucester's, and the miserable welcomes on the heath. With all the anxiety contained in Elizabethan gests, Lear expresses his impatience with the preparations: "Let me not stay a jot for dinner; go get it ready" (1.4.8). Lear, Mack admits, "is not an easy domestic guest: this we know from his conduct in the first scene, and from however much we may choose to believe of the list of grievances his daughter catalogues to Oswald in I, iii."[17] No one who has ever seen Peter Brook's interpretation of "Lear as guest" will ever forget the flying plates, pounding, yelling, and belching. Mack certainly has not, and he objects to the interpretation by recalling "the visible courtesy of their spokesman earlier (I, iv, 54–78), Albany's significant unawareness of what Goneril is complaining about, and Lear's explicit description of his knights" (pp. 31–32). Mack takes Brook's interpretation of the scene as one more bizarre attempt to make Lear a probable character, a task Mack believes best left undone. Mack's defense may miss the point. Surely, royalty need not be "probable." Queen Elizabeth, whose own fantasies of hosting haunt the decorums of this play, seems to have given no thought to probability in her own actions as guest. We know that the good queen insulted her hosts, changed her plans many times, committed one host to prison, and presided over a retinue famous for plucking plate, vessels, and deer. The queen's party could always be counted on to destroy hedges and ruin the grass.[18] Lear is finally most probable and most royal.

His kingdom divided, Lear attempts to enter his fantasy in Goneril's household. A playwright given to the depiction of welcomes, Shakespeare makes the fascinating choice not to show us Lear's arrival. The destruction of old hospitality is everything. We discover the royal guest after he has become subject to an aristocratic hostess, and his identity is challenged immediately. One of Lear's knights approaches: "My lord, I know not what the matter is; but to my judgment your Highness is not entertained with that ceremonious affection as you were wont" (1.4.55–57). Long before Lear rants in the storm, a servingman signals a tragic breach in the fabric of the Renaissance world. We can only imagine what Elizabeth would have done—the imprisonments, the trimming of ears—at such an announcement. Lear's response suggests the importance of ceremonial decorums when he responds: "Thou but rememb'rest me of mine own conception" (1.4.64).

As we have already seen, Lear's conception owes its construction to pamphlet ideals. Lear may only be properly conceived in relation to his entertainment, to his soil and his service. To remember Lear's conception is to place his hundred knights in the context of Vincent's defense of custom. Without a retinue of servants, Vincent asks, "How should we furnish our halls? how should we be ready for quarellers?" Playing her tactical advantage, Goneril knows the answers to these questions and attacks her father's conception in service:

> Not only, sir, this your all-license'd fool,
> But other of your insolent retinue
> Do hourly carp and quarrel, breaking forth
> In rank and not-to-be-endured riots. Sir,
> I had thought by making this well known unto you
> To have found a safe redress, but now grown fearful,
> By what yourself too late have spoke and done,
> That you protect this course, and put it on
> By your allowance; which if you should, the fault
> Would not 'scape censure, nor the redresses sleep,
> Which, in the tender of a wholesome weal,
> Might in their working do you that offense,
> Which else were shame, that then necessity
> Will call discreet proceeding. (1.4.191–204)

In this brilliantly tortured syntax, Goneril weaves a language of hospitality in sympathy with the revisionary views of Vallentine even as it subverts a householder's traditional responsibilities. To understand the proximity of comedy to tragedy, one need only compare Goneril's practicing to that of the Lord in *The Taming of the Shrew*. Like Sly, Lear is to be molded by his host's hospitality. To grasp the neighborhood of pamphlet and tragedy, one need only compare Vallentine and the converted Vincent to Goneril as she points to the "insolent retinue" as a breach of household decorum. Like the speakers in the pamphlet, her speech is marked by ellipsis, by the unsaid that, instead of deleting difficulties, threatens a discrete violence. Lear's own code of custom, his example of the barbarous Scythian, has been turned against him, for Goneril has shaped the monarch's traditional and rightful retinue into a barbarous horde. The monarch's very notion of himself (his origins in womanly conception as well) must now derive from the realization of hospitable care offered by women, a state that in the civil discourse of the day must have seemed more rash than the kingdom's division.

In Goneril's hands, hospitality becomes a trap. Certainly, the idea that hospitality could serve as a dramatic snare was commonplace on the Renaissance stage.[19] A play that epitomizes Renaissance notions of deceit, Christopher Marlowe's *The Jew of Malta* depends on Barabas's manipulation of the speech genres that define hospitable practice. When he complains of the government's appropriation of his possessions, he hoards pieces of a now familiar speech genre, the formulaic complaint of hospitality: "And whether I would or no, / [the authorities] Seized all I had, and thrust me out-a-doors."[20] Barabas's revenge comes through his manipulation of hospitable invitations. In Occidental culture, no one expects to die over dinner—but they do. To Lodowick, he offers: "I pray, sir, be no stranger at my house, / All that I have shall be at your command" (2.3.141–42). In order to craft the two suitors' jealousy, the host invites Mathias: "Come to my house; / Think of me as thy father; son farewell" (2.3.153–54). Perverting the formula invoked by Clunch in Peele's *The Old Wives Tale* and the Shepherd in Shakespeare's *The Winter's Tale*, Barabas enjoins his daughter to "entertain" Lodowick, to "bid him welcome for my sake" in order to lime the trap (2.3.228–36).

Shakespeare could hardly have ignored such dramatic possi-bilities. Plunging into an ever-expanding spiral of violence, his *Titus Andronicus* plays host at a grisly banquet, more trap than triumph: "And welcome all: although the cheer be poor, / 'Twill fill your stomachs; please you eat of it" (5.3.28–29). Titus has baked Tamora's sons in a pie, and every ounce of terror finds tactical nuance in the speech genres of welcome and good cheer. With a more complex set of motives than Marlowe's protagonist and not unlike the Lord practicing on Sly, Hamlet assumes the role of the Earl of Leicester or the Earl of Hertford or Hieronimo in Kyd's *The Spanish Tragedy:* he provides courtly entertainment for the mon-arch. In the spirit of Hieronimo, Hamlet calls his hospitality *The Mousetrap;* and though it succeeds only in the oblique fashion of every other action in Denmark, Hamlet's blending of house, the-ater, snare, and irony prepares the way for Jonson's and Middle-ton's comic traps. In plays such as *Epicoene, Michaelmas Term,* and *A Trick to Catch the Old One,* Wotton's theater of hospitality enables elaborate programs of comic deceit tinged with the hospitable sen-sibilities of Shakespearean tragedy.

At the heart of Shakespeare's tragic vision, these dangerous domestic precedents assemble in a castle. In *Macbeth,* Lady Mac-beth waits to play hostess to military victors, contemplating "the fatal entrance of Duncan / Under my battlements" (1.5.37–38). Lady Macbeth's position at the play's beginning seems most pro-vocative. In an age that had given up the building of fortified houses, the hostess presiding over the castle gestures back at the old practice of hospitality cataloged by Vincent.[21] In counter-point, the woman's plotting seems all the more horrible. Whereas the society encourages Macbeth to take "bold strokes" of direct action, the castle confines the woman to a subculture such that the only avenue for attaining power lies in a violent exploitation of household decorums. Whereas the pamphlet texts devoted to hospitality typically imagine a host in charge of the arrangements, Shakespeare foregrounds a woman's "horrible imaginings."

As in *King Lear,* the horror of the scene builds through the for-mulaic speech genres of hospitality. The audience would no doubt bring to the moment the traditional expectations of progress hos-pitality after the fashion of Norwich or the noble host Cecil. Shakespeare's own dramatic practice confirms such expectations in *Troilus and Cressida* when Agamemnon welcomes his enemy Aeneas:

> let me touch your hand;
> To our pavilion shall I lead you first.
> Achilles shall have word of this intent;
> So shall each lord of Greece, from tent to tent.
> Yourself shall feast with us before you go,
> And find the welcome of a noble foe. (1.3.304–9)

In Occidental culture, even noble foes can count on a welcome and a feast. Banquo speaks out of this military tradition, contributing to the effect with a gentle allegory of householding, a fine *comprobatio* worthy of a pamphlet author:

> This guest of summer,
> The temple-haunting martlet, does approve
> By his loved mansionry that the heaven's breath
> Smells wooingly here. No jutty, frieze,
> Buttress, nor coign of vantage, but this bird
> Hath made his pendent bed and procreant cradle.
> Where they most breed and haunt, I have observed
> The air is delicate. (1.6.3–10)

On such short notice, Lady Macbeth can hardly arrange an elaborate welcoming device. In an abbreviated form, Banquo's allegorical tableau of the martin's hosting serves her purpose. In this spirit of welcome, Duncan places his safety in the hands of "our honored hostess": "Fair and noble hostess, / We are your guest tonight" (1.6.24–25). Lady Macbeth answers with the proper speech genre: "Your servants ever / Have theirs, themselves, and what is theirs, in compt" (1.6.25–26).

To measure the currency of this formula, one has only to note its repetition in nearly every town visited by Elizabeth and James during their reigns. In the pamphlet texts reporting these hospitalities, the mystification of unequal allocation is complete. Subjects happily acknowledge that all they have comes from the monarch. Prestation, as Mauss would call it, ensures that an exchange of gifts will preserve communal order. As Banquo reports to Macbeth, Duncan has played his part faithfully in the old system:

He [Duncan] hath been in unusual pleasure and
Sent forth great largess to your offices.
This diamond he greets your wife withal
By the name of most kind hostess, and shut up
In measureless content. (2.1.13–17)

Unfortunately for Duncan, Lady Macbeth has imagined the role of hostess otherwise. Like Lear, Duncan is blind to the possibility of such imagining because he believes completely in the security of hospitable decorums supported by the larger system of prestation: "our honored hostess"; "Conduct me to mine host"; "By your leave, hostess" (1.6.10, 29, 31).

The tradition of the banquet, in Renaissance tragedy, evokes the split between private political aims and public duties of care. At the same time, it demonstrates the source of a ruler's vulnerability in the gap between hospitable strategies and tactics. The host submits his designs to the ideal of hospitable feasting. The progression of dramatic action pauses over this confluence of hopes and fears; and the host finds that he cannot control the entertainment, that hospitality has enabled his tragic end. I think, for example, of Thomas Preston's *Cambises*, of the King's feast set carefully by Preparation but usurped by Ambidexter. There is the spectacular end of Barabas in *The Jew of Malta* as he falls into the cauldron that waited for his "honored" guests. I think, too, of Arden's ill-fated feast in *Arden of Feversham* or Giovanni's bloody appropriation of Soranzo's banquet of revenge in John Ford's *'Tis Pity She's a Whore*. Above all, I return to *Titus Andronicus*. In the middle of the play, this tragic leader of men offers a banquet as tactical preservation: "So, so, now sit; and look you eat no more / Than will preserve just so much strength in us / As will revenge these bitter woes of ours" (3.2.1–3). Dressed as a cook, Titus later finds his revenge in the baking of a pie. The host explains his attire: "Because I would be sure to have all well / To entertain your highness and your empress" (5.3.31–32). In every case, the banquet ought to contain the host's enemies, but time and again the action expands to permit an undoing of the host. The banquet does not digest its divergent courses. It only heightens vulnerability.

In reference to *Macbeth*, critics talk about "the banquet scene." In fact, the play has *two* banquet scenes that stand apart, mirroring each other, echoing and anticipating many such hospitable

affairs on the Renaissance stage. A sewer passes, then more servants with many dishes. Emotional intensity builds as expectations clash. The host should, as King James would have done,
remain at the feast's center, a volatile nexus of authority. But
Macbeth, as he will do later in the play, removes himself from
the scene of hospitality to weigh his conflicting sense of himself as
noble host, kinsman, and villainous usurper:

> First, as I am his kinsman and his subject,
> Strong both against the deed; then, as his host,
> Who should against his murderer shut the door,
> Not bear the knife myself. (1.7.13–16)

This speech exemplifies the function of represented hospitalities in
tragic action. Moral statement appears in the inverted commas of
awkward time, moments stolen from the pressing responsibilities
of host. The hospitable practice allows for a pause; moral positions
are juggled. Am I kinsman? host? murderer? Macbeth is summoned by the hostess:

> LADY: He has almost supped. Why have you left the chamber?
> MACBETH: Hath he asked for me?
> LADY: Know you not he has? (1.7.29–30)

The irony is subtle and effective. Lady Macbeth wants to summon
a murderer, but Macbeth responds out of his meditation with
a host's instinctual concern for the entertainment: "Hath he
asked for me?" His rationalization could well come from the
lips of the Earl of Hertford or Sir Henry Lee or Lord Burghley:
"He hath honored me of late, and I have bought / Golden opinions from all sorts of people" (1.7.32–33). Were it not for the
hostess, Macbeth's hospitality would conclude in the fashion of
all such Elizabethan and Jacobean events. But Shakespeare's
woman is unsexed by the proximity of power in hosting: "What
cannot you and I perform upon / Th' unguarded Duncan?"
(1.7.69–70). In a manner all too close to that of the Lord in *The
Taming of the Shrew*, who will "practice" upon the sleeping Sly,
Lady Macbeth takes advantage of "swinish sleep" to "perform" on
Duncan.

As Macbeth explains to the murderers, "The valued file /
Distinguishes the swift, the slow, the subtle, / The housekeeper,
the hunter, every one" (3.1.95–97). Having assumed the part of
royal host in order to celebrate his rule, Macbeth turns out to be a
bad conflation of every one, simultaneously swift, slow, subtle,
housekeeper and hunter. In this famous banquet scene, Duncan's
fate has prepared the way for Banquo's as Macbeth decants the
fatal speech genre: "Here's our chief guest" (3.1.11). As he does in
King Lear, Shakespeare takes care to frame the violence as bad
hosting:

> *LADY:*   If he [Banquo] had been forgotten,
>   It had been as a gap in our great feast,
>   And all-thing unbecoming.
> *MACBETH:* To-night we hold a solemn supper,
>   sir, And I'll request your presence. (3.1.11–15)

Lady Macbeth's imaginings spin out of control as Banquo does
indeed become the gap in the feast. Macbeth longs to "mingle with
society / And play the humble host." He speaks the part of housekeeper: "Now good digestion wait on appetite, / And health on
both!" But in Renaissance tragedy, the banquet promises nothing
but indigestion of strategic purposes. The ghost of Banquo suggests that gaps cannot be anticipated. In the end, Macbeth is a bad
host and vulnerable in the bad hosting. Lady Macbeth serves nothing but irony when she complains: "My royal lord, / You do not
give the cheer."

For his part, Thomas Middleton seems to have found in such
action a paradigm for tragedy. The arrival of the stranger Alsemero in Middleton and Rowley's *The Changeling*, like an arrival in
one of Shakespeare's romantic comedies, awakens an immediate
desire. Though she must marry Alonzo in days, Beatrice adopts
the language of hospitality to hold on to the new man:

> I am beholding to this gentleman
> Who left his own way to keep me company,
> And in discourse I find him much desirous
> To see your castle.[22]

Though the names are Spanish, the decorums are most English as Vermandero inquires: "I must know / Your country. We use not to give survey / Of our chief strengths to strangers . . ." (157–59). When the stranger's rank and family have been determined, Vermandero assures his guest: "My best love bids you welcome" (166). On the heels of this welcome, Alonzo arrives to claim his bride; and the playwright, having outlined Beatrice's predicament, envisions her recourse in the same language of hospitality. When Beatrice turns to DeFlores as a means of removing Alonzo permanently, the servant offers Alonzo the same hospitality shown Alsemero. DeFlores promises to entertain the guest with the "ways and straits of some of the / Passages" in the castle (3.1.162–63). The household becomes, in the guise of hospitality, a perfect trap for Alonzo as DeFlores murders him by a casement. Andronicus, Hamlet, and Barabas all offer snares in the guise of hospitality, but a woman's hospitality ensnares *and* unmans.

Perhaps the definitive treatment of this pattern (next to that in *King Lear*) appears in Middleton's *Women Beware Women*, a play that practically wallows in the hospitable occasion, toying with every treacherous nuance of hospitable concern. The play's first scenes establish Bianca as a beauty whose capacity for awakening desire torments her young husband; he shuts her up in his mother's house. When the Duke, in procession, spies Bianca, he turns to the widow Livia for assistance. Playing the part of hostess, Livia proves to be the most effective agent of entrapment. She welcomes the Mother:

> Faith, I must chide you, that you must be sent for!
> You make yourself so strange, never come at us,
> And yet so near a neighbour, and so unkind
> Troth y' are to blame, you cannot be the more welcome
> To any house in Florence, that I'll tell you.[23]

In the use of "neighbour," Livia couches her welcome in the language of the masses, of Stow and *George a Greene*. She weaves her guest's perceptions by carefully playing on the formulas of welcome, assuring the Mother that she is no stranger. Middleton lingers melodramatically over this bit of hospitable practice until women appear to be the essence of precariousness. Livia spins out neighborhood terms in order to elaborate a seeming warmth:

> Say I should entreat you now
> To lie a night or two, or a week with me,
> Or leave your own house for a month together—
> It were a kindness that long neighbourhood
> And friendship might well hope to prevail in.
> (2.2.196–200)

With a charge to guard her daughter-in-law hanging over her head, the Mother naturally hesitates over such an ample invitation. When the hostess includes Bianca in the invitation, the Mother simply becomes more confused.

In a fine rhetorical borrowing, Middleton makes Livia's motivated invitation a matter of pamphlet complaint:

> LIVIA: Oh what's become
>   of the true hearty love was wont to be
>   'Mongst neighbours in old time?
> MOTHER: And she's [Bianca's] a stranger, madame.
> LIVIA: The more should be her welcome. When is courtesy
>   In better practice, than when 'tis employed
>   In entertaining strangers? (218–22)

England's idealization of the host/guest relationship here meshes perfectly with the subterfuge of the hostess. Writers like Stow have taught the age how to succumb to representations of "better practice." Who among a contemporary audience could have faulted the Mother for believing in the "true hearty love" of the past? Why should the Mother be any different than the age's monarchs? Why should Bianca, any more than Alsemero and Alonzo, distrust a tour of the household? Why should she fail to praise the "welcome of strangers" as she is led upstairs to the waiting Duke? Livia entertains the Mother with a game of chess, a Shakespeherian Rag, a glossing of Bianca's rape.

Goneril and Regan join Livia and Lady Macbeth as the age's arch hostesses. No one recalls Madge's fine hosting in *The Old Wives Tale*; everyone recollects Lady Macbeth's housekeeping. Indeed, such bad hosting moved Maynard Mack to dogma: "The motivation of the sisters [Goneril and Regan] lies not in what Lear has done to them, but in what they are. The fact that they are paradigms of evil rather than (or as well as) exasperated spoilt children whose patience has been exhausted gives them their stature and dramatic force" (p. 32). Would it be possible, however, to pass through this moral judging to ask why woman-as-hostess should be such an effective version of tragic anarchy and suffering on the Renaissance stage? We may also return to my initial questions, raised in Chapter 1, concerning the usurpation of women's authority as hostesses in early modern England. Knowing only too well that my own contextualization cannot contain the manifold nuances of Goneril and Regan's actions, I suggest that we return these women to their households in the English countryside where paradigms of evil may appear to be paradigms of a failed royal progress. As social historians have made clear, the failure of the countryside may easily become the failure of woman.

As a prologue to Macbeth's arrival, Shakespeare evokes this topical significance through the First Witch's tale:

> A sailor's wife had chestnuts in her lap
> And mounched and mounched and mounched.
> "Give me," quoth I.
> "Aroint thee, witch!" the rump-fed ronyon cries.
> Her husband's to Aleppo gone, master o' th' Tiger:
> But in a sieve I'll thither sail
> And, like a rat without a tail,
> I'll do, I'll do, and I'll do. (1.3.4–10)

This creature's complaint has less magic in it than bad hospitality. If women, as Hyde says, are at times the special collectors and distributors of gifts, then the witch's need to do evil really responds to a failure of giving. Historians have begun to confirm this anthropological perspective. Keith Thomas points out that the old woman turned away from the gate without the traditional care of hospitality was practically an emblem for the age's neglect of hospitality.[24] Alan Macfarlane has argued that the identification of witches in the culture proceeded from communities' perceptions that traditional ties were crumbling. Since women were seen as vessels of such ties, they became the targets of anxiety and resentment.[25] Woman was a sign of failing tradition. Felicity Heal offers a splendid plebeian version of this prevailing perception: "Neighbours expected that they would be junketed on these [hospitable] occasions, and any who were not bidden to share in the generosity showed vigorous resentment. When the wife of one Malter was not asked to her neighbour's sheep-shearing dinner in 1570 she allegedly 'bewitched two of his sheep; for immediately after they were taken with sickness.'"[26]

Failed hospitality and feminine evil come together in a drama of bad invitation. This is precisely the economy governing playwrights' appropriations of woman and hospitality in tragedy. When Shakespeare assembled the age's deepest anxieties over cultural change, "hostess" offered itself to the male imagination as a fictional agent of destruction, particularly evocative because centuries of socialization confirmed woman's responsibility for domestic care.[27] If men of rank fidget in contemplation of their own vulnerability in an age of nascent capitalism and fading ceremony, representations of hospitable practice mystify the origins of that vulnerability. We may therefore recognize the truth of Mack's evaluation for our experience of the performance, but such an insight must not displace the cultural context of the tragedy's appropriation of the idea of hostess. Shakespeare creates "evil" out of the contradictions, hopes, and fears of Jacobean culture. Evil emerges from the condition of traditional ties.

In the ghastly pause that is Goneril and Regan's entertainment of their father, further examples of the age's hospitable practice come to mind, situations that re-gender Mack's essentialized "paradigms." The predicament of Sir Thomas Posthumous Hoby, a Puritan magistrate in the North Riding of Yorkshire, illustrates the point. Hoby was an ambitious intruder (via marriage to a local heiress) in the local structure of authority. His Puritan customs grated on his Catholic neighbors, who eventually came up with the perfect plan for abusing a Puritan. A wild group of tall fellows, allies, and kinfolk originating from the neighboring household of Ralph, Lord Eure, swooped down on the Hoby household one summer evening in 1600—demanding hospitality.[28] So heavily did the protocols of the model weigh on this Puritan (who could hardly have accepted this version of the model) that Hoby admitted the party and entertained the whole to the letter. What followed would make Brook's version of *Lear* pale by comparison. Cards, dice, and drink flowed through the house. The happy guests disrupted the singing of the psalms and assaulted a servant

as well as Lady Hoby in her bedchamber. Windows were broken
and a courtyard destroyed. Hoby protested such treatment—after
his duties as host were discharged. In fact, the Puritan approached
the Star Chamber, complaining that hospitality was a strict code
that *his guests* had violated.[29]

As a context for the household confrontation between Goneril,
Regan, and Lear, the case is startling. So powerful were the protocols of hospitality that Eure's household could count on using
them as a weapon against a householder whose religious beliefs
denied a like interpretation. So powerful were the protocols that
Hoby and his wife endured countless abuses rather than forego
the model. Compared to Hoby's example, Goneril's violation of
Lear's expectations and her complaints about her father's retinue
achieve their full, contextualized dramatic force.

In the language of hospitality, in the midst of these fraught
exempla, *King Lear* comes down to a series of what Dalechamp
would call *discourteous dismissions or deductions.* Goneril and Regan
preside over bad households more concerned with entrapment
and expulsion than with convivial entertainments. In what Wilson
Knight would no doubt term a grotesquely comic inversion of
hospitable ideals, the daughters' trap begins to close as Lear succumbs to a condition that Vincent (with some pride) admits to
having experienced when he "was driven out of mine own bed, to
lie at some tenants' house of mine, for a night or two: Notwithstanding, I took it for no great trouble, so long as my friends found
themselves content and welcome" (p. 33). In an uncanny foreshad-
owing of Lear's sojourn on the heath near a tenant's hovel, Vincent
prepares the way for Vallentine's questioning: "But, sir, are you
sure they were all your friends?" (p. 33). The skeptic goes on to
point out the vulnerability of the host in the practice of liberality
and charity: "For as his true friends do seek him for love and
honour, so are there others that do it for flattery or fear: Thus you
see how easily you may be deceived in the love of your neighbours, and that haunting your house, may be for other cause or occasion, as well as love" (p. 33).

Quite in keeping with tradition, Lear has sought love through
household practice only to be driven out of his own bed—permanently. Lear seems to know very little about "his friends" and so
enters the trap "easily deceived," hoping to salvage Regan's care,
assuring himself that above all it is not in her "to oppose the bolt

/ Against my coming in" (2.4.171–72). With Lear's belief so completely condensed into this brief exchange, Regan denies the entertainment that he, like Vincent, seeks: "I am now from home, and out of that provision / Which shall be needful for your entertainment" (2.4.200–201). Like the householders chided by Elizabeth and James and by countless pamphleteers, Regan keeps a small buttery; she avoids hospitality by leaving home. Pamphlet complaint directed toward male householders has become tragic peripeteia managed by hostesses.

Lear's horrible dismission moves toward climax through the daughters' attack on what Vallentine calls (in coincidence with the play's stress on "need") "needless men." Regan thus makes the final move: "How in one house / Should many people, under two commands, / Hold amity? 'Tis hard, almost impossible" (2.4.235–37). Surgically, in the next twenty lines, Goneril and Regan toss his followers back and forth until—"What need one?" The hostesses have reduced the guest. Lear comes to a point of recognition perhaps only available to the beggar at the gate: *need*. Hospitality's capacity to refashion guests becomes a weapon as Lear senses his own alteration: "O reason not the need! Our basest beggars / Are in the poorest thing superfluous" (2.4.259–60). At the outer limits of civilization, lurking about the gate of the household, the shadows of the least creatures seem by virtue of their continued existence to possess some superfluity, to be in some slight degree independent of hosts. A king's desire to be an eternal guest means becoming the lowest of beggars. In the act's final lines, Goneril and Regan bring about the pamphlets' worst nightmare: "This house is little; the old man and's people / Cannot be well bestowed" (283–84). The dismission is complete: "Shut up your doors."

Thrust out of the thin world of pamphlet ideal, Lear's progress confronts heath and storm, a terrible rage filled with the hyphenations and collisions of a pamphleteer's pen:

> Blow, winds, and crack your cheeks. Rage, blow.
> You cataracts and hurricanoes, spout
> Till you have drenched our steeples, drowned the cocks.
> You sulph'rous and thought-executing fires,
> Vaunt-couriers of oak-cleaving thunderbolts,
> Singe my white head. (3.2.1–6)

Bereft of the lavish entertainment offered in pamphlet accounts, Lear's complaint reaches back into Samuel Harsnett's pamphlet diatribe for expression. The king has lost exactly what the author of *Civil and Uncivil Life* assured us must not be lost: the direction of one's mind. This is not madness, but neither is it sanity. Pamphlet composition draws the unhosted mind out in so many hyphenations, vain attempts at complaint in words that neither feed nor shelter. The ideal has failed the fantasy.

As Nashe termed it, The Tragedy of Hospitality is played out in this center as one more obdurate tax on the audience's senses, one more scene of arrival, bad welcome, violent deduction. Not unlike the author of a progress narrative, Kent tests the countryside to see if any alternative to the daughters' bad households exists:

> Gracious my lord, hard by here is a hovel;
> Some friendship will it lend you 'gainst the tempest.
> Repose you there, while I to this hard house
> (More harder than the stones whereof 'tis raised,
> Which even but now, demanding after you,
> Denied me to come in) return, and force
> Their scanted courtesy. (3.2.61–67)

Contrary to the claims of the contemporary progress narratives, the country offers no help. The imagination staggers through a contemplation of metaphysics, grand moralities. The sense is stone, a hard house. Like Edgar and Lear, Kent determines to force a "scanted courtesy." When he returns, he announces: "Here is the place, my lord" (3.4.1). Which place? Certainly not the hard house. In the absence of hospitality's paradigms, lodgings blur. Three times Kent commands without ceremony: "Enter." The age's speech genres of welcome have been pared to this kernel command. Though his mind has begun to turn, Lear grasps the nature of his predicament with a clarity tuned by the mode of his first rantings: "but I'll go in. / In, boy; go first. You houseless poverty" (25–26).

In Lear's miserable progress, only Gloucester's housekeeping preserves the old ways. What has the subplot to do with the main action? I suggest that Gloucester exists as the only functioning remnant of aristocratic hospitality and its maintenance of tradition.

In a genre practically defined by its investment in destruction, the hospitable practice represented in the subplot remains. When he finds Lear in his houseless poverty, Gloucester asks, "What, hath your Grace no better company?" (3.4.133). Marion D. Perret has written persuasively of this concern, describing it as an evolving model of charity in the play. Finally, it is the old householder, "like Edgar, [who] becomes 'pregnant to good pity' (4.6.224)."[30] But Gloucester is more. In terms familiar to Vincent, Gloucester registers the lack of simple care and a conflict of duties:

> my duty cannot suffer
> T' obey in all your daughters' hard commands.
> Though their injunction be to bar my doors
> And let this tyrannous night take hold upon you,
> Yet have I ventured to come seek you out
> And bring you where both fire and food is ready.
> (3.4.139–44)

Gloucester maintains the whole complex of hospitable duty— against "hard commands," against the example of the "hard house," wandering out into the storm to offer what the pamphlets demand, fire and food for the monarch. Old Hospitality could not have done better.

In a play prone to metaphysical musing, Gloucester speaks the language of neighbors' fires. His sense of wrong comes from no grand speculation but a simple belief in the old models and the right to complain:

> If wolves had at thy gate howled that [stern] time,
> Thou shouldst have said, "Good porter, turn the key."
> All cruels else subscribe. But I shall see
> The wingèd vengeance overtake such children.
> (3.7.63–66)

Gloucester describes Lear's dismission with an angry incredulity reminiscent of Hoby's: a good host would minister to wolves before neglecting the ancient practice. The grounds of indictment serve equally well as the material of the householder's own complaint:

> Naughty lady,
> These hairs which thou dost ravish from my chin
> Will quicken, and accuse thee. I am your host.
> With robber's hands my hospitable favors
> You should not ruffle thus. (3.7.36–40)

Gloucester's presence asserts: "I am your host." He demands some reverence for the keeper of hospitable favors and suffers for it. The bad hostesses punctuate his blinding with one more cruel dismission: "Go thrust him out at gates, and let him smell / His way to Dover" (3.7.93–94).

As in the case of Lear, attachment to hospitable ideals leaves the householder vulnerable; but, unlike his monarch, Gloucester's assertion is not fetishism. His maintenance of the old ways does not die. Outside the gates, Gloucester's good housekeeping is demonstrated by the proffered care of an old tenant. In Gloucester's words, the man offers "ancient love," a love confirmed through traditional ceremony, something Lear cannot find. Indeed, perhaps most importantly, Gloucester's hospitality and its nurture of "ancient love" live on in Edgar:

> Here, father, take the shadow of this tree
> For your good host. Pray that the right may thrive.
> If ever I return to you again,
> I'll bring you comfort. (5.2.1–4)

In this instant, the dramatic action must pause awkwardly and finally over the figure of the blind old man, hosted by the shadow of a tree.

Tragic Destruction and Hospitable Remnants

What remains at the end of the age's great tragedies? *King Lear* has, of course, a hundred, perhaps a thousand, agendas to pursue; and reckoning the significance of hospitable crusts will hardly tie up these varied sufferings into a single, universal statement. My focussing on representations of hospitable practice and its fetishism in *King Lear* leaves out much. Surely, we cannot dismiss the final meeting of Lear and Cordelia in a catalog of "what remains," nor can household stuff comprehend the many nuances of the play's dialogue with history and contemporary politics, the heterodox sources and the classical models. One must acknowledge, finally, the deep challenges to any meaningful construction of social order that practically define the genre of tragedy in Renaissance England.

Since Aristotle, we have taken catastrophe to be central to tragedy's working. Recent scholarship has only heightened our awareness of the genre's emphasis on destruction. Franco Moretti demonstrates that "the historical 'task' effectively accomplished by this form was precisely the destruction of the fundamental paradigm of the dominant culture. Tragedy disentitled the absolute monarch to all ethical and rational legitimation."[31] Jonathan Dollimore has gone so far as to conclude that, by the end of the play, recuperation of value is simply impossible.[32] If I conclude my discussion of *King Lear* with an examination of the remains of hospitality amid the remains of Lear's world, it is done with the knowledge that the play's greatness and the genre's vicissitudes humble every movement of closure. With these caveats, I want to concentrate on the difference the representation of Gloucester's "food and fire" makes to the genre's thirst for destruction.

I suggest that Gloucester and Edgar haunt the play's conclusion as a moral sentence, as an obdurate bundle of hospitable values that, instead of triumphing over vulnerability, simply refuse to be assimilated by the vortex. The play begins with a fantasy of the ideal hospitality, a manifestation of the ideal described in *The True Narration* wherein "every entertainment seemed to exceed others," a version packaged in the unstable pamphlet *Civil and Uncivil Life.* Bound to his fantasy, Lear has looked for hospitality after the fashion of Queen Elizabeth and King James, Nashe's Summer and Shakespeare's Duncan. At the play's end, the fetish is exhausted but not, I think, "the fundamental paradigm of the dominant culture." Pamphlet ideal and traditional practice continue to swirl around Shakespeare's theater in the early seventeenth century, regardless of Lear's fate. Indeed, the destruction of fantasy in *King Lear* can only drive its fretful audience back to the old ideals manifested in the practice of Albany, Kent, and Edgar, the keepers of the play's final scene. At the play's end, ironically, *the audience* has become more vulnerable, for its catharsis depends on the subtle mystifications of hospitality, mystifications of un-equal allocation and woman's place in early modern England. At the play's end, audiences of tragedies always go back to house-keeping.

NOTES

1. For a discussion of the motion of "'poisonous' gifts and gifts from evil people" in systems of prestation, see Hyde, "Some Food We Could Not Eat," 34. For an analysis of James I's confu-sion of prestation and capitalism (which makes, by the way, a fine preface to *King Lear*), see Peck, "'For a King not to be bountiful were a fault,'" 49.

2. Roberts, *The Most Royal and Honourable Entertainment of the Famous and Renowned King Christian the Fourth, King of Denmark*, 435.

3. Knight, *The Wheel of Fire*, 179.

4. Kahn, "The Absent Mother in *King Lear*," 33–49.

5. Scholarship suggests that such fantasies frequently emerge in decidedly male configurations. See, for example, Snow, "Sexual Anxiety and the Male Order of Things in *Othello*," 384–411; and Adelman, "'Born of Woman,'" in *Cannibals, Witches, and Divorce*, 90–121.

In his *James I and the Politics of Literature*, Goldberg brilliantly details James I's own tremulous fetishizing of the age's re-presen-tations of royal power.

6. The term "subject position" signifies the cultural and psychological constructs that a human being may adopt in order to act. To adopt the subject position of host is to seek access to the agency bequeathed by society on hosts.

7. Marcus, in *Puzzling Shakespeare*, draws a concise link be-tween *King Lear*, the old custom of Stephening, James's interest in holiday custom, and political agenda concerning the Scots: "The 1606 *King Lear* performed before King James I was, in contempo-rary political terms, a demand for what had not been offered generously and freely, a morality play enforcing the king's argu-ments for naturalization and acceptance of the alien on the basis of liturgical and customary holiday injunctions" (156).

8. Samuel Taylor Coleridge, *Coleridge's Shakespearean*

Criticism, ed. Thomas Middleton Raysor (London: Constable, 1930), 1:59.

9. Bradley, *Shakespearean Tragedy,* 205.

10. In "'Service' in *King Lear,*" Barish and Waingrow argue that "by refusing to honor the reciprocal force of the bond tying him to his inferiors, Lear cuts the bond, 'cracks' it, and so lets loose the forces of disorder, division, and disservice that are to overwhelm the kingdom" (348). Strier explores the "limits to obedience" in "Faithful Servants," in *Historical Renaissance,* 104–33.

11. Hinman, Introduction, *The Life of Timon of Athens,* in *William Shakespeare,* 1139.

12. Quoted in Nichols, *Elizabeth,* 1:308.

13. See Greene, "Magic and Festivity at the Renaissance Court," 636–59.

14. For a discussion of how Kent entertains, holds together, character and spectator in the play, see Egan, "Kent and the Audience," 146–54.

15. Goldman, *Shakespeare and the Energies of Drama,* 97–98.

16. Ibid., 81–85. See Chapter 1 above for a discussion of the pamphlet.

17. Mack, *King Lear in Our Time,* 31.

18. For a discussion of these trials, see Chambers, *The Elizabethan Stage,* 1:113–15.

19. Hospitality certainly functioned as a trap in the real life of kings. James remained ever watchful. When, in 1607, the Merchant Taylors hosted James and Henry at their hall, the master and wardens made a careful search to prevent "villainy" (Nichols, *James,* 2:142).

The motif of the hospitable trap figures, too, in city comedies such as Jonson's *Epicoene* and Middleton's *Michaelmas Term* and *A Trick to Catch the Old One.*

20. Marlowe, *The Jew of Malta,* 2.3.79–80. Subsequent references to the play will appear parenthetically in the text and be from this New Mermaids edition.

21. Indeed, the general emphasis on castles in the period's greatest tragedies makes this gesture all the more meaningful. I thank David Evett for bringing this pattern to my attention.

22. Middleton and Rowley, *The Changeling,* 1.1.152–53. Subsequent references to this play will be from this Regents edition and appear parenthetically in the text.

23. Middleton, *Women Beware Women*, 2.2.139–43.

24. Thomas, *Religion and the Decline of Magic*, 560–69.

25. See Macfarlane, *Witchcraft in Tudor and Stuart England*. On the relation of witches and social order, see also Belsey, *The Subject of Tragedy*, 188–91 and David E. Underdown, "The Taming of the Scold: The Enforcement of Patriarchal Authority in Early Modern England," *Order and Disorder in Early Modern England*, 116–36.

26. Heal, *Hospitality*, 357–58.

27. Two fine discussions of domestic tragedy and women's struggle for subject positions are Catherine Belsey's "Alice Arden's Crime" and Frances E. Dolan's "Gender, Moral Agency, and Dramatic Form in *A Warning for Fair Women*," *Studies in English Literature* 29 (1989): 201–18.

For a stimulating discussion of how Shakespeare seems to be reclaiming the old system of prestation through particularly female giving, see Erickson, "Patriarchal Structures in *The Winter's Tale*, 819–29.

28. My account derives from the editorial labors of Meads, *Diary of Lady Margaret Hoby, 1599–1605*, and Heal's "Hospitality and Honor in Early Modern England," 321–23.

29. A truly illustrative record of representational difference occasioned by gender difference is Lady Hoby's diary entry recording this vicious hospitality. Whereas her husband filled pages with his complaints, Lady Hoby reduced the whole to a contained incident:

> After priuate praier I did worke some thinge, and, after, praied and medetated often : some thinge I did eate, and then did reed, and made prouision for som strangers that Came : after I went to priuate examenation and praier, then I went to priuate, supper, and after to bed. After I was readie I spake with Mr Eure, who was so drunk that I soon made an end of that I had no reason to stay for: and after, praied, break my fast, praied, and then dined. *(Diary of Lady Margaret Hoby 1599–1605*, 141)

It would seem that women did perceive hosting differently than men, but this woman's representation of hospitable practice makes the male versions appear positively hysterical.

30. Perret, *"Lear's* Good Old Man," 92.

31. Moretti, "The Great Eclipse," in *Signs Taken for Wonders,* 42.

32. Dollimore, *Radical Tragedy,* 203.

DEDUCTION

Often the most difficult task in hospitality is what Dalechamp termed *dismission or deduction*, "a liberal and charitable bestowing of necessary things for the journey."[1] What must we let go of and what can we know in the letting go? "Deduction" means "farewell" and "therefore." Shakespeare understood it. Hermione and her family in *The Winter's Tale* suffered for it. Antony in *Antony and Cleopatra* never *did* get it right. In attempting to conclude this discussion of the representations of hospitable practice in theatrical genres, I find the task of deduction doubly difficult. How hard to release such an amorphous project. How impossible to determine the point of departure, since it seems certain that hospitality, the idea of the practice, fades after England's Civil War even as it continues to haunt modern literature.[2] What can a writer bestow for such an imprecise journey beginning at the end of the book? I will offer, tentatively, *a cabinet*.

Entering the twilight of public theater in the Renaissance, Thomas Heywood assembled a curious and heterogeneous text he called *Pleasant Dialogues and Dramas*. Five years later, in 1642, the public stage would be silent. In the aftermath of the Revolution, theater returned, but the culture's intense fascination with hospitality did not. Heywood's text appears on the threshold of immense change and exists as a provocative if opaque sign of the times. Filled with translations of classical writers, emblems, elegies, epitaphs, epithalamiums, anagrams, acrostics, and "divers speeches" that focus on hospitality, Heywood's book seems to defy categorization. When they merge with comedy or the progress or tragedy, hospitality's primary genres trigger immense ideological forces latent in the genres. When hospitality merges with Heywood's odd collection, it makes a jingle or a clink: one more curiosity on the pile.

In presenting the work to his patron Lord Henry Carey, Earl of Dover, Heywood must have searched for a generic principle to tie the bundle together. His choice is most instructive: *"This is a small Cabinet of many and choice, of which none better than your noble*

*self can judge, some of them borrowing their luster from your own vir-
tues, vouchsafe therefore (great Lord) their perusal."*[3] Hospitality comes
in a cabinet bursting with other curiosities. What are we to make
of Heywood's generic container? I think of the Renaissance Wonder Cabinet. In a most provocative discussion of the fashion, and
Walter Cope's cabinet in particular, Steven Mullaney recounts a
list of contents: a sea mouse, a Madonna made of Indian feathers,
a unicorn's tail. . . .[4] Hospitality, for better or worse, takes its place
in such a collection, perhaps between mouse and Madonna.

Mullaney contends that the cabinet is indicative of what he
calls the period's "collective activity": "The late sixteenth and early
seventeenth centuries collected and exhibited not only the trap-
pings but also the customs, languages, and even the members of
other cultures on a scale that was unprecedented" (p. 63). Mullaney suggests that the cultivation of wonder cabinets participated
in both the maintenance and production of an Other (p. 64), a process quite akin to Greenblatt's notion of "recording" discussed in
Chapter 4. The value of "producing" an Other is summed up by
Michel de Certeau in his excellent discussion of Montaigne: "The
discourse about the other is a means of constructing a discourse
authorized by the other."[5] In a sense, people conquer by reproduc-
ing what they intend to conquer and by making it appear that the
conquered are narrating the activity. But what do such strategies
have to do with hospitality and genre?

In a hundred ways, Renaissance hospitality was the special
province of the aristocracy and the monarchy. Of course, it was
possible to conjure images of plebeian entertainment after the fashion of Stow or Greene, but hospitality was first and foremost a
male hosting in a great hall. Hospitality meant the possibility of
advantageous marriages. If one had erred seriously in the eyes of
the monarch, as the Earl of Hertford or Nicholas Bacon had done
before Elizabeth, one could host fantastically and salvage a position. Hospitality meant Theobalds and Lord Burghley. Insofar as
it was old, hospitality meant the habits of old power, mystifying
the means of control and unequal allocation, naturalizing the origins of dominant constructions. Heywood captures something of
this fact in one of his speeches:

> Amongst the Grecians there were annual feasts,
> To which none were invited as chief guests,
> Save princes and their wives.[6]

Hosting was as old as culture, or so it seemed to Heywood; and the power it promised had always been conserved for "chief guests." By the first decades of the seventeenth century, the aristocracy could look back at and cultivate anew such "precedents" as signs of authority.

Lawrence Stone's title *The Crisis of the Aristocracy* has become a kind of signature for these years, the last years of old hospitality, of old monarchy, of old theater—a time of wonder cabinets. In scrutinizing this moment, we must avoid becoming too attached to a notion of "crisis." As Stone noted, the patterns of flux and drift at work in the society were subtle, difficult to fathom. Contemporaries noticed, according to Stone, "basic insecurity" and "hypersensitive" nobles who stumbled over themselves "calling in the past to redress the balance of the present."[7] Certainly the pamphlet literature devoted to hospitality participates in this phenomenon. And Heywood's speeches follow the pattern, as in the following Candlemas epilogue for Carey:

> you and your lov'd wife
> > Have to dead hospitality given new life.
> Still cherish it: old Christmas almost starv'd
> Through base neglect, by you hath been preserv'd.
> O give him still like welcome, that whilst he
> Hath name on earth, you may his harbourer be.
> > > (8300–8305)

Echoing the period's tragedies and borrowing from the pamphlets, Heywood casts hospitality as an old man whose ways persist in aristocratic care, the nurture of Gloucester and Edgar. The pamphlets—consistently and confidently—linked the fate of hospitality to the fate of the aristocracy, but from our perspective, the connection seems ominous.

In gazing back at the past, the tone of a funeral elegy seems more fitting. Heywood has collected the following specimen dedicated to Sir George Saint Poole:

> He kept about him still not like this age,
> Changing his traine, to a foot-boy or a page.
> Free hospitality exil'd the realme,
> He took charge, which like a plenteous streame
> On his full tables flow'd (now a strange thing)
> It rather seem'd a torrent than a spring,
>   His hand was ever open, but before
> All others, to the vertuous and the poor;
> Not as most men are bounteous now; to those
> That either need not, or with cunning glose.
>   (8565–74)

The old thrice-noble gentleman kept full tables—not like this age. Hospitality recedes and so, it seems, does the character of the nobility. Heywood's cabinet is nothing but indigestion, and so the primary genres of hospitable discourse dotter by themselves. Polonius advises Laertes: "Those friends thou hast, and their adoption tried, / Grapple them unto thy soul with hoops of steel" (1.3.62–63). England's nobility, certainly its monarchs, took Hospitality as a tried old friend, attaching themselves, and finding themselves hooped to, in Heywood's terms, *a strange thing*.

As people sometimes do, cultures become strange to themselves. Hospitality, that most heterodox of customs, gradually became a strange thing, a thing fit for a wonder cabinet. People certainly entertained after 1642, and such entertainments found their way into literary texts. But the kind of persistent attention to hospitality, as an economic, social, and political form, as idea and practice, gradually became estranged. This metamorphosis shadows, I think, the transformations of the aristocracy and monarchy during the period, for in their attachment to the old practices, England's ruling elites helped to fashion themselves into an Other whose habits and artifacts were subject to collection and rehearsal in the most important genres of the day. Tossed about in the ebb and flow of generic digestion, hospitality could be mused over and toyed with by the lower orders. The process of "making strange" went forward, as did the redistribution of power in England. My deduction of Renaissance theatrical genres and hospitality comes thus in the shape of the cabinet that "none better" than a "noble self" can judge, for the cabinet borrows its "luster" from aristocratic, even royal, virtues. Hospitality hardly "explains" England's civil conflict; rather, the idea's appropriations by various writers working in distinct and volatile genres suggest how the culture came to imagine weakness in the traditional fabric and the powerful as Other.

Genre is no esoteric entanglement. Between literary text and culture, genre marks a passage—sometimes a gutter or a casement, sometimes a gateway or vomitory, even the king's highway—between the restricted world of the elites and the allocated world of the lower orders, between literature and the other domains of cultural activity. Even as they seem to exclude, theatrical genres enable a certain parasitical digestion. As Michel Serres puts it, "Every parasite that is a bit gifted, at the table of a somewhat sumptuous host, soon transforms the table into a theater."[8] At the heart of Renaissance theater, displacing modes of control attributed to monarchs, Kemp and Nashe—gifted but marginal writers—join with Shakespeare, Greene, and Dekker to turn the table of the great into a parasitical theater. A clown may write a progress narrative. A pinner may host in a comedy. A woman may edit and augment male housekeeping. Such intrusions travel along the boundaries marked by genre, suggesting a vocabulary of critical thought quite distinct from notions of "containment" and "subversion." We may think, instead, of *diminution, resistance, feeding and la perruque, vulnerabilities,* and *other powers.* The cumulative vision of such concepts is something less than revolution, something closer to *critical symbiosis.*

In his diary of 1571, Lord Burghley notes: "The Queen's Majesty came to Theobalds, where some verses were presented to her Majesty, with a Portrait of the House."[9] The following September day, Hugh Fitz William wrote to the Countess of Shrewsbury: "They say the Queen will be at my Lord of Burghley's house beside Waltam on Sunday next, where my Lord of Oxford shall marry Mrs. Anne Cecil his daughter."[10] Casual notations of power multiply, the hosting of marriages, alliances and jealousies, news for the court, feasts and soul-ravishing music, an ambassador or two, pools in the shape of moons, dryads and nymphs, verses and countless representations of houses—houses most of all. Look again and hospitality sits on a shelf beside a sea mouse. The powerful are strangers all.

NOTES

1. Dalechamp, *Christian Hospitality*, 24.
2. Consider, for example, Jane Austen's *Pride and Prejudice*, Charles Dickens's *Bleak House*, Kate Chopin's *The Awakening*, Harold Pinter's *The Caretaker*, Edward Albee's *Who's Afraid of Virginia Woolf?*, and Marilynne Robinson's recent *Housekeeping*. The English film *High Hopes* (1988) offers a painful, poignant, and satiric vision of hospitality under Margaret Thatcher's government.
3. Thomas Heywood, *Pleasant Dialogues and Dramas*, ll. 10–14.
4. Mullaney, *The Place of the Stage*, 63.
5. Certeau, "Montaigne's 'Of Cannibals,'" in *Heterologies*, 68.
6. Heywood, *Pleasant Dialogues and Dramas*, ll. 8016–18. Cf. Annabel Patterson's discussion of the cabinet as a symbol of privacy in *Censorship and Interpretation: The Conditions of Writing and Reading in Early Modern Europe* (Madison: University of Wisconsin Press, 1984), 5–8.
7. Lawrence Stone, *The Crisis of the Aristocracy, 1558–1641* (Oxford: Clarendon, 1965), 751.
8. Serres, *The Parasite*, 211. J. Hillis Miller imagines critical theory in just these terms in "The Critic as Host," *Deconstruction and Criticism* (New York: Seabury Press, 1979), 217–53.
9. Nichols, *Elizabeth*, 1:291.
10. Ibid.

BIBLIOGRAPHY

Primary Sources

Beaumont, Francis. *The Knight of the Burning Pestle*. Edited by Michael Hattaway. London: Ernest Benn, 1969.

The Brewer's Plea: Or a Vindication of Strong Beer and Ale. London, 1647.

Calendar of State Papers Venetian. Vols. 17 and 23. Edited by Allen B. Hinds. London: Her Majesty's Stationery Office, 1911, 1921.

Chamberlain, John. *The Chamberlain Letters: A Selection of the Letters of John Chamberlain Concerning Life in England from 1597 to 1626*. Edited by Elizabeth McClure Thomson. Vol. 2. London: John Murray, 1966.

Charles I. *The Royal Proclamations of Charles I, 1625–1640*. Vol. 2 of *Stuart Royal Proclamations*. Edited by James F. Larkin and Paul L. Hughes. Oxford: Clarendon, 1983.

Churchyard, Thomas. *A Discourse of the Queen's Majesty's Entertainment in Suffolk and Norfolk*. In *The Progresses and Public Processions of Queen Elizabeth*, by John Nichols. Vol. 2. London, 1823.

Clifford, Lady Anne. *The Diaries of Lady Anne Clifford*. Edited by D. J. H. Clifford. Wolfeboror Falls, N.H.: Alan Sutton Publishing, 1991.

Dalechamp, Caleb. *Christian Hospitality*. London, 1632.

Dekker, Thomas. *The Shoemakers' Holiday*. Edited by D. J. Palmer. London: Ernest Benn, 1975.

Elizabeth I. *The Late Tudors, 1588–1603*. Vol. 3 of *Tudor Royal Proclamations*. Edited by Paul L. Hughes and James F. Larkin. New Haven: Yale University Press, 1969.

The Elizabethan Home Discovered in 2 Dialogues. Edited by Muriel St. Clare Byrne. London: Frederick Etchells & Hugh Macdonald, 1925.

Garter, Bernard. *The Joyful Receiving of the Queen's Most Excellent Majesty in Her Highness' City of Norwich*. Reprinted in

Norwich, 1540–1642, edited by David Galloway. Records of Early English Drama. Toronto: University of Toronto Press, 1984.

Greene, Robert. *Friar Bacon and Friar Bungay*. Edited by Daniel Seltzer. Lincoln: University of Nebraska Press, 1963.

———. *George a Greene, The Pinner of Wakefield*. In *The Plays and Poems of Robert Greene*, edited by J. Churton Collins. Vol. 2. Oxford: Clarendon, 1945.

Grevious Groans for the Poor. London, 1621.

Harman, Thomas. *A Caveat for Common Cursitors, London, 1566*. In *Cony–Catchers and Bawdy Baskets: An Anthology of Elizabethan Low Life*, edited by Gamini Salgado, 79–153. Middlesex: Penguin, 1972.

Heywood, John. *John the Husband, Tyb his Wife, and Sir John the Priest*. Edited by John S. Farmer. London: Barnes & Noble, 1966.

Heywood, Thomas. *Pleasant Dialogues and Dramas*. Edited by W. Bang. Materialien zür Kunde des Älteren Englischen Dramas. Lovain, 1903.

———. *Londini Emporia, or Londons Mercatura*. In *Thomas Heywood's Pageants, A Critical Edition*, edited by David M. Bergeron, 53–70. New York: Garland, 1986.

Hoby, Lady Margaret. *The Diary of Lady Margaret Hoby, 1599–1605*. Edited by Dorothy M. Meads. London: George Routledge, 1930.

Humphrey, Laurence. *The Nobles: or, Of Nobility*. London, 1563.

James I. *The Works of the Most High and Mighty Prince, James*. London, 1616.

———. *The Poems of James VI of Scotland*. Edited by James Craigie. Vol. 2. Edinburgh: William Blackwood, 1958.

———. *The Royal Proclamations of James I, 1603–1625*. Vol. 1 of *Stuart Royal Proclamations*. Edited by James F. Larkin and Paul L. Hughes. Oxford: Clarendon, 1973.

Jonson, Ben. *Ben Jonson*. Edited by C. H. Herford and Percy and Evelyn Simpson. 11 vols. Oxford: Clarendon Press, 1925–52.

———. *Selected Masques*. Edited by Stephen Orgel. Vol. 2. New Haven: Yale University Press, 1970.

Kemp, William. *Kemp's Nine Days Wonder*. Edited by Alexander Dyce. London, 1840.

Lupton, Donald. *London and the Country Carbonadoed and Quartered.* London, 1632.

Markham, Gervase. *The English Housewife.* London, 1615.

Marlowe, Christopher. *The Jew of Malta.* Edited by T. W. Craik. London: Ernest Benn, 1966.

The Merry Devil of Edmonton. Edited by William Amos Abrams. Durham: Duke University Press, 1942.

Middleton, Thomas. *A Trick to Catch the Old One.* Edited by Charles Barber. Berkeley: University of California Press, 1968.

———, and William Rowley. *The Changeling.* Edited by George W. Williams. Lincoln: University of Nebraska Press, 1966.

———. *Women Beware Women.* Edited by J. R. Mulryne. London: Routledge & Kegan Paul, 1970.

Munday, Anthony. *The Downfall of Robert, Earl of Huntingdon.* In *The Huntingdon Plays: A Critical Edition of the Downfall and the Death of Robert, Earl of Huntingdon,* edited by John Carney Meagher. New York: Garland, 1980.

Nashe, Thomas. *The Works of Thomas Nashe.* Edited by Ronald B. McKerrow. 4 vols. 1905. Reprint, with editorial additions by F. P. Wilson. Oxford: Basil Blackwell, 1958.

Nichols, John. *The Progresses and Public Processions of Queen Elizabeth.* 3 vols. London, 1823.

———. *The Progresses, Processions, and Magnificent Festivities of King James, the First.* 4 vols. London, 1828.

Norwich, 1540–1642. Edited by David Galloway. Records of Early English Drama. Toronto: University of Toronto Press, 1984.

Porter, Henry. *Two Angry Women of Abington: A Critical Edition.* Edited by Marianne Brish Evett. New York: Garland, 1980.

Peele, George. *The Old Wives Tale.* Edited by Patricia Binnie. Manchester: Manchester University Press, 1980.

R. R. *The House–holders Helpe, For Domesticall Discipline.* London, 1615.

Roberts, Henry. *The Most Royal and Honourable Entertainment of the Famous and Renowned King Christian the Fourth, King of Denmark.* In *Harleian Miscellany.* 1606. London, 1812.

Roper, William. "The Life of Sir Thomas More." In *Two Early Tudor Lives,* edited by R. S. Sylvester and D. P. Harding. New Haven: Yale University Press, 1962.

Savile, John. *King James, his Entertainment at Theobalds.* In *Stuart*

Tracts, edited by C. H. Firth, 53–63. 1603. New York: Cooper Square Publishers, 1964.

Shakespeare, William. *William Shakespeare: The Complete Works.* Edited by Alfred Harbage. New York: Viking/Pelican, 1969.

Sidney, Sir Philip. *The Complete Works of Sir Philip Sidney.* Edited by Albert Feuillerat. Vol. 3. Cambridge: Cambridge University Press, 1923.

————. *The Countess of Pembroke's Arcadia.* Edited by Maurice Evans. Middlesex: Penguin, 1977.

Smith, Sir Thomas. *De Republica Anglorum.* Edited by Mary Dewar. Cambridge: Cambridge University Press, 1982.

Stafford, William. *A Compendious or Brief Examination of Certain Ordinary Complaints.* London, 1581.

Stow, John. *A Survey of London.* Introduction by Charles Lethbridge Kingsford. 1603. Reprint. Oxford: Clarendon, 1908.

T. M. *The True Narration of the Entertainment of his Majesty from his departure from Edinburgh till his receiving at London.* In *Stuart Tracts,* edited by C. H. Firth, 11–51. 1603. New York: Cooper Square Publishers, 1964.

Topsell, Edward. *The Householder.* London, 1610.

Tusser, Thomas. *Five Hundred Points of Good Husbandry.* Edited by W. Payne and S. Heritage. 1573. Reprint. London, 1878.

Vaughan, William. *The Golden–grove, moralized in three books.* London, 1600.

Walker, Gilbert. *A Manifest Detection of Dice–Play. London, 1552.* In *Cony–Catchers and Bawdy Baskets: An Anthology of Elizabethan Low Life,* edited by Gamini Salgado, 27–58. Middlesex: Penguin, 1972.

Wandesford, Christopher. *A Book of Instructions.* London, 1777.

Wheler, George. *The Protestant Monastery: or, Christian Economics.* London, 1698.

Williams, C. H., ed. *English Historical Documents, 1485–1558.* London: Eyre & Spoltiswoode, 1967.

Wilson, Jean, ed. *Entertainments for Elizabeth I.* London: D. S. Brewer, 1980.

Wotton, Sir Henry. *The Elements of Architecture.* Introduction by Frederick Hardt. 1624. Facsimile reprint. Charlottesville: University of Virginia Press, 1968.

York. Records of Early English Drama. Vol. 1. Edited by Alexandra F. Johnston and Margaret Rogerson. Toronto: University of Toronto Press, 1979.

Secondary Sources

Adelman, Janet. "'Born of Woman': Fantasies of Maternal Power in *Macbeth*." In *Cannibals, Witches, and Divorce: Estranging the Renaissance*, edited by Marjorie Garber, 90–121. Baltimore: Johns Hopkins University Press, 1987.

Anglo, Sydney. *Spectacle Pageantry, and Early Tudor Policy*. Oxford: Clarendon, 1969.

Bakhtin, M. M. "Discourse in the Novel." In *The Dialogic Imagination*, edited by Michael Holquist and translated by Caryl Emerson and Michael Holquist. Austin: University of Texas Press, 1981.

———. *Rabelais and His World*. Translated by Helene Iswolsky. Bloomington: Indiana University Press, 1984.

———. "The Problem of Speech Genres." In *Speech Genres and Other Late Essays*, translated by Vern W. McGee. Austin: University of Texas Press, 1986.

Barber, C. L. *Shakespeare's Festive Comedy*. Princeton: Princeton University Press, 1959.

Barish, Jonas A., and Marshall Waingrow. "'Service' in *King Lear*." *Shakespeare Quarterly* 9 (1958): 347–55.

Barroll, Leeds. "A New History for Shakespeare and His Time." *Shakespeare Quarterly* 39 (1988): 441–64.

Belsey, Catherine. *The Subject of Tragedy: Identity and Difference in Renaissance Drama*. London: Methuen, 1983.

Bergeron, David M. *English Civic Pageantry 1558–1642*. Columbia: University of South Carolina Press, 1971.

———. *Pageantry in the Shakespearean Theater*. Athens: University of Georgia Press, 1985.

———. "Patronage of Dramatists: The Case of Thomas Heywood." *English Literary Renaissance* 18 (1988): 294–304.

———. "Representation in Renaissance English Civic Pageants." *Theatre Journal* 40 (1988): 319–31.

Bonnard, George A. "Shakespeare's Purpose in *A Midsummer Night's Dream*." *Shakespeare Jahrbuch* 92 (1956): 268–79.

Booth, Stephen. *King Lear, Macbeth, Indefinition, and Tragedy*. New

Haven: Yale University Press, 1983.

Booth, Wayne C. *The Rhetoric of Fiction.* Chicago: University of Chicago Press, 1963.

Bordieu, Pierre. *Outline of a Theory of Practice.* Cambridge: Cambridge University Press, 1977.

Bradbrook, M. C. *The Growth and Structure of Elizabethan Comedy.* London: Chatto & Windus, 1955.

Bradley, A. C. *Shakespearean Tragedy.* London: Macmillan, 1960.

Bristol, Michael. *Carnival and Theater: Plebeian Culture and the Structure of Authority in Renaissance England.* New York: Methuen, 1985.

Brooks, Harold. Introduction to *A Midsummer Night's Dream,* by William Shakespeare. London: Methuen, 1979.

Brownstein, Rachel M. *Becoming a Heroine: Reading about Women.* New York: Viking, 1982.

Brunvand, Jan Harold. "The Folktale Origin of *The Taming of the Shrew.*" *Shakespeare Quarterly* 17 (1966): 345-59.

Burke, Kenneth. *Rhetoric of Motives.* Berkeley: University of California Press, 1969.

Burke, Peter. *Popular Culture in Early Modern Europe.* New York: Harper & Row, 1978.

Burt, Richard A. ""'Tis Writ by Me': Massinger's *The Roman Actor* and the Politics of Reception in the English Renaissance Theatre." *Theatre Journal* 40 (1988): 332–46.

Campbell, Mildred. *The English Yeoman under Elizabeth and the Early Stuarts.* New Haven: Yale University Press, 1942.

Carroll, William C. *The Metamorphoses of Shakespearean Comedy.* Princeton: Princeton University Press, 1985.

Certeau, Michel de. *The Practice of Everyday Life.* Translated by Steven F. Rendall. Berkeley: University of California Press, 1984.

———. "Montaigne's 'Of Cannibals': The Savage 'I.'" In *Heterologies: Discourse on the Other,* translated by Brian Massumi. Minneapolis: University of Minnesota Press, 1986.

Chambers, E. K. *The Elizabethan Stage.* Vol. 1. Oxford: Clarendon, 1923.

Charlton, H. B. *Shakespearean Comedy.* London: Methuen, 1938.

Chartier, Roger. *Cultural History: Between Practices and Representations.* Translated by Lydia G. Cochrane. Ithaca: Cornell University Press, 1988.

Chodorow, Nancy. *The Reproduction of Mothering*. Berkeley: University of California Press, 1978.

Cohen, Walter. *Drama of a Nation: Public Theater in Renaissance England and Spain*. Ithaca: Cornell University Press, 1985.

Coleridge, Samuel Taylor. *Coleridge's Shakespearean Criticism*. Edited by Thomas Middleton Raysor. Vol. 1. London: Constable, 1930.

Colie, Rosalie L. *The Resources of Kind: Genre Theory in the Renaissance*. Edited by Barbara K. Lewalski. Berkeley: University of California Press, 1973.

Cooper, Helen. "Location and Meaning in Masque, Morality and Royal Entertainment." In *The Court Masque*, edited by David Lindley, 135–48. Manchester: Manchester University Press, 1984.

Creevy, Patrick J. "Hospitality in the Old Testament and English Literature: Some Points of Connection." *Publications of the Mississippi Philological Association* (1984): 14–36.

Crewe, Jonathan V. *Unredeemed Rhetoric: Thomas Nashe and the Scandal of Authorship*. Baltimore: Johns Hopkins University Press, 1982.

Culler, Jonathan. *The Pursuit of Signs: Semiotics, Literature, Deconstruction*. Ithaca: Cornell University Press, 1981.

Cunliffe, J. W., ed. "The Queenes Majesties Entertainment at Woodstocke." *PMLA* 26 (1911): 92–141.

Daley, A. Stuart. "The Dispraise of the Country in *As You Like It*." *Shakespeare Quarterly* 36 (1985): 300–14.

Darnton, Roger. *The Great Cat Massacre and Other Episodes in French Cultural History*. New York: Basic Books, 1984.

Dobson, R. B., and J. Taylor. *Rymes of Robin Hood: An Introduction to the English Outlaw*. Pittsburgh: University of Pittsburgh Press, 1976.

Dollimore, Jonathan. *Radical Tragedy: Religion, Ideology, and Power in the Drama of Shakespeare and His Contemporaries*. Brighton: Harvester, 1984.

———, and Alan Sinfield, eds. *Political Shakespeare: New Essays in Cultural Materialism*. Introduction by Jonathan Dollimore, 2–17. Ithaca: Cornell University Press, 1985.

———. "Transgression and Surveillance in *Measure for Measure*." In *Political Shakespeare: New Essays in Cultural Materialism*, edited by Jonathan Dollimore and Alan Sinfield, 72–87.

Ithaca: Cornell University Press, 1985.

Dubrow, Heather. "The Country–House Poem: A Study in Generic Development." *Genre* 12 (1979): 153–79.

———. *Genre.* London: Methuen, 1982.

Dunlop, Ian. *Palaces and Progresses of Elizabeth I.* London: Jonathan Cape, 1962.

Eagleton, Terry. *William Shakespeare.* Oxford: Basil Blackwell, 1986.

Egan, Robert. *Drama within Drama: Shakespeare's Sense of His Art.* New York: Columbia University Press, 1975.

———. "Kent and the Audience: The Character as Spectator." *Shakespeare Quarterly* 32 (1981): 146–54.

Elias, Norbert. *The Civilizing Process: The History of Manners.* Translated by Edmund Jephcott. Vol. 1. New York: Urizen Books, 1978.

———. *The Civilizing Process: Power and Civility.* Translated by Edmund Jephcott. Vol. 2. New York: Pantheon Books, 1982.

Elsky, Martin. *Authorizing Words: Speech, Writing, and Print in the English Renaissance.* Ithaca: Cornell University Press, 1989.

Erickson, Peter B. "Patriarchal Structures in *The Winter's Tale.*" *PMLA* 97 (1982): 819–29.

Felperin, Howard. *Shakespearean Representation: Mimesis and Modernity in Elizabethan Tragedy.* Princeton: Princeton University Press, 1977

———. "'Tongue–tied our queen?': The Deconstruction of Presence in *The Winter's Tale.*" In *Shakespeare and the Question of Theory,* edited by Patricia Parker and Geoffrey Hartman, 3–18. New York: Methuen, 1985.

Ferguson, Charles W. *Naked to Mine Enemies: The Life of Cardinal Wolsey.* Boston: Little, Brown, 1958.

Fowler, Alastair. *Kinds of Literature: An Introduction to the Theory of Genres and Modes.* Cambridge: Harvard University Press, 1982.

Friedman, Alice T. *House and Household in Elizabethan England: Wollaton Hall and the Willoughby Family.* Chicago: University of Chicago Press, 1989.

Frye, Northrop. *The Anatomy of Criticism.* Princeton: Princeton University Press, 1957.

Galloway, David. *Norwich 1540–1642.* Records of Early English Drama. Toronto: University of Toronto Press, 1984.

Garber, Marjorie. *Shakespeare's Ghost Writers: Literature as Uncanny Causality.* New York: Methuen, 1987.

Gass, William. *Habitations of the Word.* New York: Simon and Shuster, 1985.

Genette, Gerard. *Narrative Discourse: An Essay in Method.* Translated by Jane E. Levin. Ithaca: Cornell University Press, 1980.

Geuss, Raymond. *The Idea of a Critical Theory: Habermas and the Frankfurt School.* Cambridge: Cambridge University Press, 1981.

Gilligan, Carol. *In a Different Voice: Psychological Theory and Women's Development.* Cambridge: Harvard University Press, 1982.

Ginsburg, Carlo. *The Cheese and the Worms: The Cosmos of a Sixteenth-Century Miller.* London: Routledge, 1980.

Goldberg, Jonathan. *James I and the Politics of Literature: Jonson, Shakespeare, Donne, and Their Contemporaries.* Baltimore: Johns Hopkins University Press, 1983.

———. "Shakespearean Inscriptions: The Voicing of Power." In *Shakespeare and the Question of Theory,* edited by Patricia Parker and Geoffrey Hartman, 116–37. New York: Methuen, 1985.

Goldman, Michael. *Shakespeare and the Energies of Drama.* Princeton: Princeton University Press, 1972.

Greaves, Richard L. *Society and Religion in Elizabethan England.* Minneapolis: University of Minnesota Press, 1981.

Greenblatt, Stephen. *Renaissance Self-Fashioning.* Chicago: University of Chicago Press, 1980.

———. "The Circulation of Social Energy." In *Shakespearean Negotiations.* Berkeley: University of California Press, 1988.

———. "Invisible Bullets." In *Shakespearean Negotiations.* Berkeley: University of California Press, 1988.

Greene, Thomas M. "Magic and Festivity at the Renaissance Court." *Renaissance Quarterly* 40 (1987): 636–59.

Greenfield, Peter H. "'All for your delight / We are not here': Amateur Players and Nobility." *Research Opportunities in Renaissance Drama* 28 (1985): 173–80.

Griffin, Alice V. *Pageantry on the Shakespearean Stage.* New York: Twayne, 1951.

Guillén, Claudio. "Poetics as System." *Comparative Literature* 22 (1970): 193–222.

Gurr, Andrew. *Playgoing in Shakespeare's London.* Cambridge: Cambridge University Press, 1987.

Haselkorn, Anne M., and Betty S. Travitsky. *The Renaissance Englishwoman in Print: Counterbalancing the Canon.* Amherst: University of Massachusetts Press, 1990.

Heal, Felicity. "The Archbishops of Canterbury and the Practice of Hospitality." *Journal of Ecclesiastical History* 33 (1982): 544–63.

———. "The Idea of Hospitality in Early Modern England." *Past and Present* 102 (1984): 66–93.

———. "Hospitality and Honor in Early Modern England." *Food and Foodways* 1 (1987): 321–50.

———. "The Crown, the Gentry and London: The Enforcement of Proclamations, 1596–1640." In *Law and Government under the Tudors,* edited by Claire Cross, David Loades, and J. J. Scarisbrick. Cambridge: Cambridge University Press, 1988.

———. *Hospitality in Early Modern England.* Oxford: Clarendon Press, 1990.

Hernadi, Paul. *Beyond Genre: New Directions in Literary Classification.* Ithaca: Cornell University Press, 1972.

Hibbard, G. R. "The Country–House Poem of the Seventeenth Century." *Journal of the Warburg and Courtauld Institutes* 19 (1956): 159–74.

———. *Thomas Nashe: A Critical Introduction.* Cambridge: Harvard University Press, 1962.

Hilliard, Stephen. *The Singularity of Thomas Nashe.* Lincoln: University of Nebraska Press, 1986.

Hinman, Charlton Introduction to *The Life of Timon of Athens.* In *William Shakespeare: The Complete Works,* edited by Alfred Harbage. New York: Viking, 1969.

Hollander, Paul. "Political Tourism in Cuba and Nicaragua." *Society* 23 (1986): 28–37.

Howard, Jean E. "Renaissance Antitheatricality and the Politics of Gender and Rank in *Much Ado about Nothing.*" In *Shakespeare Reproduced,* edited by Jean E. Howard and Marion F. O'Connor, 163–87. New York: Methuen, 1987.

Hulse, Clark. "Stella's Wit: Penelope Rich as Reader of Sidney's Sonnets." In *Rewriting the Renaissance,* edited by Margaret W. Ferguson, Maureen Quilligan, and Nancy J.Vickers,

272–86. Chicago: University of Chicago Press, 1986.

Hutson, Lorna. *Thomas Nashe in Context.* Oxford: Clarendon Press, 1989.

Hyde, Lewis. "Some Food We Could Not Eat: Gift Exchange and the Imagination." *Kenyon Review* 1, no. 4 (1979): 32–60.

———. *The Gift: Imagination and the Erotic Life of Property.* New York: Random House, 1983.

Iser, Wolfgang. *The Act of Reading: A Theory of Aesthetic Response.* Baltimore: Johns Hopkins University Press, 1978.

Jameson, Fredric. *The Political Unconscious.* Ithaca: Cornell University Press, 1981.

Kahn, Coppélia. "The Absent Mother in *King Lear.*" In *Rewriting the Renaissance,* edited by Margaret W. Ferguson, Maureen Quilligan, and Nancy J. Vickers, 33–49. Chicago: University of Chicago Press, 1986.

Kaplan, Steven L., ed. *Understanding Popular Culture: Europe from the Middle Ages to the Nineteenth Century.* Berlin: Mouton, 1984.

Kastan, David Scott. "Workshop and/as Playhouse: Comedy and Commerce in *The Shoemakers' Holiday.*" *Shakespeare Quarterly* 84 (1987): 324–37.

Knight, G. Wilson. *The Wheel of Fire.* Oxford: Oxford University Press, 1930.

Knights, L. C. *Drama and Society in the Age of Jonson.* 1937. Reprint. London: Chatto & Windus, 1962.

Krieger, Elliot. *A Marxist Study of Shakespeare's Comedies.* London: Macmillan, 1979.

———. "Social Relations and the Social Order in *Much Ado about Nothing.*" *Shakespeare Survey* 32 (1979): 49–61.

Labarge, Margaret Wade. *Medieval Travellers.* New York: Norton, 1982.

Leggatt, Alexander. *Shakespeare's Comedy of Love.* London: Methuen, 1973.

Levin, Richard. *New Readings vs. Old Plays.* Chicago: University of Chicago Press, 1979.

Levy, F. J. "How Information Spread among the Gentry, 1550–1640." *Journal of British Studies* 21, no. 2 (1982): 11–34.

Lewis, C. S. *English Literature in the Sixteenth Century.* New York: Oxford University Press, 1954.

Lucas, Caroline. *Writing for Women: The Example of Woman as Reader in Elizabethan Romance*. Milton Keynes, England: Open University Press, 1989.

MacCabe, Colin. "Abusing Self and Others: Puritan Accounts of the Shakespearean Stage." *Critical Quarterly* 30, no. 3 (1988): 3–17.

McClung, William A. *The Country House in English Renaissance Poetry*. Berkeley: University of California Press, 1977.

Macfarlane, Alan. *Witchcraft in Tudor and Stuart England*. London: Routledge & Kegan Paul, 1970.

Mack, Maynard. *King Lear in Our Time*. Berkeley: University of California Press, 1972.

Marcus, Leah S. *The Politics of Mirth: Jonson, Herrick, Milton, Marvell, and the Defense of Old Holiday Pastimes*. Chicago: University of Chicago Press, 1986.

———. *Puzzling Shakespeare*. Berkeley: University of California Press, 1988.

Martines, Lauro. *Society and History in English Renaissance Verse*. London: Basil Blackwell, 1985.

Mauss, Marcel. *The Gift: Forms and Functions of Exchange in Archaic Societies*. New York: Norton, 1967.

Mertes, Kate. *The English Noble Household: Good Governance and Politic Rule*. London: Basil Blackwell, 1988.

Miller, Ronald F. "Dramatic Form and Dramatic Imagination in Beaumont's *Knight of the Burning Pestle*." *English Literary Renaissance* 8 (1978): 67–84.

Moeslein, M. E. Introduction to *The Plays of Henry Medwall: A Critical Edition*. Edited by M. E. Moeslein. New York: Garland, 1981.

Moi, Toril. *Sexual/Textual Politics: Feminist Literary Theory*. London: Methuen, 1985.

Montrose, Louis A. "Gifts and Reasons: The Contexts of Peele's *Araygnement of Paris*." *English Literary History* 47 (1980): 433–61.

——— "*A Midsummer Night's Dream* and the Shaping Fantasies of Elizabethan Culture: Gender, Power, Form." In *Rewriting the Renaissance*, edited by Margaret W. Ferguson, Maureen Quilligan, and Nancy J. Vickers, 65–87. Chicago: University of Chicago Press, 1986.

Moretti, Franco. "The Soul and the Harpy: Reflections on the Aims and Methods of Literary Historiography." In *Signs Taken*

for Wonders: Essays in the Sociology of Literary Forms, translated by Susan Fischer, David Forgacs, and David Miller.
London: Verso, 1988.

Morrill, J. S. *The Revolt of the Provinces.* New York: Barnes and
Noble, 1976.

Moxey, Keith P. F. "The Function of Peasant Imagery in German
Graphics of the Sixteenth Century: Festive Peasants as
Instruments of Repressive Humor." In *Print and Culture in
the Renaissance: Essays on the Advent of Printing in Europe*,
edited by Gerald P. Tyson and Sylvia S. Wagonheim, 151–
88. Newark: University of Delaware Press, 1986.

Muchembled, Robert. *Popular Culture and Elite Culture in France,
1400–1750.* Translated by Lydia Cochrane. Baton Rouge:
Louisiana State University Press, 1985.

Mullaney, Steven. *The Place of the Stage: License, Play, and Power in
Renaissance England.* Chicago: University of Chicago Press,
1988.

Nares, Rev. Edward. *Memoirs of the Life and Administration of the
Right Honourable William Cecil, Lord Burghley.* 3 vols. London, 1831.

Nevo, Ruth. *Comic Transformations in Shakespeare.* London:
Methuen, 1980.

Newman, Karen. "Renaissance Family Politics and Shakespeare's
The Taming of the Shrew." *English Literary Renaissance* 16
(1986): 86–100.

Novy, Marianne L. "Patriarchy and Play in *The Taming of the
Shrew.*" *English Literary Renaissance* 9 (1979): 264–80.

Ochshorn, Judith. *The Female Experience and the Nature of the Divine.*
Bloomington: Indiana University Press, 1981.

Orgel, Stephen. "Prospero's Wife." In *Rewriting the Renaissance*,
edited by Margaret W. Ferguson, Maureen Quilligan, and
Nancy J. Vickers, 50–64. Chicago: University of Chicago
Press, 1986.

Palmer, D. J. *Comedy: Developments in Criticism.* London: Macmillan, 1984.

Palmer, Daryl W. "Entertainment, Hospitality, and Family in *The
Winter's Tale.*" *Iowa State Journal of Research* 59 (1985): 253–
61.

———. "William Kemp's *Nine Daies Wonder* and the Transmission
of Performance Culture." *Journal of Dramatic Theory and*

Criticism 5 (1991): 33–47.

Patterson, Annabel. *Shakespeare and the Popular Voice.* London: Basil Blackwell, 1989.

Pearson, D'Orsay W. "'Unkinde' Theseus: A Study in Renaissance Mythography." *English Literary Renaissance* 4 (1974): 276–98.

Peck, Linda Levy. "'For a King not to be bountiful were a fault': Perspectives on Court Patronage in Early Stuart England." *Journal of British Studies* 25 (1986): 31–61.

Perret, Marion D. "*Lear's* Good Old Man." *Shakespeare Studies* 17 (1985): 89–102.

Polan, Dana B. "'Above All Else to Make You See': Cinema and the Ideology of Spectacle." In *Postmodernism and Politics*, edited by Jonathan Arac. Minneapolis: University of Minnesota Press, 1986.

Quilligan, Maureen. "The Comedy of Female Authority in *The Faerie Queene.*" *English Literary Renaissance* 17 (1987): 156–71.

———. "Sidney and His Queen." In *The Historical Renaissance: New Essays on Tudor and Stuart Literature and Culture*, edited by Heather Dubrow and Richard Strier, 171–96. Chicago: University of Chicago Press, 1988.

Sacks, David Harris. "Search for 'Culture' in the English Renaissance." *Shakespeare Quarterly* 39 (1988): 465–88.

Salingar, Leo. *Shakespeare and the Traditions of Comedy.* Cambridge: Cambridge University Press, 1976.

Samuelson, David A. "The Order in Beaumont's *Knight of the Burning Pestle.*" *English Literary Renaissance* 9 (1979): 302–18.

Sanford, John Langton, and Meredith Townsend. *The Great Governing Families of England.* Edinburgh: William Blackwood, 1865.

Serres, Michel. "The Origin of Language: Biology, Information Theory, and Thermodynamics." In *Hermes: Literature, Science, Philosophy*, edited by Josué V. Harari and David F. Bell. Baltimore: Johns Hopkins University Press, 1982.

———. *The Parasite.* Translated by Lawrence R. Schehr. Baltimore: Johns Hopkins University Press, 1982.

Sharp, Buchanan. *In Contempt of All Authority: Rural Artisans and Riot in the West of England, 1586–1660.* Berkeley: University of California Press, 1980.

Sharp, Ronald A. "Gift Exchange and the Economies of Spirit in *The Merchant of Venice." Modern Philology* 83 (1986): 250–65.

Sharpe, Kevin. *Criticism and Compliment: The Politics of Literature in the England of Charles I.* Cambridge: Cambridge University Press, 1987.

———. *Politics and Ideas in Early Stuart England: Essays and Studies.* London: Pinter Publishers, 1989.

Silverman, Kaja. *The Subject of Semiotics.* New York: Oxford University Press, 1983.

Smuts, R. Malcolm. *Court Culture and the Origins of a Royalist Tradition in Early Stuart England.* Philadelphia: University of Pennsylvania Press, 1987.

Snow, Edward A. "Sexual Anxiety and the Male Order of Things in *Othello." English Literary Renaissance* 10 (1980): 384–411.

Stallybrass, Peter. "'Drunk with the Cup of Liberty': Robin Hood, the Carnivalesque, and the Rhetoric of Violence in Early Modern England." In *The Violence of Representation: Literature and the History of Violence,* edited by Nancy Armstrong and Leonard Tennenhouse, 45–76. London: Routledge, 1989.

———, and Allon White. *The Politics and Poetics of Transgression.* London: Methuen, 1986.

Stokes, James D. "Robin Hood and the Churchwardens in Yeovil." *Medieval and Renaissance Drama* 3 (1986): 1–25.

Stone, Lawrence. *The Crisis of the Aristocracy, 1558–1641.* Oxford: Clarendon, 1965.

Strier, Richard. "Faithful Servants: Shakespeare's Praise of Disobedience." In *The Historical Renaissance: New Essays on Tudor and Stuart Literature and Culture,* edited by Heather Dubrow and Richard Strier, 104–33. Chicago: University of Chicago Press, 1988.

Strong, Roy. *Art and Power: Renaissance Festivals of State.* Berkeley: University of California Press, 1984.

Tennenhouse, Leonard. *Power on Display: The Politics of Shakespeare's Genres.* New York: Methuen, 1986.

Thomas, Keith. *Religion and the Decline of Magic.* New York: Scribners, 1971.

Thompson, E. P. "Patrician Society, Plebeian Culture." *Journal of Social History* 7 (1973–74): 395–96.

Timbs, John. *Nooks and Corners of English Life, Past and Present.*

London: Griffith and Farran, 1867.

Todorov, Tzvetan. "Typology of Detective Fiction." In *The Poetics of Prose,* translated by Richard Howard. Ithaca: Cornell University Press, 1977.

Turner, Myron. "The Disfigured Face of Nature: Image and Metaphor in the Revised *Arcadia." English Literary Renaissance* 2 (1972): 116–35.

Underdown, D. E. "The Taming of the Scold: The Enforcement of Patriarchal Authority in Early Modern England." In *Order and Disorder in Early Modern England,* edited by Anthony Fletcher and John Stevenson, 116–36. Cambridge: Cambridge University Press, 1985.

Waller, Gary. *English Poetry of the Sixteenth Century.* London: Longman, 1986.

———. "The Countess of Pembroke and Gendered Reading." In *The Renaissance Englishwoman in Print: Counterbalancing the Canon,* edited by Anne M. Haselkorn and Betty Travitsky. Amherst: University of Massachusetts Press, 1990.

Weimann, Robert. *Shakespeare and the Popular Tradition in the Theater: Studies in the Social Dimension of Dramatic Form and Function.* Edited by Robert Schwartz. Baltimore: Johns Hopkins University Press, 1978.

———. "Towards a Literary Theory of Ideology: Mimesis, Representation, Authority." In *Shakespeare Reproduced,* edited by Jean E. Howard and Marion F. O'Connor, 265–72. New York: Methuen, 1987.

Wellek, René, and Austin Warren. *Theory of Literature.* New York: Harcourt Brace, 1942.

Westfall, Suzanne R. *Patrons and Performance: Early Tudor Household Revels.* Oxford: Clarendon Press, 1990.

Whigham, Frank. *Ambition and Privilege: The Social Trope of Elizabethan Courtesy Theory.* Berkeley: University of California Press, 1984.

Wickham, Glynne. *"Love's Labor's Lost* and *The Four Foster Children of Desire,* 1581." *Shakespeare Quarterly* 36 (1985): 49–55.

Wiesner, Merry E. "Spinsters and Seamstresses: Women in Cloth and Clothing Production." In *Rewriting the Renaissance,* edited by Margaret W. Ferguson, Maureen Quilligan, and Nancy J. Vickers, 191–205. Chicago: University of Chicago Press, 1986.

Williams, Penry. *The Tudor Regime.* Oxford: Clarendon Press, 1979.
Williams, Raymond. *The Country and the City.* New York: Oxford University Press, 1973.
———. *Marxism and Literature.* Oxford: Oxford University Press, 1977.

INDEX